Women at the Well, Volume II

Meditations for Quenching Our Thirst

D1468983

Women at the Well, Volume II

Meditations for Quenching Our Thirst

Edited by Linda-Marie Delloff and
Bernadette Glover-Williams

Judson Press •Valley Forge

Women at the Well, Volume 2:
Meditations for Quenching Our Thirst
© 2003 by Judson Press, Valley Forge, PA 19482-0851
All rights reserved.

Judson Press has made every effort to trace the ownership of all quotes. In the event of a question arising from the use of a quote, we regret any error made and will be pleased to make the necessary correction in future printings and editions of this book.

Unless otherwise noted, Bible quotations in this volume are from the New Revised Standard Version of the Bible, copyright ©1989 by the Division of Christian Education of the National Council of the Churches of Christ in the United States of America. Used by permission. All rights reserved. (NRSV)

Where noted, Bible quotations are also from: *The Holy Bible*, King James Version. (KJV); *The Message*. Copyright © 1993, 1994, 1995. Used by permission of NavPress Publishing Group (The Message); The New American Bible, copyright ©1970, 1986, 1991 by the Confraternity of Christian Doctrine, 3211 Fourth Street, N.E., Washington, D.C. 20017. All rights reserved. (NAB); HOLY BIBLE: *New International Version*, copyright © 1973, 1978, 1984. Used by permission of Zondervan Bible Publishers. (NIV); The New King James Version. Copyright ©1972, 1984 by Thomas Nelson Inc. (NKJV); The *Holy Bible,* New Living Translation, copyright © 1996. Used by permission of Tyndale House Publishers, Inc., Wheaton, IL 60189. All rights reserved. (NLT); The New American Standard Bible, © 1960, 1962, 1963, 1968, 1971, 1972, 1973, 1975, 1977 by The Lockman Foundation. Used by permission. (NASB); The Revised Standard Version of the Bible, copyright © 1946, 1952, 1971, by the Division of Christian Education of the National Council of the Churches of Christ in the U.S.A. Used by permission (RSV).

Library of Congress Cataloging-in-Publication Data
Original data for Volume 1:
Women at the well : meditations on healing and wholeness / edited by Mary L. Mild.
    p. cm.
    ISBN 0-8170-1245-1 (pbk. : alk paper)
    1. Women—Prayer—books and devotions—English. 2. Spiritual healing—Meditations. 3. Health—Religious aspects—Christianity—Meditations. 4. Devotional calendars. I. Mild, Mary L., 1944–.
    BV4844.W654 1996
    242'.643—dc20   96-29296
    Volume 2, edited by Linda-Marie Delloff and Bernadette Glover-Williams; ISBN 0-8170-1404-7

Printed in the U.S.A.
10 09 08 07 06 05 04 03
5 4 3 2 1

Acknowledgments

Such an ambitious endeavor as this—blending the voices of many into a unified whole—has required the faithfulness and diligence of many, some of whom deserve special mention:

Lonnie Lane for organizing this effort in its early stages.

The National Council of Churches' Justice for Women Working Group, which provided an extensive list of contributors and will receive a portion of the royalties from book sales.

Sandy Schmidt, who was so moved by the first volume that she became a faithful advocate and recruiter for the second.

Lisa Blair for being the best organizer and support person anyone could ask for.

Diane Vescovi and Victoria McGoey for their care-filled attention to editorial detail.

The contributors who shared their insights, their hurts, their hopes, their inspiration, and their wisdom—in a word, their lives.

Contents

Foreword

This collection of deeply spiritual writings draws us into a hope. This hope is neither uncommon nor immodest. It is the hope that most of us rest on, the hope that somehow in answering the call of God in our lives that we—through praying together, opening our lives as food for the journey for each other, and living out our faith relentlessly—will be healed and renewed to touch the world. This touch, like the hope that grounds it, is one that reaches out from the depths of our souls to bring love, justice, and mercy into our lives and into the lives of others. This is no small task, but this is the way of faith.

The women in this collection are not afraid to talk to and with God. They know that God can bear all that we have to say and more. From joy and thanksgiving to despair and anger, this collection invites you to stand before God and experience holy boldness. This boldness folds ever deeper into God's unyielding spirit of justice and mercy. God's spirit showers us morning by morning with the ways in which truth and righteousness are not options or idle flights of fancy. God meets us in the roaring whirlwind our lives can become as well as in those moments of quiet stillness. Through our fears, tears, searching, and finding, God stands with us with a spirit of thundering grace.

As you read, you will find a deep-walking journey that bonds both Scripture and life witness. Indeed, the story and image of the woman at the well inspires much in us. It has been used as the name for spiritual discernment ministries and also for re-entry programs for recently released women inmates. It has been drawn on by women who are traditionalists as well as by feminists; by those who consider themselves conservative, liberal, or somewhere in between. It has been used in other literary collections that range from spiritual direction to menopause. There is something about the well and the Samaritan woman's question, "Where do you get this living water?" and then her plea "Give me this water, so that I may never be thirsty or have to keep coming here to draw water" that speaks to our search for both comfort and sustenance for the work our souls must have as women of faith. This thirst-quenching collection is a refuge for learning, comfort, encouragement, and growing through God's grace and love. You will even find moments of humor and whimsy.

I invite you to spend some of your prayer and meditation time with this collection. The words and lives you will find here are not meant to solve your problems, nor is this book to be a how-to manual for spiritual growth and enrichment. No, this collection seeks to comfort and challenge in the same breath. This, I believe, is closer to the ways in which the gospel calls to us each day. We see both judgment and grace as ongoing witness to the power and fortitude of the word. This word not only provides bread for the journey; it also quenches parched spirits and dry souls with a water gushing up to eternal life.

—*Emilie M. Townes*
New York City

Introduction

With this volume, we meet for a second time at the well. We are women from various walks of life; we are young and old, rich and poor, leaders and followers. We represent a variety of vocations, ethnic groups, faith traditions, and political viewpoints, but we hold in common the desire, the thirst, to encounter Christ anew.

Some have come to the well to teach, others to inspire with their testimonies of hope and faith. Some have come to pour out their pain, to confess their struggles and doubts. Still others have come to the well to challenge their sisters to extend a hand of mercy—to be a well of hope, understanding, or comfort in the desert of someone else's life. These motivations are represented by the seven categories grouping these devotions: spiritual formation, testimonies of faith, the quest to be whole, a call for justice, called to serve, words of hope, and living faithfully. All serve in one way or another to quench our individual and collective thirst for understanding and renewal.

Compiling this collection has been a long and sometimes arduous journey, one that has taken several years to complete. To say that our world has changed during the time this volume has developed is an understatement that borders on the absurd. Many of these devotions were written prior to September 11, 2001. During the weeks and months following that fateful day, as we reread the earliest contributions, many seemed dated, not so much because of what they said, but because of what they didn't say—or didn't assume—about the precarious nature of the world in which we live.

Our world never stands still. As this volume goes to press, our nation is deeply engaged in military action in Iraq. Ironically, our responses to the events of 9-11 may now seem dated. Perhaps the lesson here is that no matter the time, place, or external circumstances, our lives are always in some sense precarious. However, the truths based on this realization are timeless.

The testimony of these reflections is that our struggles—our grief and our pain—are infused with hope, life-changing hope to which the first woman at the well testified. She encountered the living Christ, and in so doing gained access to the well that quenches even the deepest of thirsts and that never runs dry. Our hope and prayer is that this volume will enable you, in some measure, to do the same. Come gather at the well. Come quench your thirst.

—The Editors

A Deeper Spirituality

Needing God

As a deer longs for flowing streams,
so my soul longs for you, O God.
—Psalm 42:1

There is a hymn, written more than two hundred years ago, based on the words of this Psalm and echoing the King James language of its day: "As pants the hart for cooling streams, when heated in the chase, So longs my soul, O God, for thee, and thy refreshing grace." I love this hymn, not only because it is a perfect blend of melody and text, but also because the image is such a good one for my busy modern life. Sometimes I feel like a hart: panting, running from or to something all the time, hoping for a sip of cool water, hoping not to get eaten by whatever it is I'm hurrying away from.

It is a powerful image—to think of thirsting for God with the same intensity as the physical thirst one experiences after a long run. Thirst is hard to ignore. Like hunger, it can make you postpone all other matters until it is satisfied. But how many of us really feel that way about our need for God? The closest I can come is how I feel about my solitude, for which I do often feel a thirst.

As a chaplain and mother of two teenage boys, I don't have a lot of time that isn't spoken for. Yet without quiet solitude I get harried and out of balance. I forget why it is I'm doing all the things I'm doing. My solitude is my time with God: I am never alone or lonely. I may consciously pray or not. I may think or not. I don't want or need noise of any kind, except perhaps the sound of rain or wind, or the creaking of the chains on my porch swing. The point is that the need for God—the desire to be someplace quiet and uninterrupted long enough to feel restored—is as urgent as thirst.

Loving God, help us to recognize when we are thirsting for you. Help us to remember where the cooling streams of your grace are, so that we might seek them out and drink, and feel restored for love and service. Amen.

Amy E. Greene

His Eye Is on the Sparrow

"I know my own and my own know me..."
—John 10:14b

It was a cold, rainy day, and I was home recuperating from the flu. Feeling better, I moved from my bed to the living room. After inserting a worship CD in the player, I closed my eyes and meditated on the songs so skillfully played by these modern-day Levites. Suddenly there was a commotion outside the window. Opening my eyes, I saw a group of sparrows flying nervously around the window and chirping loudly. Walking to the window, I saw what the noise was about. Somehow, a little sparrow had trapped himself between the storm window and window. He was frantically throwing his little body against the glass to escape.

I groaned. Since purchasing our seventy-year-old home, we had been unable to open this window. The dampness of the day would only make any effort to open it even more futile. Breathing a prayer, I unlocked the sash. To my surprise, the window glided open with ease.

How would I safely remove the bird? I began speaking in soothing tones as I attempted to guide him into my hand. It was not working. Now my words of comfort switched to prayers. "Dear Father, how am I to do this?"

Impulsively, I grabbed the tiny bird by the tail feathers and grasped him with my other hand, forming a cell for the frightened captive. He reacted more violently than I expected. I could barely hold him with both hands, so how was I to open the doors to release him?

I continued to alternately speak to him and pray. Unexpectedly, we made eye contact, and his struggle ceased. I was able to hold him with one hand and open the doors with the other. Seconds later, he was free and I was left in wonder and amazement.

We all get into difficult situations. Do we immediately hear God's gentle voice trying to guide us? Or does God have to grab us by the "tail feathers"? Had the little sparrow known me, would he have trusted me immediately? Yeshua said, "My sheep listen to My voice, and I know them, and they follow Me..." (John 10:27, American Translation).

Abba, in the midst of many voices, may I learn to know yours. When you rescue me, help me not to struggle. May I always seek your face and not fear your hand. Amen.

Terri Gillespie

The Spirituality of Compost

*For he grew up before him like a young plant,
and like a root out of dry ground.*
—Isaiah 53:2a

Out back, on the shady side of our long and narrow city garden, sit the compost heaps in their wooden bins. A few weeks ago the compost was still partially frozen, but now it is loose and crumbly, ready to nurture the new plants that have just arrived by mail. Spring is also the time for clearing out the vegetable bed, pulling up last summer's broccoli, and digging up the sad row of leeks that we didn't harvest.

At such times, when I have to throw out some of the vegetables we've grown, I take comfort in being able to take them out to the compost heap where they will live again, in a sense. There they become part of a new life-form: the mysterious and magical mixture of dead and decaying plants, bits of soil and manure, and a lively crew of earthworms and other creepy crawlies that will give life and health to other plants in the garden. Compost is true alchemy (if only all those medieval philosophers had realized it!), turning dross into gold, death into the very essence of life on this planet.

The plants that serve as food and fodder, along with the plants whose glorious beauty brings us joy, are all dependent on soil; and soil, to state it bluntly, is not possible without death and decay: "flesh, fur, and faeces," as my beloved T.S. Eliot puts it. Thus our whole earthly existence expresses the connections among death, life, and rebirth.

As Christians, we are nourished by receiving Christ, who "grew up…like a young plant, a root out of dry ground" and, like the plants in my garden, died, was buried, and then was reborn as a new kind of nurturing life. The Paschal Victim/Priest is also the Tree of Life nourished by its own death. Creation abounds with sacramental signs and symbols. Holiness is everywhere.

God of new beginnings, help us to notice daily the reminders that, even in seasons of death, life springs forth. Amen.

Nancy Adams

Caging God

I am about to do a new thing;
now it springs forth, do you not perceive it?
—Isaiah 43:19a

Five-year-old Kathy sat down with her new markers. "What are you drawing?" I asked.

"This is the jungle," she said, "and these are the animals in cages."

"Oh," I responded. "I know there are animals in cages in the zoo. But I didn't know animals were in cages in the jungle."

Kathy looked up at me. With a hint of exasperation in her voice, she replied, "Grandma, this is the petting jungle." Kathy didn't understand that few jungle animals are ever truly tamed or controlled, and that taming them changes their very nature.

We often want to put God in a cage, to control God's actions in our world and in our lives. We want God to speak to us in the accustomed places and through familiar people. We want our prayers answered right now, and in a particular way. We may think that if we make certain offerings or worship often enough, God is almost obliged to do what we ask. We may forget that a God we could manipulate would not really be God. The only limit on what God can do is God's nature.

If we allow God to be "God uncaged," God can surprise us. God startles us by loving those we consider unlovable and calling us to do the same. God surprises us by gifting those society least expects to do God's work and wanting us to celebrate their ministry.

Whenever someone walks out of worship because a woman is preaching, that person is attempting to cage God. Whenever someone declines to listen to the poor or dispossessed, he or she is attempting to limit God. Whenever we consider the words or needs of a child to be less important than those of adults, we are attempting to confine God. When we turn away from others because of their ethnicity or religion, we close our eyes to the fact that God can surprise us.

The God of surprises invites us to be astonished, enraptured, and filled with a sense of wonder and hope and love. Will we let God be God?

Amazing God, forgive us when we try to manipulate you. Come to us through people and in places where we least expect to find you. Surprise us with the abundance of your love. Amen.

Wilda K. W. (Wendy) Morris

Dry Bones

He said to me, "Mortal, can these bones live?" I answered, "O Lord GOD, you know." Then he said to me, "Prophesy to these bones, and say to them: O dry bones, hear the word of the LORD. Thus says the Lord GOD to these bones: I will cause breath to enter you, and you shall live. I will lay sinews on you, and will cause flesh to come upon you, and cover you with skin, and put breath in you, and you shall live; and you shall know that I am the LORD." So I prophesied as I had been commanded; and as I prophesied, suddenly there was a noise, a rattling, and the bones came together, bone to its bone. I looked, and there were sinews on them, and flesh had come upon them, and skin had covered them; but there was no breath in them.

—Ezekiel 37:3-8

Our lives are filled with many memories that make us who we are today. At times we experience events that plague us and weigh us down—even after we seemingly forget about them. But when we don't deal with these kinds of challenges properly, they accumulate within us and become as dry bones in our spirits. Eventually one day we find that our hearts and our spirits are heavy all of the time because we have collected so many of these bones. It feels as if we are in the valley of dry bones that Ezekiel spoke of in the Scripture. The Lord desires that we follow the lesson in 1 Peter 5:7 by casting all of our anxieties on him. For he cares for us and removes the stumbling blocks.

Our part is to speak to the dry bones in our lives. No one can do that for us. If Ezekiel had not spoken to those bones, they would have remained scattered across the entire valley. But they did nothing until he spoke to them. He could have tried to put them together himself as we try to do with so many situations in our lives, but it would have taken years until he figured out what part goes with which body.

Ezekiel had only to speak to the bones in faith, as God had commanded, and God did the rest. When Ezekiel spoke, he heard a rattling sound and then he saw the bones coming together. He witnessed them assume flesh and skin. Imagine what would have happened if Ezekiel never spoke to the bones.

Lord, teach me to be obedient that I might see the miracles you perform. Let my eyes remain fixed upon you and my heart clean and pure that I may speak your word to dry bones in my life and thus be spiritually restored. Amen.

Tawanda N. Tucker

Quenching Our Thirst

Jesus said to her, "Everyone who drinks of this water will be thirsty again, but those who drink of the water that I will give them will never be thirsty. The water that I will give will become in them a spring of water gushing up to eternal life."
—John 4:13-14

For many years I suffered with three very annoying ailments. My right eye was frequently dry and painful; my nose was dry and itchy; and I had a dry cough in my throat. One doctor said I suffered from stress. Other doctors gave me allergy medicine or told me I had asthma.

One day, out of the blue, after flying cross-country and having more trouble than usual breathing, it occurred to me that if the "common denominator" with my ailments was dryness, then maybe, just maybe, I was thirsty. Within five minutes after drinking about a quart of water, all of my uncomfortable symptoms disappeared. This has been a wonderful discovery. Now whenever my eye hurts or I start coughing, I take a big drink of water and am soon feeling fine.

In the same way, I believe, many of our problems in life are caused because we do not recognize that we are spiritually thirsty. Are we fearful or anxious? Are we lonely? Do we feel inadequate to meet life's daily challenges?

When I am fearful or anxious, which happens far too often, I know it is because I am not putting my trust in God. When I ask for God's presence in my life, my fears and anxieties go away just like my dry eye after a drink of water.

When I am lonely, it is because I am walking my daily journey by myself instead of choosing to walk with God. When I feel inadequate to do the task that is before me, it is because I have lost sight of the one who has promised to sustain me.

Jesus said that everyone who drinks of the water he gives them will never be thirsty. There is plenty of water at the well. But we must remember to drink it, or we will still suffer the consequences of our spiritual thirst.

> *The Lord is my shepherd, I shall not want.*
> *He makes me lie down in green pastures;*
> *he leads me beside still waters;*
> *he restores my soul.*
> *You prepare a table before me in the presence of my enemies;*
> *you anoint my head with oil; my cup overflows.*
> *—Psalm 23:1-3,5*
>
> *Thank you. Amen.*

Mary L. Mild

"I Am Epaphras"

*Epaphras, who is one of you, a servant of Christ Jesus,
greets you. He is always wrestling in his prayers on
your behalf, so that you may stand mature and fully
assured in everything that God wills.*
—*Colossians 4:12*

When I first discovered this verse, I was so impressed. As a child would claim to be her favorite superhero, I began to declare proudly, "I am Epaphras!" My family laughed at my excitement and, although I agreed that it sounded hilarious, I was sincere. I had discovered in the Scriptures a personal hero. The testimony of the apostle concerning this diligent warrior of prayer spoke immediately to my desire. The verse reflected and still reflects what I would want to be said of me. It is an excellent legacy.

Prayer is the most powerful component of our lives as Christians. Few would debate that the best way to get to know someone is to talk with that person. So it is with God. Prayer, although diverse in postures, levels, and types, is constant in that it always involves talk between God and his children. To pray in general is essential, but Epaphras did more. He prayed for others.

We live in a society so consumed with self. Even as Christians, considering others before ourselves can be a challenge. It excites me to know that Epaphras cared enough about others' destinies to commit his time to pray for them. There are two points worthy of note. First, the Scripture says that Epaphras prayed with all his might. Second, the plural of prayer is used, indicating that Epaphras used many kinds of prayers for the church. He must have prayed prayers of intercession, thanksgiving, petition, praise, and more. It is also striking to think that Paul mentions Epaphras's zest for prayer, as well as the subject matter of his prayers. Epaphras prayed that the saints would come into perfection and completion in all of God's will. He desired that they come into the fullness of God.

The name Epaphras means "lovely." Paul teaches us a powerful lesson by using this man's prayer life as an example. It is an example we would all do well to heed. May we become like Epaphras in our zeal for prayer. That would be lovely.

Lord, we thank you for the gift of prayer. Please draw us by your spirit into a deeper relationship not only with you but with one another. Amen.

Jéneen N. Barlow

Talking to God

Then when you call upon me and come and pray to me,
I will hear you. When you search for me,
you will find me; if you seek me with all your heart,
I will let you find me, says the LORD...
—Jeremiah 29:12-14a

The day my friend Sondra committed suicide, I quit praying. I had been a fervent prayer warrior for Sondra: I prayed for her family, her relationships, her mental health, and above all, for God to protect her from her suicidal feelings. In the days and months following her death, I was spiritually shattered. I felt betrayed by a capricious God. My reasoning went like this: sometimes God answered prayer, sometimes he didn't, and sometimes God gave me things I wanted without my even asking. Why, I concluded, should I even pray if God is just going to do whatever he wants anyway? I was mad at God, and to show him just how mad, I stopped talking to him.

A year later our family was camping in Colorado. My eight-year-old son, Matthew, had just returned from an off-trail hike around Turquoise Lake with his cousins. He was overflowing with reports of his adventures: how he almost got stuck in undergrowth, what animals they had seen. As we lay on sleeping bags and talked and laughed, I was gratified that he wanted to share this experience with me. I realized that while sometimes I give him what he asks for, sometimes I don't, and sometimes I give him good things without his asking. I guess I am lucky that he does not get mad and stop talking to me.

That day in my tent, I began to see that prayer is about so much more than requests to God, however unselfish they may be. Prayer is also about building a relationship with God like that of a mother and son sharing stories under the pine trees. Prayer is about getting to know God's heart. On that day of recognition I began to ask God to help me understand and deal with Sondra's death. And I began, ever so slightly, to trust again.

Loving Father, help me to trust you with the same confidence and love that my children feel for me. Help me to pray, both for the sake of our relationship and for the sake of conforming my life to your image. I love you. Amen.

Jeanne L. Williams

Unsittable Rocks

The steadfast love of the LORD never ceases,
his mercies never come to an end; they are new
every morning; great is your faithfulness.
—Lamentations 3:22-23

The first several days of a conference at a university, I found myself depressed. In my wanderings around campus, I discovered an interactive sculpture of Mary, surrounded by large rocks intended for sitting. So I sat. Depressed. Homesick. My seat was jagged and uncomfortable but appeared to be the best available. The next day I returned, looking for a rock. None seemed sittable. Choosing one anyway, I perched precariously at prayer. I kept returning to those rocks, always finding them unsittable.

Early on the sixth day, a day of retreat, I went to those persistently unsittable rocks but abandoned them for comfort elsewhere. At day's end, a time intended for thanksgiving, I returned to Mary. I found a comfortable flat-top rock! Glancing around me, I saw other flat rocks. Startled, I actually believed for a moment that someone had switched the rocks! Ten rocks in all, half very sittable now. It was a grace-filled moment when I sensed, more than any other time, God's abiding presence.

God is ever-faithful, ever-present. Like those granite rocks, God is always fully present. The invitation offered is for us to be fully present to God. Sometimes our desire to be with God is obstructed by depression, anger, fear, loneliness, the chaos of our lives, material possessions. I knew no one had changed the rocks. Nothing changed God's presence. It was I who had changed after a very intentional day at prayer that helped free me from obstacles keeping me from being fully present to God.

Just as I kept going back to the rocks those first days, we are ever drawn back to our source of life. Sometimes the pathway is smooth stone; sometimes it is jagged. What matters is that we keep coming back. Again and again and again.

We need to create spaces in our lives—sacred spaces—where we go to rest in God. Spaces where we relinquish our burdens. Spaces where we find comfort, and where we can trust in the presence of God, our life source. Even when we find ourselves not fully present. Even when the rocks seem unsittable.

Source of life, great is thy faithfulness. Help me to be faithful to you, to always seek and find sittable rocks. Amen.

Emilie J. Aubert

Give Me the Soup

"...you shall love the Lord your God with all your heart, and with all your soul, and with all your mind, and with all your strength."
—Mark 12:30

For I am not ashamed of the gospel; it is the power of God for salvation to everyone who has faith, to the Jew first and also to the Greek.
—Romans 1:16

The difference between chicken soup and chicken broth is obvious. The first contains substantive flavor weighted with healing properties. The second is more of a flat rinse with a smidgen of taste. If we wouldn't expect a broth-fed body to respond as though soup had been its diet, why are we surprised when a spiritually undernourished Christian or church bears no significant evidence of a living faith?

Undiluted "Gospel Soup" strengthens the entire being from the inside out! "Gospel Rinse"—a highly particularized thematic extract—though offered out of sincerity, fails to yield an authentic, balanced Christian life. Accordingly, a grasp of social ethical responsibility shouldn't negate an embrace of vertical intimacy. Doing something for God isn't a substitute for being with God.

Lord Jesus, give me courage to both receive and offer the substance of the whole faith so that spiritual malnutrition will not be known. Amen.

Bernadette Glover-Williams

Motherhood of God

So God created humankind in his image, in the image of God he created them; male and female he created them.
—Genesis 1:27

It is all too rare that as a woman I find myself characterized in the divine image or even as resembling the divine image. But increasingly, feminist theologians have recognized and articulated the andro-centric perspectives and patriarchal biases of Holy Scripture and the church. How wonderfully refreshing that both female and male, taken together, are named in the divine image.

This piece of Scripture is an invitation to image God as female as well as male. And there are other Scripture passages that identify female forms: God as Dame Wisdom, Bakerwoman God, the Godhead as a woman in the process of giving birth, God as Mother Bear, God as Female Beloved, God as Mother Hen, and God as female searcher for the lost coin.

My own experiences of the holy are centered on Mother God, Loving Creator, a protective, safe, secure, and nurturing womb. Our Creator is like an accepting, loved-no-matter-what home, a place of solid and fertile ground, a holy dwelling place.

Images help me approach God, frame my experience of God,

and assist me in thinking and talking about God. To some extent images of God shape and influence my experience of God. Metaphors operate not simply at the cognitive level but at the emotional level as well.

I recognize my own human limitations in imaging God in human terms. But this is a struggle of enormous importance (and worthy of the effort) in the life of the church and in our own spiritual lives. The way we image and imagine God, the person of God, and the gender of God influences how we imagine one another, the world, and ourselves.

Holy One of Blessing, with full and thankful hearts we honor that you created us all in your image. Strengthen us to affirm the dignity you have given all human beings. Work through our struggles and confusion to accomplish your purposes in this life. Help us to be open to your presence in which we dwell, however we name you. In Jesus' Name. Amen.

Nancee Martin-Coffey

Free Gift

"Look at the birds of the air; they neither sow nor reap nor gather into barns, and yet your heavenly Father feeds them. Are you not of more value than they?"
—Matthew 6:26

Two men stand side by side, their right arms outstretched, heads to the sky. Pointing? At what? Brilliant blue and green autumn beach afternoon. Surf breaks on the shore, washing sand, chasing children. The men stand still. Young seagulls fly, dive, circle, hover, land, lift off, fly a bit, circle back, calling as they play and scavenge, not mindful of the humans, save the two men standing still, arms outstretched.

They are not pointing—they are offering: inviting the gulls to take and eat. Pieces of food held by fingertips entice the gulls to draw near and nearer. The birds of the air approach, hesitate, hover, back away. Save one. It inches toward one of the men, wings positioned to keep it aloft, holding still in mid-air, ready to fly with the faintest adjustment. Got it! The gull takes the food from the young man's fingertips! My spirit leaps to join the gifted adventurer.

Will the others follow its lead? Will they repeat its achievement? Will they dive, hover, ponder, then take? Will they learn from their companion to accept the invitation to become guest rather than scavenger? Will any of them take the gift of nourishment so rarely provided in such a manner? No, not one. They are witnesses of the invitation and acceptance, and even approach the giver, but they do not take it for themselves. Instead, they continue with the familiar and normal routine. Truly, they will feed well in their usual manner, but they will never know just what they have missed—not the taste, not the act of acceptance, not the full relationship with the gift giver.

But that single gull returns for another morsel, still careful, tentative until the moment of "Yes." My heart embraces the little gull whom I watch in this precious hour. I've given this time to myself to sit at the beach in the middle of the week because I long for rest and tranquility. I want to be like you, young gull, not your friends. I want to allow myself boldly yet humbly to take the good and perfect gift even when it is offered in challenging modes of invitation.

Gracious Lord, thank you for your invitation to receive abundant life, and for your patience in not withdrawing when we merely hover. May we dare to be your honored guests, rather than mere scavengers of scraps from your table of blessing. Amen.

Linda Kirkland-Harris

The Desires of Your Heart

Take delight in the LORD, and he will give you the desires of your heart.
—Psalm 37:4

This verse has nourished me for many years, speaking to something deep within me, though I wasn't always sure I understood it. It seemed to clash with other Scriptures, such as "The heart is desperately wicked above all things." I once believed that whatever my heart deeply desired was probably contrary to God's will.

But now I am learning that I am created in the image of God. That is the first word the Scriptures speak about what it means to be human: created in God's likeness, created good, with power and responsibility. That is my true essence. Genesis 1 is followed by Genesis 3, the account of Adam and Eve's disobedience, but the disobedience is not the definition of what it means to be human. Adam and Eve followed a voice external to them and then followed a path not authentic to them, departing from their true essence.

I have come to learn that the deepest desires of my authentic self, my heart, truly lead me to God and God's will, and often are consistent with God's desire for me. Both Teresa of Avila and Thomas Merton said something to this effect: "Find God and you find yourself; find yourself and you find God."

To "deny" ourselves, to take up the cross to follow, isn't denying the essential self created in the image of God, but the inauthentic self that has conformed to the external voices of culture, unhealthy family messages, sexism, racism, agism, prejudice against sexual minorities, and other misguided tendencies. And since God never violates our true authentic being—because God created it in the first place—we can trust.

I do not need to fear what God will take away from me or what God will ask me to give up. I can listen to my heart and listen to God at the same time and find congruence, peace, healing, direction, and joy. There is always danger that I might rationalize or be willful, substituting my disordered, externally-directed self for my authentic self. But silencing that still, small voice within me is even more dangerous. So embrace your heart and let it lead you to God.

Creating God, give me the courage to listen to my heart and to you my Creator, thereby finding the wholeness and the calling of my heart. Amen.

Joy A. Bergfalk

Let Life Flow

May the Lord direct your hearts to the love of God
and to the steadfastness of Christ.
—2 Thessalonians 3:5

Have you ever wondered how water can seem to find its way around any barrier, through any crack, over any obstacle? Water has the unique ability to adapt to and transcend any restricted space. Sometimes life presents us with obstacles, barriers, or narrow spaces that seem insurmountable. We must learn to let our lives flow in ways that allow us to meet our trials, tribulations, and temptations, and to be transformed by the experience.

Recently, while meditating on a picture of a snow-capped mountain in Japan, I left behind my present state of being and envisioned myself standing at the foot of the mountain, overwhelmed by its massiveness and chilled by its coldness. My spirit did not know whether to run and hide, to negotiate my position, or to accept being overwhelmed. Suddenly, I felt myself communing with the mountain. It was now equal with me in size; I could feel crystals of snow blowing on my face. The mountain and I met and agreed that we were co-created to exist in peace and harmony. Fear left me, and the mountain carried on with its existence.

The mountain was symbolic of real obstacles in my life. With any problem I encounter, once I have gotten beyond short periods of self-pity and doubt, something in me takes over, fortifying me for the journey. Faith reminds me of my God-given abilities to meet stumbling blocks and turn them into steppingstones.

Let your own life flow. God is directing the currents. Whether your life is whitewater rafting or smooth sailing, make sure your soul is anchored in the Lord. Then bask in the flow of life.

O Great Navigator, guide me into the sea of life. Make my anchor hold while showing me each mountain I pass. Let me rest knowing that I am sailing free. Let the waters flow, for I am blessed in thee. Amen.

Christine Dean Keels

Loving Our Enemies

"You have heard that it was said, 'You shall love your neighbor and hate your enemy.' But I say to you, Love your enemies and pray for those who persecute you, so that you may be children of your Father in heaven; for he makes his sun rise on the evil and on the good, and sends rain on the righteous and on the unrighteous. For if you love those who love you, what reward do you have? Do not even the tax collectors do the same? And if you greet only your brothers and sisters, what more are you doing than others? Do not even the Gentiles do the same? Be perfect, therefore, as your heavenly Father is perfect."
—Matthew 5:43-48

I recently learned an important lesson on loving your enemies. I find that learning to love your enemy is one of the hardest concepts in the Bible to understand. The message is quite clear. But reading it is one thing; doing it is another.

I sat one night, peering out at a raging thunderstorm. The lightning and thunder were scary, destructive forces of nature, and yet in a way, they were beautiful. I thought to myself, "How could something that has killed people and was so scary to me as a child be so beautiful?" The typical human answer seemed obvious: the color and shape of the lightening bolts. I tried to make myself dig deeper. God created the thunder and lightning. In Genesis, we read that when God created the world, everything was good in his eyes. That means everything! Even the most repulsive creatures on earth have some hidden beauty in them because they are from God.

I tried out my new theory. I thought of snakes. I think they're disgusting, but I was able to find beauty in their bright colors and intricate patterns. I moved on to the harder challenge of people. I sat on my bed thinking of all the people I seriously loathed and tried to think of one good trait about each of them. It took me a couple of days to think up a legitimate trait for some people, but in the end I came up with a trait for everyone. I realized that loving your enemy was just learning to appreciate a person's good qualities. I mean, that's what you do with your friends. You see their good and bad traits, but you dwell on the good and forgive the bad.

Loving your enemy does not mean you are becoming their best friend. It's being able to look at them as you do any other human, not as a creature from the black lagoon but as a worthwhile creation formed and loved by God. They have faults just like every other human being. They have good points also, just like you, your mom, your best friend, and every other human in this world. Understanding this is important for me, and it changed my entire view on other people.

Dear God, we know it is difficult for us to love those who have wronged us and who do not like us, but help us to remember that they were made by you. Help us re-learn the "Golden Rule" and with your grace, help us carry it out in the name of Jesus. Amen.

Kelli Shermeyer (age 13)

The Two-Day Wait

"Did I not tell you that if you believed,
you would see the glory of God?"
—John 11:40

"Draw near to God, and he will draw near to you" (James 4:8). That's what the Bible says. That's the way it's supposed to work. It's a timely, measured result: a cause-and-effect promise. Well, that was certainly what I expected as the Lord started to strip away another layer of my self-constructed securities when I lost my job. Where am I supposed to be? When is the next door going to open? I surrender to your ways, God. Now will you come and rescue me? Soon!

John 11 describes the struggle of a family who was very dear to Jesus. This was the family of Mary, who engaged in the intimate act of pouring perfume over Jesus' feet (John 12) and whom Jesus complimented for doing what was right in sitting at his feet (Luke 10:42). The Gospels also mentioned how Jesus loved Martha,

Mary's sister, and their brother Lazarus (John 11:5). Yet when they sent word to Jesus that Lazarus had become seriously ill, Jesus waited two more days—enough time for Lazarus to die.

Jesus was hit hard by the reality of Lazarus's death when he got there, and he grieved deeply. Yet it seems that before he knew Lazarus would die, he prayed foremost for a greater work: that they would believe. He announces that Lazarus's illness will not end in death, but the Son will be glorified by it (verse 4), and he gives thanks to his father for hearing his prayer (verse 41). But it was not without tremendous cost to himself and his dear loved ones.

There are times when we who are intimate with our Lord call upon him in crisis, and we find that a funny thing happens: he waits two more days. Does he answer our prayers? Sometimes in greater ways than we can imagine. Is it at a cost to us? You bet. Is it at a cost to him? Most definitely.

Prayer has no easy formula. When we ask for something, even something that is part of what the Lord wants, there is still more to consider. Are you in a two-day period? Remember that great works do come, but not without a cost.

Help us, God, to be patient for "two more days"; to realize that our desire may yield to your greater goal. Amen.

Carolyn Iga

Will You Let Me Help You Now?

*"Blessed are the poor in spirit,
for theirs is the kingdom of heaven."
—Matthew 5:3*

My daughter takes piano lessons. I listen to her practice but I rarely intrude. Sometimes she struggles to figure out a piece of music, but she is tenacious and independent, preferring to wrestle with the problem herself. There are times, however, when she faces a challenge she does not yet have the tools or experience to figure out on her own. I watch her frustration build, tears brimming in her eyes, as each thing she tries ends in failure. At those times, I stay somewhere nearby, agonizing, because I know I can help her—but not until she's ready to let me.

As a parent, my heart yammers away inside: "Let me help. I can show you, teach you. I can help you through this." I don't mind watching my child work hard to learn something, but when I know the thing she is wrestling with is simply beyond her ability to handle, I ache to help her. That's when I have to remind myself, "Stop hovering! She'll let you know when she's ready."

My daughter nearly exhausts herself before she'll let me step in. It is not until I see her literally slumped over the piano that I ask, "Will you let me help you now?"

There is much about the piano that my child can manage on her own, but there are also pieces of knowledge that she does not yet have. When she finally acknowledges her need for help, she has access to all of my experience and knowledge. Admitting she doesn't have everything she needs to do it herself allows me to enrich her with my abilities.

The awesomeness and extent of God's power become so wonderfully vivid to us when we realize our own limitations. When we are slumped over in defeat, we start looking around for the resources of the kingdom of heaven! It is then that we are most able to hear God saying, "Will you let me help you now?"

Lord, may the poverty in my own spirit awaken me to the resources in yours. Amen.

Kelly S. Moor

A Day on the Beach

Some went down to the sea in ships,
doing business on the mighty waters.
—Psalm 107:23

It is the end of August and I am feeling "antsy." I have not yet been to the ocean, and my soul is parched. Some summers it is a beach retreat with a spiritual director for guidance and discernment. Some summers it is a family vacation with sun and sea and surf.

Some summers it is friends with fun and food and fellowship. Some summers it is a gathering of the women with giggles and "girl talk."

Tomorrow I am going to the beach. Like the woman at the well, I will find physical and spiritual renewal and refreshment there. Long, lazy days on a beach towel on the sand will give me the rest I need. Playing in the waves will revive my spirits. Eating seafood and boardwalk fries will feed my body. Talking and being with friends will nourish my psyche. Meditating on the shore to the steadfast ebb and flow of the waves will restore my soul.

Whatever it is that connects us to the "living water" that Jesus offers us, it is essential that we avail ourselves of the nourishment we need. For me, it is time at the beach. All too often, women become too focused on "doing" and neglect the "being" that is so important for our well-being. My hope for all of us is that we will recognize our life-giving sources and incorporate them into the routines of our lives. May it be so.

Dear God, thank you for all the "living water" that you offer us. Help us in the midst of hectic lives and busy schedules to drink deeply from your well. We pray in Jesus' name. Amen.

Janet K. Hess

Pentecost Moments

Peter said to him, "Even though I must die with you, I will not deny you." And so said all the disciples.
—Matthew 26:35

I am at war. Having accepted Jesus Christ as my Lord and Savior, and having been duly ordained into the ministry, I still fight the battle of faith. My war is quiet and stealthy. I neglect prayer. The days skip by like stones on the water, only brushing the surface.

I am in too much haste to drink deeply. I feel rushed, pressured, and guilty, conscious of my failings but too absorbed in the every-day whirlwind to deliberately seek the calm. Oh, I have good intentions, but somehow the simplicity and beauty of faith are tangled and nearly strangled in webs of my own weaving.

When I find myself spending too much time on the unimportant, when I find myself sidetracked, exhausted, and ever-so-thirsty, I think of Peter. Peter, the disciple with the best of intentions. Peter, who said he would never deny Jesus. Peter, the all-too-human disciple who found himself doing the unthinkable: denying Christ not once, but three times. Peter knew the pain of falling short, of disavowing that which was nearest to his heart. On that dark day in Jerusalem, Peter lost the battle of faith. He wept bitter tears.

Yet Peter's story does not end there. He gathers the pieces of his own failure, regroups, and goes on. The risen Christ commissions the disciples, and the Holy Spirit comes to them at Pentecost. Peter will rediscover his calling as leader, as preacher, as follower of Christ. God's grace and renewal will bless Peter and the other disciples, enabling them to spread the Good News. Those who have tasted the bitter fruits of failure will somehow find themselves planting the seeds of faith once more. Their harvest will continue.

It occurs to me that Pentecost is more than just the birth of the church. It is also the receiving, again and again, of the Holy Spirit. I fail to be the Christian I want to be, yet it is precisely here, in my rueful, repentant acknowledgment of failure, that I am once again graced with the desire and ability to go on, to try again, to fight the good fight. Like Peter, I am blessed by these Pentecost moments. Like Peter, I go forth to follow Christ.

Lord, help me to drink deeply of your waters, to bathe in your grace, and to linger in your Holiness. Forgive me and heal me. Amen.
Becky Tornblom

Liberty and Justice for All

"So if the Son makes you free, you will be free indeed."
—John 8:36

I was on a public health nurse study tour in the former Soviet Union when the words "with liberty and justice for all" from the Pledge of Allegiance to the United States flag flashed through my mind. During my professional visit I was not free from rules or restrictions.

Although I was able to shop, walk in town, go to church, ride the subway or take a taxi, there were certain circumstances that made me aware that I was not free. The militia and soldiers were everywhere—on the streets, in doorways, cars, and restaurants, blowing whistles if I moved outside the white lines, using a sound system from their automobiles or from towers on the highway.

Each time I registered in a hotel I had to surrender my passport and visa until I checked out of the hotel. I was not going very far without these credentials! In each hotel a floor lady was on duty twenty-four hours a day. The hotel room keys were under her control. I presented my guest card to her, and she gave me the key to my room. I returned the key to her when I left my room for the day. I felt as if my every move was monitored. I did not feel free although I was not confined to a specific place.

Dear Lord, every day Christian women around the world experience the constraints that I felt for a few weeks. Thank you for the spiritual freedom that is ours through your Son, regardless of our physical circumstances. Amen.

Marilyn O. Harris

On Being Birthed Again, from Above

"What is born of the flesh is flesh, and what is born of the Spirit is spirit. Do not be astonished that I said to you, 'You must be born from above.'"
—John 3:6-7

I'll never forget the joy of studying Scripture with the late and legendary Father Raymond Brown. Learning about all the double meanings of the words used in John's Gospel was terribly liberating to me. This passage in particular stood out, because growing up in the Bible belt I was used to hearing "You must be born again" as an excuse to bully people into a certain type of profession of faith. That profession didn't fit me very well. When people asked me if

I'd been born again, I'd say, "Yes, and again, and again." Even as a child, I was never able to feel like my "decision" for Christ was a one-time event. I felt that the process of spiritually growing up required renewing those vows often.

When I learned that the Greek words actually contained a double meaning, I was intrigued. "Born again" or "born from above"— either and both meanings were probably intended by the writer. They make clear that a spiritual birth is different from a physical one, but that there are similarities from which we can learn. The words bring me comfort whenever I feel the birth pangs of something new ready to come forth. It isn't always comfortable; I know from past experience that birthing is hard, messy, unpredictable.

Sometimes I feel as if I'm giving birth to something, and sometimes I feel as if I'm the one being birthed again: squeezed and shoved out into a new place that is no longer warm and safe. I'm comforted by the knowledge that we have been counseled, "You must be birthed again, from above."

Loving God, help us to be encouraged when we feel the birth pangs begin. Help us to trust that you are birthing something new in us that will glorify you. Amen.

Amy E. Greene

Busyness

For freedom Christ has set us free. Stand firm,
therefore, and do not submit again to a yoke of slavery.
—Galatians 5:1

Some of my retired friends were talking about how surprised they were to be so busy in retirement: traveling, volunteering, spending time with grandchildren, housekeeping, yard work, hobbies, church work, civic activities, community events. One friend said she had never been this busy while employed.

Busyness can consume us. Busyness crowds our calendars and misleads us into believing we are making a contribution, that we are helping others, that we are living. But we also have the freedom to live quietly, deliberately, peacefully, even contemplatively: "Christ has set us free." We can choose to "stand firm" and claim that freedom. We don't have to "submit again to a yoke of slavery."

Those held captive to busyness vacuum their carpets every day. They volunteer for a task in every organization to which they belong. They are active in every club in town. They attend every community event. They think, "If I don't do it, nothing will get done."

Free women and men recognize that God calls them to relinquish their egos and relish life in new ways. They take time to just sit and invite God's presence with them. They schedule only one or two events a day so that they have energy for what is truly important. They don't get mired in ruts.

Often our multiple, non-stop activities interfere with the tasks God wants us to concentrate on, the things God wants us to do that only we can do. What could you do if you gave up your busyness? What would God have you do with your freedom?

Lord Christ, you set us free. Help us to learn how to reject busyness and how to serve you and your purposes in perfect freedom. Amen.

Amanda Palmer

My Redemption Flower

When Jesus saw their faith, he said to the paralytic, "Son, your sins are forgiven....I say to you, stand up, take your mat and go to your home."
—Mark 2:5,11

On my desk sits a flower. It has been there for years. I call it my redemption flower. It is really a tin can lid that a friend cut, bent, and fashioned into a beautiful piece of art—a flower with petals and leafy tendrils. It reminds me that with God, with deep-abiding faith in God, anything is possible. Even a useless piece of tin, removed from the top of a can and rescued from the trash heap, can be redeemed, set free, and made whole again.

Looking at my flower also takes my thoughts down another path. When I look at my flower, I often wonder how many cuts and nicks my artist friend had on her hands as she worked with shears and sharp metal to create this piece of beauty. Then I think about how many cuts, nicks, and bruises we all experience on the journey of life. We leave untended so many of these wounds that they paralyze us and keep us from being who God intends us to be.

With a little help from my artist friend, a seemingly worthless piece of tin was made whole and gives beauty and meaning to my day. My flower is a visible reminder of the wholeness that can be ours—in spite of the brokenness of our lives—because of our faith.

Gracious God, you sent your only Son as a ransom for our lives, to set us free so that we might live life abundantly. Help us to recognize the possibilities in every humble experience. Strengthen us in our faith that we might be visible symbols of wholeness in our broken world. We ask this in the name of Jesus. Amen.

Marjorie A. Burke

If Only

"Look at the birds of the air; they neither sow nor reap nor gather into barns, and yet your heavenly Father feeds them. Are you not of more value than they?"
—Matthew 6:26

After watching birds for more than forty years, one of my great joys this past winter was to have birds eat from my hand. I stand very still, my outstretched hand filled with sunflower seeds, and also with seeds on my shoulders and head. Chickadees, nuthatches, and tufted titmice take seeds from my hand, my head, and my shoulders. I have come to love each of the birds with a deep passion.

It has occurred to me that God might feel much as I feel: standing in the cold, knowing I have food that will keep those birds alive and well, if only they will come, if only they can trust me enough to overcome their fear, if only they can understand how much I love them and want the best for them.

I think God works very hard to show us how much we are loved. Then I realize I am like those birds—so fearful, so lacking in trust, yet wanting very much to be loved and safe and warm and fed. But it's so hard to trust, to believe that God could really love even me.

It is terribly exciting when a bird lands on me. Could it be that God is just as excited when we give even a portion of our heart to God? When we are able to trust God a little? When we find the courage to see Christ in our neighbor, if only for a moment?

Patient God, you wait for us with outstretched arms. But we hold back in fear, uncertain of what turning to you will mean. Calm our fears; still our anxious minds. Our souls long for the love you offer us. Grant us the courage simply to rest in your presence, sure of your faithfulness, content with the food and drink you offer us. We are trying, Lord. Wait for us. Amen.

Dianne L. Mansfield

In My Own Language

"...I will change the speech of the peoples to a pure speech, that all of them may call on the name of the Lord *and serve him with one accord."*
—Zephaniah 3:9

Just as there are different languages and dialects, so there are different languages that God uses to speak to each of us. We don't have to wonder or worry if God understands what we are saying because God is the designer and creator of language. Yet often we don't recognize our language when it's spoken to us. We pray eloquent prayers, we moan and we groan, we cry, we plead with God to pleeeease speak to us. We plead with our Savior to direct our paths; we plead with our Lord to hear us when we pray. We get angry at God because we feel that God is not speaking to us.

However, God does speak to us! Our problem is that we are trying to listen to God in a language that is not our own. God hears us, and God sends us a response. But because we try to comprehend in a language different from that which God gave us, we miss the blessings that are in store for us.

We need to pray for wisdom and ask God to incline our ears to find the right frequency so that we can recognize the language God has provided each of us. We ought not concern ourselves with how God speaks to anyone else. It doesn't matter how God speaks to our spouses, our friends, our pastors, or our children. We are unique individuals, and God has given each of us her or his own language. Our marvelous Creator has no problem recognizing who we are when we speak. Likewise, we should have no problem recognizing the voice of the Chosen One, who speaks to us in an individual language.

Lord, thank you for providing us with a direct channel to you. We're blessed that, once we have learned to recognize and speak it, we can communicate with you in our own language. Amen.

Inga O. Green

Uncluttering Our Lives

*Shake yourself from the dust, rise up, O captive
Jerusalem; loose the bonds from your neck,
O captive daughter Zion!*
—Isaiah 52:2

When my husband and I entered the "empty nest" phase, we both felt the Lord's urging to "simplify" our lives. Part of that process was selling our large, sprawling home and purchasing a place half its size. The task of downsizing seemed overwhelming. I am, by nature, a pack rat. I hold on to boxes, drawers, closets, and sometimes rooms full of mementos, seeming essentials, and potentials. As this mountain of belongings loomed before me, I decided to consult a friend who is one of the most organized people I know. Deborah insisted I give her permission to be severe. Optimist that I am, I enthusiastically agreed.

The test of this agreement would be her first chore, the kitchen. My most intimate domain was the culmination of twenty-five years in kitchen gadget stores. I'd been on one long continuous quest to find and purchase the next new gizmo that promised to make my life simpler and easier.

Deborah began by opening one of my many gadget drawers. It was neat and orderly; I thought she would be impressed. She paused, looked up at me in consternation, and said determinedly, "Pick four things, the rest goes."

I wailed, "NO!" Such a fuss I put up. Nevertheless, I knew it was the right thing to do. The process was liberating and became our pattern for downsizing.

At this point, I began asking myself some questions. How much time and money had I invested in things? Where did utility stop and wastefulness begin? When did the things become burdens, chains?

But removing the material things was only part of the solution. Deborah opened a drawer and helped me see the chains of material possessions. The Holy Spirit needed to open my heart and help me see the real chains. As I uncluttered my old house to move into my new one, I realized I needed to do the same with my heart daily. "Search me, God, and know my mind. Test me and know my thoughts, and see if there's anything in me that leads to pain, and lead me on the everlasting way" (Psalm 139:23-24, American Translation).

Abba, I give you permission to organize and clean my "house." Search me and help me to remove any chains of captivity in my heart. Amen.

Terri Gillespie

Fear Not

Perfect love casts out fear.
—1 John 4:18a

Somewhere I heard that "Fear not" is the phrase spoken by Jesus that appears most often in the Bible. Jesus must have known what a stumbling block fear is for us. Out of our mouths too often come the words, "I'm afraid that it's going to rain; I can't learn this assignment; I can't make this public speech." We seem to be unaware that such statements flood our energy fields with negativity and make the "feared" more likely to happen. Fear is subtle and can sneak up on us quickly. Top athletes have to let go of fear to perform.

When I was thirty-five, someone told me to "do the thing you fear and the death of fear is certain." I subsequently picked skiing as the thing most feared and went alone to challenge the slopes. Jokingly I remarked thereafter that my nail prints remain in the side of my ski instructor. What I now realize is that my many prayers to overcome fear that day were being answered with an extra bolt of love and courage. I continued to ski with enjoyment.

What is the remedy for this stance of fear? Jesus told us clearly that it is perfect love that enables trust. He also told us to ask and we shall receive. I believe he was talking about an energy flow that is always available when we become very still, very clear about our request and intention, when we focus our minds and hearts and allow ourselves to receive the quietness and energy of love. Courage will then follow.

Oh God, grant us the wisdom to take "I'm afraid" language out of our thoughts. Grant us the patience to become still and focused while requesting love energy. Thus we can allow it to flow through us, enabling us to become unafraid. Amen.

Judith Northen Eastman

Cease Striving and Know...

"Be still, and know that I am God!"
—Psalm 46:10a

Two other translations of this Scripture are "Cease striving and know that I am God" and "Pause awhile and know that I am God." All three translations call forth a desire to focus on the *being*, not the *doing*, in my life. So often the doing takes over and the being gets lost. And so do I. There needs to be a balance between the doing and the being, but the emphasis in our society today is on the doing.

Many of us who were brought up in the traditional Christian church were neither encouraged nor taught how to "be still." So for me as an adult, it has taken many years, much patience, and much grace to "be still and know that God is God" and to listen to God's still small voice that speaks to my soul in the stillness. I believe that this invitation to listen, to be with God, is vital to a deeper intimate relationship with the Holy One.

Most of us do not like to "pause awhile," because when we begin to "be still," we hear our hearts scream: "Please listen, please listen." Listen to God as God speaks to your heart. God's desire is to be with you, to sit with you with a loving gaze. "Pause awhile and know that I am God."

All of my spiritual readings, my personal experience, and the experiences of many others have taught me that it is through being still and knowing God is God that the doing unfolds.

God of balance, your desire is for us to take time to be still, to cease striving, and to know you. Give us the desire to be, so that our doing comes out of being still and knowing you. Amen.

Sara J. Davis-Shappell

How Deep Is Your Well? Is the Water Muddy?

But the wisdom from above is first pure, then peaceable, gentle, willing to yield, full of mercy and good fruits, without a trace of partiality or hypocrisy. And a harvest of righteousness is sown in peace for those who make peace.
—*James 3:17-18*

As a small child, I lived on a farm in western Colorado. We had no well. Our household water supply was stored in a large cistern my father had dug and lined with cement.

One spring our cistern went dry. We needed water. Snow was melting in the higher elevations and bringing a light gray silt from the area called Chalk Mountain. Mother was not very pleased with the thought of having our cistern filled with such murky water. Dad assured her the mud would settle and soon the water would be clear.

He siphoned water from the ditch with a long canvas hose, filling the cistern to the brim. He added the right amount of chlorine to make it safe for drinking. Then we waited.

Sure enough, in a couple of days the water ran crystal clear from the hand pump in the kitchen. Suppose Mother had tried to speed the process by stirring the water?

How often in our spiritual lives we find muddy water. And we want it to be made clear NOW! We are instructed to wait and pray. But in an action-oriented society like ours, waiting is hard.

God has promised living water when we invite Christ into our lives. He does not say it will always run clear and trouble-free. What muddies our water? We often deal with people in the real world who do not have our best interests at heart. Even those who love us may exert pressure on us that jangles our nerves and saps our energy. We may wake in the night crying, "Where are you, Lord? My water is muddy, and I thirst!" Does Christ appear at your bedside with a cup of cold water? No. But he will give you strength to pray and wait for your spiritual water to clear.

Do you ever muddy someone else's water? An unkind word or quick retort may go far deeper than we think. Who among us has not wished we had thought and prayed before we spoke? We should not be so focused on ourselves that we forget the feelings of others. An apology to one we have thoughtlessly hurt will do much to settle our own spiritual waters as well as theirs.

Gracious God, we confess we feel unsettled at times in our lives. We hurry and dash about full of troubled water. Calm our spirits and restore our souls. Please use us as vessels of living water. Help us to be patient while the turmoil settles. Amen.

Nona Kelley Carver

Sacred Places

*Extol the LORD our God, and worship at
his holy mountain: for the LORD our God is holy.*
—Psalm 99:9

When I was a child growing up in a secluded rural area, miles from the nearest town and the next community, I was not allowed to venture out of our own small community. So my four cousins and I spent enjoyable weekend afternoons hiking up our sacred mountain to sit on our high cliff. There, we could look out and see three other communities and wonder aloud what exciting activities were taking place "over there."

Then we would lie on the warm rocks in the cool mountain breeze and dream our futures. That mountain was my haven, my place to dream in what I thought was an otherwise mundane, boring life. Those experiences taught me to appreciate solitude and to seek out other mountains where the voices of my ancestors whisper in the wind and the awesomeness of God's creation stirs my deepest emotions and brings me inner peace.

Just as certain mountains were holy to people of biblical times, we Native Americans have our sacred mountains where we can cleanse our minds, where visions and dreams come with greater clarity. Our Great Creator dwells not only in synagogues and sanctuaries but can also be found upon the pinnacles of high places. It is there that we are given power and strength as we come face to face with our Creator. Mountains also give us a towering image of Mother Earth touching Father Sky.

Black Elk, a great Sioux visionary, expressed our feelings well:

> We should understand well that all things are the works of the Great Spirit. We should know that He is within all things: the trees, the grasses, the rivers, the mountains, and the four-legged animals, and winged people; and even more important, we should understand that He is also above all these things and peoples.

Great God, whose spirit is in the earth among us, help us never to forget to seek our sacred mountains and places for dreaming.

Create within us a spirit of responsibility to care for all of your creation and to bring justice to a world full of chaos so that those who are treated unjustly may experience your love and saving grace. Amen.

Evangeline W. Lynch

A Peaceful Place

He leads me beside still waters; he restores my soul.
—Psalm 23:2-3

While attending a retreat for interim ministers at Green Lake, Wisconsin, I took many walks every day. It was good exercise and a time for meditation and prayer. One day before going on my walk, I decided to take a pencil and paper to write notes for sermon preparation. As I walked out to the Point, I experienced the power of God's presence. He was speaking to me in the rippling of the waters, in the wind, in the smell of the atmosphere. The very air I breathed was full of God's spirit. Moreover, I experienced the peace of God as never before. I sat down on the bench and began writing:

I heard the sound of peace.
And saw the waters playing among the rocks and branches.
I felt the joy of the wind on my face and
Saw the color of peace on the lake.
I could smell peace in the atmosphere as it rushed out to sea.
That was a peaceful place.

As I pondered this experience, I affirmed to myself that the real peaceful place is in the heart: the place where God dwells within you and me. Have you found that place where you know that God is waiting to speak to you? It is a place deep within, where you experience the presence of God. Have you gone to that peaceful place where you see the face of God? I cannot take that journey to Green Lake every day, but I can experience my peaceful place as I sit quietly and listen to the voice of God within.

O God, who is both father and mother, thank you for providing the places that nourish our souls, and places of rest and relaxation for the mind and body. We give you thanks for caring for our needs. Lord, we thank you for your love and mercy. Teach us to love one another as you have loved us. We pray in Jesus' name. Amen.

Blanche Clipper Hudson

Simply Ask and God Will Quench Your Thirst

The woman said to him, "Sir, give me this water, so that I may never be thirsty or have to keep coming here to draw water."
—John 4:15

There have been times and seasons in my life and ministry when my to-do list seems to get longer and longer rather than shorter and shorter. Times when the more I do, the more there is left to do. When my days and nights are filled with comings and goings, deadlines and appointments. When my mind has absorbed and given out all that it conceivably can. Physically, I feel drained, empty and dehydrated. Surely, during these times I have pushed my body and mind to their limits, and more than anything I need renewing.

This fall, I listened very attentively to the signals in my body and spirit and decided to retreat to the mountains to spend time with my Creator. Humbly I asked God to replenish my spirit, to revive my body and soul. I must admit I had no idea of the blessing that would come simply because I asked for and was open to receiving all that God had for me.

My journey began on a Sunday, following morning worship. I packed my bags and food to prepare for seven days. I scheduled mornings for meditating and praying, afternoons for exercise, and evenings for writing and relaxing.

What joys I experienced during that week. I granted God permission to "minister to his minister," to rearrange my schedule and my priorities, to heal me in places where I was covering open wounds with smiles, and to forgive me for my shortcomings. It seemed that the more of me I offered to God the more God received and blessed me. I remember leaving the mountain a different person. I understood completely why Jesus spent so much time alone in communion with the Father.

It is you, Lord, during times when we are empty and our souls have gone dry, and our spirits and bodies have grown weary, who speaks to our condition and offers us healing. Thank you, God, for quenching our thirst when we humble ourselves and ask. Amen.
Judy L. Brown

The Cactus

Jesus said to her, "I am the resurrection and the life.
Those who believe in me, even though they die,
will live, and everyone who lives and believes
in me will never die."
—John 11:25-26

Two years ago I purchased a small cactus from K-Mart for $1.95. I was drawn to it because it pictured perfectly the desert dryness I was experiencing. By this spring, the cactus was four feet tall with its fragile top bending toward the sun. It was ugly and had outgrown the pot. I took it to the florist, who promptly turned it over to her husband, the cactus expert.

After repotting it, he returned it with the suggestion that I cut off the top and plant it. Then, he said, I would have two healthy plants. He cut off the top, and I took it to my basement floor, where it lay for six weeks before I planted it. Both parts of the plant oozed a white milky substance that gave them a deathly appearance. I was sure I'd made a mistake and was even more convinced of this when early summer winds tore the plants from the soil, necessitating several replantings.

When I left on vacation in July, neither cactus resembled anything I would want to bring into the house. The top portion especially was withered with only a thin strip of green about six inches long up one side. The base held no beauty or character. I felt certain they were both destined for the trash.

However, upon returning from vacation, the cacti caught my eye. The bottom portion was thriving. In fact, it was beautiful! The small green portion of the top had grown and branched out with new life. The florist was right!

As I contemplate the cactus, I see a picture of life. We all have wounds that appear as though they will lead to death. We grieve and sometimes lose hope. But when cared for and brought into the light, we can thrive once again.

God, come to us in our dryness and fill us with light and life. Heal our woundedness and guide us to become your catalysts for healing others. Amen.

Jo Ellen Witt

It's Hard to Wait

But those who wait for the LORD shall renew their strength, they shall mount up with wings like eagles, they shall run and not be weary, they shall walk and not faint.
—Isaiah 40:31

Imagine the disciples' emotional meters in the days following Easter. From the depths of despair, they begin to wonder and hope because the tomb is empty. Then they reach the heights of marvel and joy when they see the risen Jesus. They understand God's plan, revealed in the Scriptures, and are caught up in the excitement of it all. They receive a glorious commission. With miracles behind and promises ahead, they must certainly have been poised for action. And then Jesus tells them to wait.

Jesus could not have asked anything harder of them. In the midst of such earth-shattering news, how could he suggest doing nothing?

Whenever we are told to wait, we suffer the same frustration. Waiting is just plain hard. We want things fixed, we want questions answered, we want to get on with it, whatever "it" is. It is so difficult simply to be and not to do. But waiting is often necessary in order to be filled with the Spirit and empowered to reach new levels of doing. We need to be with our thoughts and sort them, to be with our emotions and honor them, to be with God and trust him.

Gracious God of action and of pauses, fill us with excitement as we await your next instructions. And fill us with your Spirit as we go about obeying your commission. Amen.

Darla Dee Turlington

Leaving the Water Jar Behind

Just then his disciples came. They were astonished that he was speaking with a woman.... Then the woman left her water jar and went back to the city. She said to the people, "Come and see a man who told me everything I have ever done! He cannot be the Messiah, can he?" They left the city and were on their way to him.
—John 4:27-30

If you enter the story of the Samaritan woman at the same point the disciples do, you really don't know much about her. All you know is that she is "different" and that she seems to have some sort of relationship with the Savior. Someone might well have said, "Who does she think she is? Doesn't she know her place?"—not realizing that Jesus personally invited her to be a disciple.

Having accepted and counted the cost, the woman risks heavily and becomes vulnerable. She leaves her water jar behind and with it she leaves behind her old self. She moves forward trusting in God, no longer concerned about the naysayers.

Can you identify with this woman? Can you count the times you have been criticized or misunderstood? As he knew the woman in this story, Jesus knows your pain. Jesus has set you free; you are truly free indeed. You see, the woman doesn't need the water jar anymore. She has exchanged it for a spring that is internal and eternal and will never run dry. What part of your life is God calling you to leave behind with the water jar you keep trying to fill with things of this world? Have you forgotten what water flows within?

Dear God, empower us to leave our empty water jars behind. We continually dip into them and come up dry. Remind us that spiritual, fulfilling water will be granted only through our relationship with you. Amen.

Susan R. Street-Beavers

A New Spirit

*Create in me a clean heart, O God, and put a new and right spirit within me. Do not cast me away from your presence, and do not take your holy spirit from me.
Restore to me the joy of your salvation,
and sustain in me a [generous] spirit.*
—Psalm 51:10-12

Ever since I became a mother, my spiritual life has changed radically, along with everything else! There was a time, which I shall call pre-child, when I aimed to find at least twenty minutes every morning to commune with God in meditation and prayer. All that went completely out the window when I gave birth to this beautiful new life, my daughter. In those early months I was totally focused on meeting her needs, and I found it virtually impossible to maintain the kind of devotional life I had prior to motherhood.

No one could have told me how exhausted I would feel as a parent. Sleep deprivation saps my liveliness, spark, get-up-and-go—but I still keep going. One of the results is that I feel not only physically depleted but also spiritually bereft. I am giving just about every ounce of myself, but my gift is lacking in grace. A spirit of generosity evades me.

One day my husband asked me, "Do you feel closer to God now than you did before our daughter was born?" I realized that on one level, I felt the most profound gratitude to God for answering my prayers and bringing this incredible blessing into my life. But on another, deeper level, I found that I was yearning for a renewed relationship with God. God felt distant. I wasn't communicating with God very much. And I wasn't taking time to listen for God's word for me. I felt "cast away from God's presence." I felt disconnected from the Holy Spirit.

Amidst the demands of parenthood, I've had to redefine spiritual growth. I slowly discovered that it takes place in moments, and I have to be on the lookout for such opportunities to encounter God. Those precious moments when my daughter laughs, I choose to remember that God is the source of all our joy. My ideas about prayer have evolved, too. In many ways my prayer is more contextual. I am challenged to give just as much validity to the prayers that I can say in snatches of time as to those that I arrive at in twenty minutes of sitting meditation. As I take my daughter for a walk in the stroller, I use the time for a kind of walking meditation, breathing in the beauty of creation.

There are times when only a dose of solitude will restore me to some equilibrium. When I need explicit solitude with God, my husband watches our daughter to give me the time and space that I need.

I find these words from Psalm 51 particularly comforting and strengthening. Simply repeating these words is a prayer for restoration. It gives me a spiritual energy boost. I am seeking a new spirit within me! I am asking God to take away my spirit of exhaustion, lack of reserves, crankiness, and to put a new and generous spirit within me. These are words of assurance. God can restore me to joy and give me a spirit of perseverance that will sustain me.

Generous and loving God, restore joy to my soul, refresh my spirit, and give me the strength I need to care for myself and for my family. Grant me a spirit of generosity and steadfastness in all I do. Amen.

Kolya Braun-Greiner

Choosing Mary and Martha

"Mary has chosen the better part…"
—Luke 10:42 (For the full context, read Luke 10:38-42.)

Several times in recent years I have heard the story of Martha and Mary spoken of as if it were about choosing between doing and being. But both these women live in me: the busy doer and the contemplative learner. How do I balance this reality?

That day in Bethany, Jesus declared that Mary had chosen the better part. But perhaps the full truth of that statement is that Mary had chosen what was right for the moment. She knew what was called for on that particular day when Jesus came to teach and to be present in love. But how would Mary respond in a time of natural disaster? What would Mary do in the situations mentioned in Matthew 25, when people need to be fed, clothed, or visited in prison? Martha would obviously excel in that moment. Would Mary? We can't tell from Luke's short story.

Both these women live in me. Can I be "well-balanced" in my doing and my being? I believe I can, but only if I remain attentive, in the moment, to what Jesus is doing and being. Doing and being cannot be separated; they exist simultaneously. Keeping a balance between the two is predicated on the presence and power of Jesus Christ.

As I write this, I can hear a baby crying in another part of the church. I know it's okay for me to ignore that cry (which has stopped now) because other people are tending that child. But if God were calling me to child-care today, all the silent reflection in the world would be without merit. And likewise, if I rush each morning to do the work of ministry without spending my quiet, listening time with God, what is the worth of my work?

Mary and Martha. You and me. Jesus Christ invites us into a loving relationship that brings wholeness and balance to our lives. May we choose wisely, today and every day.

Lord God, Giver of this moment and of eternity, Who am I? I am nothing but what your grace has made me. My doing, my being, my thinking, my praying—all come from you. Help me lose myself in you that I may be found in all that you lead me to be and do. Amen.

Karen Ann Selig

The Fruit of the Spirit

By contrast, the fruit of the Spirit is love, joy, peace,
patience, kindness, generosity, faithfulness,
gentleness, and self-control.
—Galatians 5:22-23

For the hundredth time since I began my job at the factory five years ago, I sat in my cubicle staring at the verse on the bulletin board. "The fruit of the Spirit..." No matter how hard I stared at the bulletin board I couldn't get "frustration" onto the list.

I manage the marketing communications group for a manufacturer in my hometown. Three members of the staff are designers; all five are younger men. I have been variously challenged managing this group, but it helped to post the verse. It was another workingwoman, the conductor of our local symphony, who gave me the idea.

Last fall I attended a women's professional development conference where this conductor was listed as a keynote speaker. She was new in town, and her predecessor had been rumored to be notoriously talented and egotistical. I had no reason to expect her to act any differently.

Midway through her speech, I began to be surprised. I began to notice her many references to a spiritual life and her straightforward statements about God's role in her daily transactions as a musician and leader.

I was amazed that a prominent woman would risk alienating those of other beliefs and cultures by doing something so un-"politically correct" as to not only mention, but give full credit to her Christianity as a primary motivator in her life. In explaining how she dealt with the difficulties of being a woman in a man's field, she quoted Galatians, listing the qualities of the fruit of the Spirit.

When I returned from the conference, I found the verse, printed it out with a border, and tacked it on the bulletin board. When I want to test my reaction to a situation, I see if what I feel is a fruit of the Spirit or if it is something I need to ignore or get over. With God's help, the Holy Spirit is working more in my life than ever before, and daily I hope to see a more bountiful harvest of his fruits.

Dear God, you have given us the Holy Spirit to work in our lives, to help us even when we don't know what to pray for. May we be ever thankful for the fruit of the Spirit. Amen.

Melinda McDonald

"I Don't Speak Norwegian"

"The reason I speak to them in parables is that 'seeing they do not perceive, and hearing they do not listen, nor do they understand.' With them indeed is fulfilled the prophecy of Isaiah that says: 'You will indeed listen, but never understand, and you will indeed look, but never perceive. For this people's heart has grown dull, and their ears are hard of hearing, and they have shut their eyes; so that they might not look with their eyes, and listen with their ears, and understand with their heart and turn—and I would heal them.' But blessed are your eyes, for they see, and your ears, for they hear."
—Matthew 13:13-16

Because of my blue eyes and blonde hair, people have often told me that I look Scandinavian. (My ancestry is Irish and German.) Recently when my husband and I enjoyed a three-week tour of Denmark, Sweden, and Norway, it wasn't unusual in shops or on the street for people to mistake me for a local, addressing me in the native tongue. This led to my embarrassment when I couldn't respond with a single word of their language, and it resulted in a rather humorous incident.

In the third week of our trip, we were staying in a hotel in Oslo, Norway. I had become somewhat resigned to not being able to understand the ordinary conversations around me. We had seen very few Americans on our trip. Therefore, when I heard the welcome sounds of English being spoken by people approaching our small elevator, I was delighted. A woman was conversing with her husband about whether or not they should wait for the next elevator because it appeared that she and her party would not fit.

Here at last was a situation in which I could fully participate, and I took pleasure in the fact that I could address these strangers and be understood. I eagerly encouraged them to join us, saying, "Come right in; there's plenty of room."

However, the woman looked at me blankly and said, "I don't speak Norwegian." Baffled, I replied, "But I'm speaking English!" She looked chagrined. She had already judged me to be Norwegian and was therefore fully prepared not to understand a word I said. She fooled herself into thinking that I was speaking Norwegian instead of her native American English.

This is an example of an all-too-common response we all have to our surroundings. Much of the time we go through the day oblivious to what is really going on around us. We are intent on our own agenda, and we prejudge everything according to the way in which we need to see it: "I know what you're going to say before you say it, so don't even bother!" We often hear but do not understand.

Jesus said we do this because our hearts have grown dull. When we close our ears and our eyes to what a person is actually going to say or do, we miss the opportunity of truly knowing that person and broadening our understanding. Jesus the Christ tells us that when we shut out others in this way, we miss moments when our hearts might be touched and we can experience Christ's healing. If we shut down our openness to the world around us, we shut off our access to those moments of grace that come from being touched by other souls.

Creator God, open our ears and our eyes so that we will not miss the moments you give us for understanding with our hearts. Help us to appreciate and truly to see the beautiful world that surrounds us. May we live every moment fully and be open to those around us so that we can experience your love and grace. Amen.
Carol K. McCollough

Peaceful Borders

He grants peace within your borders;
he fills you with the finest of wheat.
—Psalm 147:14

I love my children dearly, but some days being a mother is the hardest thing I do. "Mom, he hit me!" "Mom, he kicked me!" "Mom, he has my toy!" "Mom, he dumped out my marbles!" I have so much experience refereeing fights that I could hire out professionally in my spare time. I have a friend who says, "Whoever doesn't believe in original sin never had children!"

Training my sons to be Christlike can drive me to the edge of my self-control. There are days when I put one in one room, and the other in another room, and draw the boundaries. I create peaceful borders to maintain sanity for all of us. And usually, after half an hour, peace does reign. My "angelic" sons return and play enthusiastically with each other.

There is so much conflict in our adult human world. I often wonder what God's solution is as God seeks to mother us. I'm sure there are days when God despairs and would like to put us all in our own rooms, drawing peaceful borders to protect the world and to protect us from one another. At other times, we create our own borders, walling off "the other." As adults, we often still act out the power plays of our youth. But isn't that why God sent Jesus to us?

Jesus came to eradicate the warring borders we create between ourselves. He seeks to erase the walls between race, age, sex, and class. He came to show us how to restore our brokenness with each other—and with God. Letting Jesus be Lord of our life can bring peace to our inner lives, as well as to the borders of the world around us. When you pick up a newspaper and read about two warring nations, two companies in heated conflict, two families in dispute, don't despair. Remember that God, like a mother, watches us closely. And if we listen, God will offer the wisdom and solutions that we need.

God, who loves us like a mother and who cries for us when we go astray, reach out your arms and hold us tight. Open our ears to the words of correction that you would offer. Give us the wisdom to create peaceful borders in our homes, our communities, and our world. Amen.

Joyce Anderson Reed

Revelation through Interference

*A windstorm swept down on the lake, and the boat was
filling with water, and they were in danger.
They went to him and woke him up, shouting,
"Master, Master, we are perishing!"
—Luke 8:23b-24a*

It's easy to imagine this scene: the taste of salt, the sound of roaring wind, the feel of cold water washing over you and covering your feet, the panic rising within you until it is as deep as the sea water filling your boat. How could you not awaken the Master and cry out that all of you are perishing?

Yet Jesus rebukes the disciples, saying, "Where is your faith?"

Where was the lack of faith? Surely not in waking Jesus, who immediately removed the danger by calming the wind and waves. Perhaps in shouting to him, "We are perishing!" And behind that shout, the belief that he and they could perish, and God's plan for redemption could be interrupted.

What do interruptions in our plans—natural interferences and accidental errors—do to our faith? Driving to a conference one morning, I drove fifty miles out of the way and missed a session. Was I mad! "Why didn't you prevent that, Lord?" I asked. Not nearly as threatening as a swamped boat in a storm, but the same expectation that troubles or aggravations should not get in the way of good plans. Beneath my annoyance was a false faith in God as a "lucky charm" that makes things go my way. When it's smooth sailing, I'm confident God is in control. When things go wrong, I'm sure confident he has jumped ship. What foolishness!

God's gift of presence has nothing to do with earthly circumstances. Faith trusts that God's purposes will be fulfilled in spite of threats, dangers, detours, even destruction. Divine power is revealed, not in preventing trouble but in getting us through it in a way that testifies to who God is. The disciples "were filled with great awe and said to one another, 'Who then is this, that even the wind and the sea obey him?'" (Mark 4:41).

Merciful God, who knows the plans you have for us, enable us to find, even in interferences and frustrations, an opportunity to see your power at work. Amen.

Darla Dee Turlington

The Abnormal

*Jesus rebuked the demon, and it came out of him,
and the boy was cured instantly.
—Matthew 17:18*

If you read the Bible daily, you know how the passages you read on a particular day often "match" your present life circumstances. On the morning I read the passage about Jesus healing an epileptic boy, I had just recovered from a migraine headache. Medical experts say that migraines and epilepsy are related—both involve abnormal electrical activity in the brain.

Jesus' rebuke of the abnormal—the demon—brings an instant cure for epilepsy. It makes me wonder whether all cures start with divine rebukes of the "abnormal."

Our resurrection from the dead may be God's ultimate rebuke of the abnormal. According to Genesis, death was not part of God's original plan. Rather, it is a consequence of human sin. The more sins pile up, the more we sicken and die inside. Death is a gift God gave us to remind us to keep in touch with him. Without death to frighten us, without the dread of an accounting to the Supreme, many people would never even look for God.

Death serves to remind us of the consequences of sin, of living our lives only for ourselves. It keeps us from being too secure, too smug, too self-reliant. It keeps our hearts from becoming too hardened against God. Facing death, one has to admit the sin—the "abnormal" in one's life—and to ask God to rebuke it in order to be cured. The twentieth century told us that sin was normal and goodness was abnormal. That is a lie. May God grant us in the twenty-first century the wisdom to plead for the normal, the healthy, the whole, the good.

Lord Jesus, we admit we live abnormally, often by our own choices. Forgive us and draw us closer to you. Rebuke the abnormal wherever it appears. Cure us, that we may be of one mind, one body, one spirit with you. Amen.

Amanda Palmer

Coming Apart

The apostles gathered around Jesus, and told him
all that they had done and taught. He said to them,
"Come away to a deserted place
all by yourselves and rest a while."
—Mark 6:30-31

It was a rare occasion when my mother misbehaved in church. Every now and then, however, she would whisper something in my ear that would set us both to giggling. One Sunday the preacher intoned with great seriousness as he read this passage from Mark. In the King James Version, it was translated, "Come ye yourselves apart for a while...." My mother leaned over and whispered to me, "They had better come apart for a while or they'll come apart for good." I knew she was onto something. My mother knew well that if you didn't "come apart" to rest, you would "come apart" in a much worse way. She was a hard worker— a nurse and an exceptional homemaker—so she knew the value of resting.

I've tried to learn from her in my work as a chaplain. If I pay attention to my need for rest, I'm much better at what I do. This may seem obvious, but it took a while for me to resist the workaholic thrust of the culture we live in: to choose a ten-minute nap over another shot of caffeine. I find that I'm much more intuitive and can listen to people on several levels if I take the time to "come apart" regularly.

One afternoon on a long drive to see a hospice patient, I decided to pull over and close my eyes for ten minutes. I dozed and awoke refreshed. When I got to the patient's bedside, she was tossing and turning, repeating the phrase "I just want to get over." Her family, loving and attentive, assumed she wanted to turn to her other side, so they kept helping her readjust her pillows. I wondered if she might be talking about a different kind of "getting over," perhaps to the life beyond this one. I took a risk and said, "Don't worry, you'll be able to get over when the time comes."

She stopped her tossing, looked deep into my eyes, and relaxed back into her bed. She died the next day. I was glad I had "come apart" before visiting her, so that I could be open to hearing her on more than one level.

Loving God, help us to know when to rest. Amen.

Amy E. Greene

In Silence

I will instruct you and teach you the way you should go;
I will counsel you with my eye upon you.
—Psalm 32:8

After reading Thomas Merton's book *New Seeds of Contemplation,* I began writing some reflections in my journal. Then out of nowhere I wrote, "Sit in the silence and allow God's Ignatius power to fill you." What was Ignatius power? I didn't know. When I asked a friend about it, she suggested I go on an Ignatius of Loyola eight-day silent retreat held near Lake Winnebago. Respecting her advice, I called and made a reservation.

As the time drew near, I began having doubts. Eight days in silence was a long time. But since I was already scheduled for a room and to meet with a spiritual director, I felt obligated to go. The first four days, after spending an hour with the director, I sat near the lake and took walks on the grounds. I read books about Ignatius and how God spoke to him in silence. In the evening I studied the Spiritual Exercises of Ignatius.

On the fifth day, I grew restless and found it increasingly difficult to sit with the other retreatants at mealtimes and not be able to talk. That night I lay in bed wanting to leave. The next morning I went into the chapel to pray. Alone and with my eyes closed, God gave me two visions. One was of myself turning into a skeleton with bones so dry they crumbled to the floor. At first it scared me, but I realized God wanted me to know I had become like the dry bones in Ezekiel. In the second vision I was handed a baby. It was Jesus. God wanted me to embrace Jesus from the cradle to the cross.

Finally God had my attention, and in the silence I learned much. He taught me that it was all right to make mistakes. He is a forgiving God. I didn't have to be perfect. And, most importantly, God taught me that my dryness came because I no longer put a priority on my time alone with God, something I really needed to do, since that is what feeds my soul.

At the end of the week, I left understanding that Ignatius's power came by trusting God in silence.

Dear Lord, may I always be willing to find your counsel in silence and never to fear my findings. Amen.

Catherine Patterson Bartell

Caution: God at Work

*Some went down to the sea in ships, doing business on
the mighty waters; they saw the deeds of the LORD,
his wondrous works in the deep. For he commanded and
raised the stormy wind, which lifted up the waves
of the sea. They mounted up to heaven, they went down
to the depths; their courage melted away in their
calamity; they reeled and staggered like drunkards,
and were at their wits' end. Then they cried to the
LORD in their trouble, and he brought them out
from their distress; he made the storm be still,
and the waves of the sea were hushed.
—Psalm 107:23-29*

In reflecting on the turmoil that sometimes invades my life, I am reminded of the sign I often see during construction on the side of the road: Caution: Men at Work. People in hard hats breaking up ground and moving foundations can be a daunting sight, an assault on the senses. When God begins to reconstruct your life, the same sensitivities apply. The breaking and reshaping of ground and the digging up of one's foundation to create something new is sometimes necessary in order to improve the construction site.

The site can also be our bodies, minds, and spirits. God often has to reshape our environment and disrupt the comfort of our surroundings in order to reshape us into the spiritually mature creatures God wants us to be.

Reconstruction can be an unsettling, noisy, and complicated process. Reconstruction is not a comfortable place to live. But if God is at the helm, you know you have the best builder on earth! After all, as a believer in the midst of trouble, don't you ask God for help? Don't you ask for God to make a way? Don't you turn the situation over to God? Don't you pray for the breakthrough?

Whenever times are unsure and the ground gets shaky, in the midst of your praying, know the breakthrough is on its way. Don't be surprised by the sight, sound, and feel of the situation when the breakthrough is near. It may even appear to be getting worse. No one said the way through and over was going to be easy. Expect some pain, some trials, and some tribulations while the situation is being remolded. God's just turning over the old soil and preparing fresh ground for you to harvest and grow.

In the midst of it all, while you are being swayed by the winds of change, know that God reigns. God controls how far you will lean to the left or right. God will never fail you. At the end of construction, you will be a renewed creature in Christ, with new possibilities, new insights, new courage, and a new spirit of wisdom. And you will be closer to the one who is the only true and living Savior. So in the midst of the chaos, be strong, be steadfast, be unmovable, have faith and fear not. It's only God at work.

Holy God, while we are in the midst of change, give us strength to endure. Give us hope and the ability to see a new vision of your will for us. Let us know that you are always in control, and even in the midst of our trials, let us see your light through the darkness. Give us peace in knowing you are always near. Amen.

Linda M. Peavy

Testimonies of God's Faithfulness.

Worshiping as One

*But now in Christ Jesus you who once were far off
have been brought near by the blood of Christ.
For he is our peace; in his flesh he has made both
groups into one and has broken down the
dividing wall, that is, the hostility between us.
—Ephesians 2:13-14*

Our new worship leader, a black man, was to arrive soon. Being a predominantly though not altogether white church, we wanted to make him and his family feel as comfortable with us as we were with hiring him. We decided to hold a welcome dinner in their honor and to wear name tags so that they could begin to associate names with faces. On these name tags there was room for each of us to write our family's nation of origin. Everyone's family did, after all, originate elsewhere, right? The idea was to emphasize our commitment to unity in diversity.

What a wonderful experience it turned out to be. We found that our blonde female associate pastor had the same Swedish background as did one of our black members, that our senior pastor's black hair and mustache were not because he was Italian but because he had Cherokee blood. In fact we found that we had more Native American tribes represented than we would ever have expected, proving that not everyone's ancestors actually did come from some other country! Over forty different nations were represented by fewer than a hundred people at the dinner. People who'd known each other for years suddenly found they had common national ancestry, resulting immediately in new levels of camaraderie.

This experience set a tone for our congregation. Today we have among our relatively small membership of two hundred, people born in thirteen different nations, including China, several African countries, and countries in South America and Europe. It is not unusual to see colorful Nigerian robes or red Chinese brocade dresses at our services, or to hear people chatting in Spanish, Swahili, or Chinese. We have folks, who identify themselves as Palestinians, fellowshiping with Jews and praying together for God's intervention in the Middle East.

I'm more personally aware that some of what I believed to be "Christian" turned out to be distinctly "American," as I've learned of the various ways in which different cultures worship the same God. I've come to regard culture as a vehicle through which we can see the manifold expressions God gives us of himself. It takes all of us, in all our varied and multi-faceted ways, over all the centuries, to make up what is the fullness of his body.

Lord, you are so far beyond anything we imagine! That you created nations with color differences and cultural variations reveals to us how multi-faceted you are in your creativity. We rejoice that you died to do away with any conditions for inclusion in or exclusion from your body. We have all been made one in you. To God be the glory. Amen.

Hannah Leafshoots

The Timber Rattler

*Devote yourselves to prayer, keeping alert
in it with thanksgiving.*
—Colossians 4:2

During a family camping trip my husband, his parents, my son, daughter, nephew, and I went out for a hike—a pleasant amble for the grown-ups, a chance to run in the woods and climb rocks for the children. Being the suburbanites we are, our wild animal contact is mostly with that ferocious beast, the backyard bunny rabbit.

All of a sudden my seven-year-old daughter, Emme, screamed the most blood-curdling scream. And then we heard rattling! Everyone except me froze. I ran up the rock and found a coiled timber rattler between Emme and me. I had never been anywhere near a rattlesnake before, yet I was strangely and completely unafraid. I simply ran around it, picked up my still-screaming daughter, and ran away.

Now you may be thinking that maternal instinct was the driving force for quick reflexes and lack of timidity. But I don't think so. As soon as we were safely out of harm's way a huge smile came across my face as I remembered something. The night before, I'd been awakened in the middle of the night with the strong sense that I needed to be prepared for something and should pray.

So, lying there in the middle of the night, I prayed that the Lord would prepare me for whatever was going to happen—for my emotions, my body, for whatever needed to be prepared—and that God would be evident in the situation. Then I felt that I needed to pray for my daughter, for her physical safety. I prayed specifically over her arms and her legs. The burden lifted and I went to sleep.

How amazing that Emme was not hurt. When she had stumbled across the snake, it was not even two feet away from her, easily within striking distance. And does she now have a tremendous fear of snakes? Not at all. Instead she knows that God woke her mommy up to pray one night. She knows that God is watching over her and protecting her, even when she is just playing in the woods.

Dear Lord, thank you for the blessing of your protection. Please give me ears always to hear when you call me to pray. Amen.

Jenny Chandler

The Back Road to China

"And remember, I am with you always..."
—Matthew 28:20b

On my eighteenth birthday, I lay paralyzed in a small Minnesota hospital. I prayed, "Lord, if you will let me walk again, I will go anywhere you want." I knew that meant Africa or China: that was where all the missionaries were serving.

I walked out of the hospital two weeks later, but my plans got sidetracked when a very handsome man named Del entered my life. (You know what life is? It's what happens while you are making other plans.) Over the years I was constantly reminded of my promise to God. But Del and I settled into a life of raising our three daughters, traveling, and being involved in our church and community. Then I again found myself paralyzed, this time with multiple sclerosis. I knew God could never use a disabled middle-aged woman. This time my prayer was, "Lord, use me in whatever way possible!"

Then my life did a complete turnaround. I saw through new eyes the hurting world around me. I was able to see that while disabilities are visible, for many the pain goes far below the surface. God, in mysterious, wonderful, magical ways, used my gifts to reach out to women though writing, speaking, and teaching. God did take me to China—by the back roads.

Our oldest daughter was unable to have children, so after much prayer she and her husband decided to adopt a baby from China. All plans and preparations were completed. Then Kris called in tears: "Mom, I can't go to China, I'm pregnant." Our second daughter, Kara, responded, "No problem, I'll go." She later called in tears of joy, "Mom, I'm pregnant." Our third daughter, Juliana, said, "No problem, I'll go." One week later, she called: "Mom, I'm pregnant."

All three daughters were pregnant, and since China is not handicapped-accessible, I could not go. Terry, Kris's husband, asked Del, his father-in-law (my husband), to go with him to China. Can you imagine sending two grey-haired men to China for three weeks to pick up an eight-month-old baby girl?

God took me by the back roads and brought China to me. Over the years, I occasionally got sidetracked on my journey, but God was always by my side carrying, guiding, encouraging, and supporting me.

Sometimes God delays the answer to our prayer in final form until we have time to build up strength, accumulate knowledge, or fashion the character that would make it possible for God to grant what we ask.

Are you struggling? Remember, God does not always send miracles down the superhighway. Be open to traveling a few back roads.

Lord, too often I pray for conditions and circumstances to change because they don't suit me, when actually the changes should take place within me. Amen.

Marlys Kroon

Complete Joy

We are writing these things so that
our joy may be complete.
—1 John 1:4

When I was young, every first Sunday afternoon was Communion day at our church. I remember that the same older people would testify about God's goodness in their lives. Some saints had the same testimony every time, so I looked forward to hearing and seeing them give their encouraging messages each first Sunday. It seemed to me they got great joy from telling and retelling how good God had been to them since the last first Sunday. Their tears, clapping, and shouting produced a powerful message of complete joy. Though the messages seemed to be the same, there was a spirit of renewed fellowship with those who gathered around the Holy Communion table to affirm that the Eternal One lives and abides in them.

Their witness of God's continuous provision, protection, and power declared to the congregation, especially to me, that since the last first Sunday God was still working miracles in their lives. I can still recall some of the testimonies: "I still have the activity of my limbs. I have a reasonable portion of health. I'm still in my right mind." I imagine that their joy was made complete repeatedly. That powerful message is written upon my heart and imprinted in my memory of those saints witnessing for Christ.

Father, teach us to testify to what we have seen and heard so that others may know you are the One who blesses us with your goodness every day. Lord, help us to know that others will come to know you and learn about your goodness through our testimony. Then let our joy be complete. In Jesus' name, we pray. Amen.

Blanche Clipper Hudson

Unknown Danger

*The LORD will guard your coming
and your going, both now and forever.*
—*Psalm 121:8, NAB*

I drove the four hundred-mile return trip from my father's funeral while my sister Maryann sat in the passenger seat reading silently from a small book of prayers. The morning sun streamed down on the road ahead, but guilt about how I hadn't spent that much time with my dad since my mother's death eight years earlier created in me a darkness I couldn't shake.

Lost in thought, I wasn't paying attention to the road signs, and I missed a sign warning me I was in a no passing zone. I came up close behind a semi-truck, and without thinking I swung out into the left lane. Instantly, my sister's voice jarred me. "Caye, go back. Don't pass."

I swung the car back in behind the truck as a car in the oncoming lane zipped by us. A dip in the road ahead had blocked my vision, and I hadn't seen the car coming toward us.

Stunned and shaken I said, "How did you know a car was there?"

"I didn't," she said. "It was just a feeling."

"Thank God," I replied, giving a sigh of relief.

Then my sister flipped the page in her book of prayers and gasped, "Caye, look."

With a quick glance I saw a picture on the left-hand page of a car passing a truck with another car coming from the opposite direction. And there above the scene stood a large image of Jesus, his hands extended in protection.

My sister read aloud the prayer printed on the right-hand page. It was for drivers. The picture and prayer convinced me that Jesus worked through my sister to save us from having a fatal accident. I also know that when Jesus allows us to see clearly his hand working in our lives, there is a reason. I believe he wanted to show me to keep my eyes on the road ahead and not let past mistakes keep me from the blessings of the present moment. My father was a loving man. He wouldn't want me to carry guilt from the past into the future.

Lord Jesus, thank you for watching over us at all times and for your everlasting help that rescues us from the unknown dangers in our path. Amen.

Catherine Patterson Bartell

The Whole Well

Jesus answered [the woman from Sychar],
"If you knew the gift of God, and who it is that is saying
to you, 'Give me a drink,' you would have asked him,
and he would have given you living water."
—John 4:10

This story of Jesus' encounter with the Samaritan woman at the well has always been one of my favorites. As I was nearing graduation from seminary, I realized how closely I related to her—and how much I had to learn.

This Samaritan woman knew *where* she had come: to the well. I knew *where* I'd come: Central Baptist Theological Seminary in Kansas City, Kansas. She knew *why* she'd come: She needed water to get her and her family through the day. I knew *why* I'd come: God had called me and I wanted to "fill up" my jar, to gather up all that I would need to fulfill that call.

She even knew *who* she was as she came. I also knew *who* I was as I came: a lay person for twenty-five years (mostly working with youth and education) and, most importantly, a child of God now willing to recognize my call to be a pastor.

She had come *prepared:* She brought a jar to fill. I, too, came *prepared*: I had brought my earthen vessel and my spirit, willing to grow. And thank God I was like her in yet one more way. Like her, I was offered not just the filling of my meager jar. I was offered the whole well.

I realized through my seminary experience that I had often limited my vision of what God intended for me. It remains easy to let other people define who I am or can become, and I sometimes bring only a "jar" that was given to me years ago. But I can remember that God offers the whole well!

The miraculous growth of an earthen jar into a whole well of living water is never easy. But blessings never cease, and I never cease to be amazed at God's goodness.

No matter how adequate I think my jar is, I live with the knowledge that there is so much more and with the assurance that God desires me to accept the whole well.

God of living water, open our eyes to the whole well of your shalom as we experience life with you, our potter and our hope. Amen.

Cheryl Gale Harader

On Trying Something New

I can do all things through [Christ] who strengthens me.
—Philippians 4:13

We all say it. Most of us say it every day: "I can't do that," "I don't know how to do that," "I don't have the ability for whatever." But Paul says that we can do all things through the power of Jesus Christ. That is a very strong statement.

When I started working for the National Ministries division of the American Baptist Churches, one of my new responsibilities was to edit a newsletter. I had never edited a newsletter, and the very idea of doing so terrified me. I was convinced I could not do it. I didn't have the foggiest notion of how to start. But this was part of my job. I confessed my fears to one of my co-workers, who wisely counseled me by saying, "The only way to do it is to start. I will show you the process, step by step."

Thanks to her, I finished my first newsletter. And thirteen years later there are hundreds of pages of newsletters, workbooks, articles, booklets, and even books that I have helped to edit. If I had listened to myself, I still would not know how to do the job.

When we confront new and scary tasks, we need to remind ourselves that with God's help we can meet the challenge. It may be true that we have never done the job before. It may be true that we're not sure how to do it. But it is not true that we cannot do the job. As long as you and I think we are not able, we will not try.

Instead of saying, "I can't do it," why not say, "Here is something new I have never tried before." Or, "This is certainly interesting. I wonder how God and I will accomplish this task!"

God, you are an awesome God. Each day you present us with new challenges that require us to put our trust in you. Give us the courage to try new things, knowing that through you all things are possible. Amen.

Mary L. Mild

Learning to Number Our Days

Lord, you have been our dwelling place in all generations. Before the mountains were brought forth, or ever you had formed the earth and the world, from everlasting to everlasting you are God. . . . So teach us to count our days that we may gain a wise heart.
—Psalm 90:1-2,12

I am reminded of the time that I chose to celebrate my fortieth birthday, an event about which I was very excited. I created a worship celebration that included "rites of passage." The worship would celebrate my passing from young adulthood into the ranks of the "elders."

I was surprised when most people I invited to join my celebration were less than enthusiastic. Some were even mean-spirited and negative. They couldn't relate to my excitement about turning forty. Nor could they imagine what kind of birthday party could be celebrated in a chapel.

But there were many reasons for my joy. In my family there were some who died before they turned forty, or soon after. When I reached forty still alive and healthy, I praised God. Secondly, for many years I had battled depression, rooted in a low sense of self-worth, even to the point of being suicidal. There was a possibility that I would never reach forty.

One Sunday, I heard the pastor of the church I had just joined dare the congregation to "try Jesus the Christ." I prayed and fasted for a week. In prayer, I dared Jesus to change me, and in response he turned my life around. He changed my name from "Fearful" to "Follower." I found hope, a new sense of self-worth and value, and a new way of living.

By age forty, I had a new sense of confidence in myself as a woman of God and as a woman in general. Even though I was single, never married, without any children, I still felt fulfilled. I still felt complete because Christ had control of my life and was molding and shaping me for his purpose. I believed that because of the new-found freedom I felt in Christ, I could do no less than to celebrate and give glory to God! I wanted to acknowledge that without Christ I would not have made it. I had grown in wisdom and was able to receive God's revelation to me through the Spirit. I was ready to cross over to full adulthood.

At this writing, I am forty-seven and getting excited about turning fifty. I can't wait. The celebration will be even better than the one I gave myself at forty!

Oh, Ancient of Days, everlasting and Holy One, we worship you today and we give praise to you for the life and the days you have given to us. Teach us to always be mindful of how you keep us in all of our ways. Grant us courage, grant us excitement, and grant us wisdom for the future. We pray this in the magnificent name of Jesus the Christ. Amen.

J. Esther Rowe

I Will Step Out on the Word of God

Your word is a lamp to my feet and a light to my path.
—Psalm 119:105

My fifth grade Sunday School teacher, Jane Sigler, was a person who stepped out on the Word of God. She didn't go around quoting the Bible. And she didn't talk her faith *at* others. Rather, she lived her faith *with* others. Her life was so steeped in service that you had no doubt who was her power source. She was the one bringing meals to the sick, organizing and cooking the church dinners, and making sure the church was clean Saturday night before Sunday worship. She faithfully attended Bible studies and prayer meetings. She opened her home to countless visitors. And she taught unruly fifth and sixth graders what the Bible was all about.

Jane Sigler's faith touched my faith. Because she immersed herself in Scripture and let God's Word light her path, she changed not only her own life, but also mine.

How does Scripture play a part in your life? Can you say without hesitation, "I will step out on the word of God"?

In my own life, so many times I have felt powerless. And God has said: "Joyce, pick up your Bible. The power is here. There are countless stories of men and women who were ordinary—just like you—and I used their faith to turn the world upside down."

So many times I have searched for the truth. And God has said: "Joyce, pick up your Bible, the truth is here. Stop relying on the world's psychology, mythology, sociology, Scientology. Seek my ways, and I will direct your paths."

So many times I have felt unloved. And God has said: "Joyce, pick up your Bible, the love is here. For all who believe in my name, I gave the right to become my children, the children of God" (See John 1:12). Set your faith in action. Say, "I WILL STEP OUT ON THE WORD OF GOD!"

Dear God, thank you for the wisdom we can find in the Bible. Challenge us to read it faithfully so that we might not only transform ourselves, but also those around us. Amen.

Joyce Anderson Reed

Who Says Angels Don't Exist?

"Take care that you do not despise one of these little
ones; for, I tell you, in heaven their angels continually
see the face of my Father in heaven."
—Matthew 18:10

I was about nine years old. It was a beautiful sunny day. Abuelo (Grandfather) had decided we would go to the beach to ride bikes. When I say that *we* would ride *my* bike, I really mean it.

Abuelo had taken off the two small safety wheels that had been part of my bike thus far and was teaching me balance so that I could ride like all the other kids. How we rode was a joke in itself. I would sit on the bike and peddle, while he would run after me holding on to my seat rail to maintain the bike's balance.

I started riding as usual that day. I could hear the wind swishing by me, feel the heat of the sun, and smell the beach. I remember feeling so happy, so free and so... lightweight? I turned my head briefly to glance at Abuelo's hand on the seat rail only to find that it wasn't there. In the distance, I saw him. He was laughing his head off and looking so proud of me. He had tricked me, but he had taught me to ride by myself.

That's just how Abuelo was. He was an intelligent, funny, and courageous person. He taught me that I, a woman, have no boundaries to what I can do. Above all, Abuelo's faith in Jesus was unshakable. I can never forget his words, "I know no fear because God is with me. When God wants me to go, I'll have no choice but to go and I shall be happy."

God called Abuelo on March 1, 2000, at age eighty-nine, three months before my wedding day. He was hit by a car while walking near his neighborhood. He wasn't able to physically be with me on my wedding day, but I know he looked at me from heaven and laughed. I hope he's still proud of me. His belief in me has helped me forget, ignore, or destroy all the boundaries I have encountered. I believe Abuelo to be my angel. He is in heaven and has seen the face of God.

Dear God, help us to understand that those we seem to lose at death, you have really won; to understand that they are happy and safe. *But most importantly, help us to know that we should not fear the toils and turns of life, because there is a place in heaven for us, too. Amen.*

Liza Marie Canino

Saints of the Household of God

Then Peter began to speak to them:
"I truly understand that God shows no partiality..."
—Acts 10:34

So then you are no longer strangers and aliens,
but you are citizens with the saints and
also members of the household of God.
—Ephesians 2:19

The move was unexpected—transplanted to an unfamiliar town, housed on a street filled with strangers. Thoughts invaded my mind: "God, what new thing are you doing here with me?"

Gradually, as I greeted people, they spoke. The Syrian family, the Russian family, the Irish Catholic couple, the German Lutheran bachelor, the young couple professing agnosticism, the old Jewish widow, the first-generation Sicilian barber and his wife. All smiled shyly, uncertain of my friendliness. They had not been neighborly by choice.

There was one vacant house. I prayed for an African American family to move in. While I was on vacation, my prayer was answered with the Goldsmiths, African American and Salvation Army people. The neighbors were certain that the new family was from Puerto Rico. That would have been more acceptable. I knew better. Taking over a plate of cookies, I welcomed them. Soon our home became a meeting place. Differences diminished as conversation sprinkled with "God talk" and children played together. Older folk joined in the fun of impromptu parades and backyard picnics.

Another job transfer was pending for us. Our neighborhood friends gave us a farewell party. A variety of ethnic foods filled the tables. Three blessings were given, followed by a chorus of "amens." My heart was overflowing as I watched the interaction. The walls and boundaries were no longer in place. The sheer enjoyment of God's saints prevailed. I pondered: "God's kingdom is here." Then I reflected on that wedding feast yet to come. Ah, what a foretaste of glory divine!

Another move; another new thing will be accomplished.

Use me, Holy One, to be a reconciler who brings the good news that Peter received long ago, news of a wondrously new world devoid of partiality. Amen.

Grace Thornton Lawrence

God's Incredible Regard

"Are not five sparrows sold for two pennies?
Yet not one of them is forgotten in God's sight.
But even the hairs of your head are all counted. Do not
be afraid; you are of more value than many sparrows."
—Luke 12:6-7

I manage four cats, and each is a one-time event in the universe. Timothy, the elder ginger and grand old male of the clan, likes to nuzzle my glasses. He purrs with delight when they fall off my face. He eats everything I eat, and if I don't give him what he wants, he whines and frets, circling my feet until I give in, which is always. The others defer to him. He is Shaman, the wise one.

The younger ginger, Jeremy, stands like a champion, sleeps at my head or across my face. He usually lets none of the others near me, likes to bite my hair, and generally hogs me and my time. I love it except when I'm busy, which doesn't deter him in the least but spurs him on to exceptional feats of distraction. One day he blew my computer by oxidizing the hard disc. He enjoyed my anger, frustration, and horror, knowing all the while that I wouldn't do anything except go out and buy another computer. Jeremy follows Timmy, but the others get out of his way.

Kepler, the only female, is a tiny little white and black thing with a big black spot on her rump. If human, she might be thought of as a Plain Jane but for her eyes, which are extraordinarily big, bright, and piercing. She is the smartest, the most independent of the bunch, and the most concerned for the others. If one is out of sorts, Keppy comes yapping to me until I do whatever she wants with the offending or offended sibling. She has actually found one or more of her brothers and brought them home when I couldn't retrieve them or they wouldn't answer my call. She does not like to be held or petted but does talk to me constantly. We have amazing conversations and a rapport that comes only with much practice by both of us.

Taiko, the black and white, is Peck's Bad Boy. He came trotting into the house one day at the tender age of two months and is still here four years later. Unlike Keppy, Jeremy, and Timmy, all of whom are more or less content to remain indoors, Taiko must go outside or my domicile pays an aromatic price. He usually stays outside no matter the weather from one to two days. I never stop worrying and believe that he does it on purpose to see if I care. When indoors, Taiko is extremely affectionate and gentle. He is shy with his brothers but secure and scrappy with his sister. There's a fragility about him that is both appealing and disconcerting. I hope he'll be around for a long time, but his frequent trips outside make me uncertain. Of all the cats, he is the most complex and ephemeral; he is our visiting angel.

So there they are—each a one-time event in this vast universe. They tell me a story of individuality in a way no ideology or philosophy can. Together they eliminate my need for books or proofs that such individuality is real and really precious. The mystery of sustaining and celebrating that uniqueness ultimately rests with God alone, with a love beyond reckoning that manifests itself in my daily routine, as Timmy paws my jeans for a bite of whatever happens to be going into my mouth. God bless God.

That you mark and know each snowflake, each leaf, each star and each person amazes me, oh God. How do you do it? How may I follow? How may I regard your world as you do? Show me the way, my God. Show me the way. Amen.

Jill Schaeffer

I Believe—Help My Unbelief!

*Jesus said to him, "If you are able!—All things can be
done for the one who believes." Immediately the father
of the child cried out, "I believe; help my unbelief!"*
—Mark 9:23-24

Yesterday, the phone rang. It was a dear friend whom I first met
forty-two years ago when we taught a Sunday school class together
in an inner-city church in Cleveland, Ohio. I was a college student,
and she was a single mother of four pre-school children.

Through the years, our paths diverged greatly and life presented
many hurdles, but somehow we remained in touch and our friendship grew stronger. Her deep, joyful faith had been an inspiration
to me over the years. She developed a career in environmental
health, and her children grew into fine young adults with successful
lives. She reached retirement age and finally could begin to travel
and enjoy a life free of crushing responsibility.

Then a bombshell hit. She was diagnosed with colon cancer. My
friend had endured and survived so many hardships. Why did she
have to develop cancer now, when it was time to rest and enjoy life?
Where was the justice in all of this? She had surgery, and was
pronounced free of cancer. But four years later, she received news
from her doctor that she had malignant tumors in her spleen, lungs,
and throat. She was given three months to live. I was devastated.
Why? Why? Why?

Her faith remained strong. She called upon the prayers of her
wide circle of friends. She struggled with weakness and pain, but
she continued to sing praises to God. Nine months later she was
still living and having surgery to remove her spleen, which was, the
doctor said, filled with cancerous tumors.

But back to yesterday's phone call! My friend said, "God is
good! He answers the prayers of righteous people. The biopsy of
the removed spleen revealed only fatty tumors, no cancer, and the
pain is gone." Jesus said, "This kind can come out only through
prayer" (Mark 9:29). I said, "I believe; help my unbelief." What a
testimony to God's great healing power to bring wholeness to one
of his faithful servants!

Almighty healing God, we thank you for your mighty deeds. You sent your son to give us life in all its fullness. Let us continually praise your name. Amen.

Norma S. Mengel

Angels of Mercy

Grandchildren are the crown of the aged.
—Proverbs 17:6a

For nine long, miserable months my husband suffered a severe, deep depression during which he seemed unaware of his surroundings and uninterested in living. Our five grandchildren, ranging in age from two to seventeen, continued to visit weekly, sharing their hugs and kisses, as well as their stories about school life, ball games, honors, and report cards. Their "Pepaw" would merely smile and say, "That's good." They never wavered in their devotion and affection, nor betrayed their sadness with the slightest downcast facial expression.

Our two-year-old granddaughter never seemed aware of how ill her grandfather was. She only knew she had a captive audience as she sang and danced her way through many impromptu stage acts. Then she and Pepaw would watch hours of cartoons featuring her latest interests, from Teletubbies to Blue's Clues. Months later, our eight-year-old grandson noticed the first breakthrough when he excitedly remarked, "Pepaw is feeling better! His voice is getting so strong."

Our five grandchildren were their Pepaw's angels of mercy as they faithfully ministered in ways that only children can. By their actions they brought me to the well of empowering love and strength many times, helping me to go on being a caregiver. They were perfect examples of how loving, non-judgmental, and loyal Jesus taught his followers to be. God can use all of us, even the youngest, as his angels of mercy to those desperately in need of comfort, a smile, or a hug.

Great God of comfort and mercy, use us as your angels of mercy to bring healing to a broken world. *Help us to acknowledge and value the spontaneous caring of children. Fill us with compassion, understanding, and patience when we minister as caregivers to loved ones. Amen.*

Evangeline W. Lynch

Friendship as Testimony

Faithful friends are life-saving medicine.
—Sirach 6:16a

My friend Belva died of cancer in the prime of her life. Members of her congregation extended sympathy to me. They knew the depths of our relationship. Together, we identified church as Christian people. Belva was a pastor in the United Church of Christ, and I am a Roman Catholic.

We had many fun times together: hiking, vacationing, praying, sharing, worshipping. Many an eyebrow was raised when one person or another found out about our different religious backgrounds. "Can you really have fun with a nun?" became a byword after we hiked the Grand Canyon together from rim to rim. Both her family and mine accepted our relationship. We all grew to love each other.

Our relationship broke down many barriers. We grew spiritually together with God always at the center. By strengthening us, God worked in the hearts of the people among whom we ministered. Results included more women in church leadership, broadened attitudes, and hearts opened to see God's presence in others. The Spirit worked in us to make us a dynamic duo of life fully lived. Though Belva now enjoys resurrection, our lives are still bonded together. My life is better for having been touched by her.

God is bonded to each of us through love. God strengthens us on our journey. God comes to us through faith, family, and friends. What beautiful gifts they are! How blessed I am for being a recipient of these gifts. When God comes into our lives and is accepted, great and wonderful things happen. Walls disappear and bridges are built.

Gracious God, loving Spirit, fill our hearts with eagerness to accept others and to love them as you love them. Open us to the gifts of each person, that hidden treasures may be found. Amen.

Mildred A. Leuenberger

Pumpkin Patch Ministry

"If you abide in me, and my words abide in you, ask for whatever you wish, and it will be done for you. My Father is glorified by this, that you bear much fruit and become my disciples."
—John 15:7-8

As a new interim pastor I wanted to communicate the idea that even in a short time together, we could plant seeds that would yield a spiritual harvest. So I brought pumpkin seeds for the children to plant. A great time was had by all, including the adults, who periodically inquired about the pumpkins.

Almost immediately I was in trouble. The seeds never germinated. A friend with a green thumb came to my rescue with three healthy plants. I planted and faithfully watered them. Soon my little pumpkin vines were loaded with blossoms. But alas the time was late for planting here in Maine, and the growing season stopped short of my hoped-for harvest. When the killer frost came, I had only one very mini pumpkin. I had to buy some pumpkins for the children as none of the harvest of our shared ministry was indeed ready for reaping.

Well, my pumpkin patch certainly didn't produce "much fruit," but even one pumpkin contains seeds for the future. Sometimes for all our efforts at ministry, we don't seem to bear much fruit either. Our timing is off, or the plants are too fragile. There may be so much resistance to change, it's a miracle anything will grow at all! The conditions are less than ideal, not to mention the limitations we ourselves bring to the many tasks of ministry. But none of that keeps God from growing a harvest, even if it's a small one. As long as the fruit endures, there's always the potential for more.

All Jesus asks of his disciples is that we abide in him and let his words abide in us. If we do that much faithfully, then there will always be a harvest. We have to trust that seeds we plant this year may not bear much fruit until many years later. In God's perfect timing, the harvest will reach its greatest potential. Let us be faithful, then, in cultivating the fruit that endures: love, joy, peace, patience, kindness, goodness, faithfulness, gentleness, and self-control. And God will give the increase!

Lord Jesus, thank you for the grace to be faithful as we tend the pumpkin patches we call your church. Bless the people we love and serve, that together we will bear much fruit for the sake of your kingdom. Amen.

Susan E. Crane

Surprised by Joy!

"I am the light of the world."
—John 9:5b

Here it was Christmas Eve, and I was at my first Christmas service since having accepted Jesus as my personal Lord and savior earlier that year. Coming from a Jewish family, Christmas carols had little meaning to me. Though we sang them in school, they were "their" songs, not ours. We would light our Hanukkah candles and sing our own songs about God's faithfulness to keep the "eternal" lamp in the restored temple lit for eight days on one day's worth of oil.

Now, sitting in the Christmas service, I was not prepared for what was to come. The musicians began the introduction to a familiar melody. Of course I knew the words—every American knows the words. And so I began to sing along with everyone else: "Joy to the world; the Lord is come; Let earth receive her king." Suddenly, the impact of what those familiar words actually meant brought me to silence. My throat swallowed the words in grateful emotion, and tears began a small waterfall from my eyes.

Jesus, the Light of the world, had restored me to God and had lit an "eternal" lamp in my heart. The Lord had come—to me! And I had received him as king.

Lord Jesus, I receive you again with renewed gratefulness this day. Come reign as king in my heart in ever-increasing measure. Amen.
Lonnie Lane

Watching Matthew with a Child

...but Jesus said, "Let the little children come to me,
and do not stop them; for it is to such as these
that the kingdom of heaven belongs."
—Matthew 19:14

Anyone can tell you that children are known for asking tough theological questions. My son, for instance, will get out of bed at night with the most important questions: "Mommy, where is heaven? Is it above the clouds? Why did God make the sky?"

On and on he'll go, my pint-sized philosopher. Usually my mind is too relaxed with the joyful expectation of sleeping (quiet!) children to expound on the mysteries of the universe or the inner workings of God's creation. However, God always proves to be the Supreme Being and occasionally does speak through the mouths of mothers with small children.

The other day my six-year-old daughter, Emily, and I were watching the video *Matthew*, which is the entire book of Matthew word for word on film. Emily was asking all sorts of questions about why and how and when. One answer in particular that came out of my mouth really surprised me. Not because it wasn't true, but because I'd never thought of things that way before. I said, "Everything you see Jesus say or do he does for one reason: to tell us he loves us.

I'll feed you (loaves and fishes) because I love you!

I'll heal you because I love you!

I forgive you because I love you!

I'll reprimand you because I love you!

I'll live with you because I love you!

I'll teach you because I love you
I will die for you because I love you!
I'll give you the Holy Spirit because I love you!
I love you! I love you! I love you!

That is what Jesus' whole life on earth was about. Every time you wonder why Jesus said or did something, realize that he is trying to show you another way he loves you."

Dear Lord, thank you for teaching us through the innocent questions of children. Please help us never to become too busy or too "grown up" to miss your message in each moment. Amen.

Jenny Chandler

Precious Memories

*One generation shall laud your works to another,
and shall declare your mighty acts.
—Psalm 145:4*

As I was driving to a meeting in Indianapolis, I was listening to George Beverly Shea sing "Precious Memories." I thought of all the very precious memories I have of family members. I remember my mother spending hours and hours in loving service to God ministering to persons in jail and prison. I remember Mother and Dad spending thousands of hours driving others to doctors, to the grocery store, to church; taking meals to those who were sick or handicapped; making visits to the hospitalized; taking me and my siblings to Sunday Evening Club, where church members gathered in homes and, after a potluck, sang praises to God.

I have a precious picture in my mind of my grandmother sitting in her rocking chair in front of the living room window, reading her Bible. I remember my grandfather chairing meetings of the Board of Deacons, often in our home. I remember, as a child, walking the three miles to church with him on Sundays.

In addition to these personal experiences that were so meaningful to me, I remember stories about ancestors who had left legacies. Before I was born, my grandfather was a minister who'd been mentored by his father-in-law. Grandfather also used to go to the jail to visit with inmates. Other stories tell of my grandmother teaching Sunday school in her home for the neighbor children who were never taken to church. Mother says that the tin cup was always hanging by the well for the stranger who came by thirsty. The welcome mat was always out for the strangers who stopped by hungry. They were invited in to eat with the family.

My great grandfather was a minister of the gospel in Kansas, baptizing people in the Saline River. He and his very large family were poor, but never too poor to help others in need, including, sometimes, those with more than he had. These are just a few of the family memories I carry in my mind and heart. What a heritage to be blessed with! I pray that I also create memories for my son, grandchildren, and others I love. I want to be a part of passing on a precious heritage to future generations!!

Creator of families, I praise you for blessing me with my family line, which is filled with persons of faith who were consistently trying to live thy will. Be my guide and strength as I endeavor to live your will for my life. Amen.

Dorinda K. W. Kauzlarich-Rupe

That's Life

Not that I am referring to being in need;
for I have learned to be content with whatever I have.
I know what it is to have little, and I know what it is to
have plenty. In any and all circumstances I have learned
the secret of being well-fed and of going hungry, of
having plenty and of being in need. I can do all things
through him who strengthens me.
—Philippians 4:11-13

She was nineteen, tall, and very beautiful. She gave birth to her first baby—a girl as lovely as her mommy—with dignity, courage, and joy. Tears of pride and happiness shone in her eyes as she held her baby daughter, just a few moments old. I had been given the great privilege of serving as her midwife. I drank in the loveliness of the moment. Then I spoke.

"Charmaine," I said quietly," You need a few stitches. It is going to hurt a little bit, but not as much as it hurt to have your baby."

Her eyes met mine with a steady gaze. "That's life," she said. It was spoken without bitterness and without resignation. It was stated simply and matter-of-factly. "That's life."

My heart was filled with admiration for this brave girl, who had already known hardships I would never know, but who remained courageous and unbroken. Thank you, Charmaine, for teaching me so large a lesson by your example. Like a tall, strong tree may you bend and never break, no matter how great the storms of life around you.

Yahweh, please give us courage and strength to receive hardship without self-pity or blame. Guard our hearts from becoming brittle with bitterness. May our trials make us both strong and flexible, bending but not breaking in our devotion and service to you and those you have placed in our care. Amen.

Lois Wilson

God Knows the Heart

But the LORD said to Samuel, "Do not look on his appearance or on the height of his stature, because I have rejected him; for the Lord does not see as mortals see; they look on the outward appearance, but the LORD looks on the heart."
—1 Samuel 16:7

Tonight Gavin had another seizure during his therapeutic riding lesson. I volunteer one day a week to help special-needs children gain the benefits from riding a horse. It is wonderful. I have learned so much about horses, special-needs kids, and how to defuse potentially difficult situations.

Gavin is particularly special. His brain did not receive enough oxygen during birth, so his life is severely compromised. He can't walk or talk or even hold his head up by himself. Some people feel there is not really a child inside his body. They are wrong.

Very intentionally Gavin lifts his spastic arm to indicate "Walk on" to the horse and to those of us who work with him. His stiff, spastic little body relaxes with the gentle motion of the horse and the person who is riding with him. Sometimes he laughs; more often he smiles. Recently he began having seizures more frequently. He will have surgery to try to stop them and salvage what brain function he has remaining. With each seizure he forever loses a few more precious brain cells.

I believe in my heart that God neither willed nor caused Gavin's condition. God's will for Gavin is health and wholeness—running, laughing, picking dandelions, playing in the mud, tormenting his brother. But Gavin in a wheelchair is the gift we have. And sometimes—just sometimes—those blue eyes look at me with a depth and wisdom that goes beyond medical diagnoses, wheelchairs, and seizures. And I am overwhelmed.

Gentle God, you love children; they are your special gifts of hope and joy to this tired world. We pray for all of them—those bound by wheelchairs and those dancing in the meadows. And we pray for ourselves. Help us to see you in every small face. Help us to celebrate the gift of life in every child. We pray in the name of Jesus, who loved children and called them to come to him. Amen.

Dianne L. Mansfield

A Mother's Love

When Israel was a child, I loved him, and out of Egypt
I called my son...it was I who taught Ephraim to walk,
I took them up in my arms; but they did not know
that I healed them. I led them with cords of human
kindness, with bands of love. I was to them
like those who lift infants to their cheeks.
I bent down to them and fed them.
—Hosea 11:1- 4

As a mother comforts her child, so I will comfort you;
you shall be comforted in Jerusalem.
You shall see, and your heart shall rejoice;
your bodies shall flourish like the grass.
—Isaiah 66:13-14a

I heard a wail in the back yard: my two-year-old son, Andrew, had skinned his knee and was looking for comfort. Andrew's daddy, David, got to him first, sweeping him into his loving arms. But Andrew's cry only got louder. He fought to get out of David's arms, yelling, "I want my Mommy!" I walked over and took Andrew into my arms. His warm body melted into mine, and his cry turned into a soft whimper. David looked at me with a smile and a shrug, and observed, "There are some times when only a Mommy will do."

My own Daddy has given me a great model of God the Father's love, and I am very grateful for that. But there are times in my life when "only a Mommy will do," and God, who created us, knows that. That is why alongside the "father" metaphors for God, Scripture gives us "mother" metaphors. God loves us like a mother, teaches us to walk, bends down to feed us, and comforts us when we need it most. Our God meets all our needs, even in those times when we cry out for a mother's love.

Dearest God, I thank you for loving me fiercely with love as potent and as passionate as the love of a mother for the child at her breast. I thirst for your love, and you quench that thirst as only you can. I love you. Amen.

Jeanne L. Williams

The Anointing

You anoint my head with oil; my cup overflows.
—Psalm 23:5

After being with Ana that day, I would never think of healing or the Trinity in quite the same way. I was making chaplain's rounds and opened the door to find Ana's beautiful eyes, weak yet strangely bright. Her request caught me off guard: "I'd like you to anoint me with oil and pray for my healing." My eyes widened. Anointing was not a part of my religious tradition. It was something "others" did, and it was a part of Ana's Latino tradition. Her eyes were pleading. I smiled awkwardly and rejoined, "I'll see what I can do."

Two hours later I was scanning the aisles of the grocery story. Sugar. Flour. Oil. "Okay," I thought, "Here's Wesson. Hain. Mazola." Not a single one said "Good for anointing." I suppose my deep sigh caught the attention of the only other person on the aisle, a pleasant-looking African American woman. My confused stare prompted her question, "Is there something I can help you find?" I told her the whole story, and she laughed and said, "You need to sprinkle her, not douse her!"

She led me to a much smaller jar of olive oil. "I have never done this," I admitted, "and I'm not sure what good it will do." "Oh, it's the good God will do, " she said. "You just shine the dishes. He'll put the food on them." And then with a gentle holiness I will never forget, there among the brownies and graham cracker crumbs, she opened the jar, and like an artist reverently stroking the canvass, she made the sign of the cross on my forehead and whispered, "In the name of Jesus, receive this healing." She embraced me and disappeared before I could ask her name.

I returned to Ana's bed and nervously gave Ana the same loving touch my anonymous friend had shared: "In the name of Jesus, Ana, receive this healing." I returned two days later to find that Ana had been discharged. I'm not sure what her medical condition was, but I know what happened to three very different women that day. They became one. Strangeness became communion. In an unexpected trinity of sisterhood, we were made whole and stood up strong together in the Body of Christ.

*God, help us to learn from one another's experiences and tradi-
tions. Give us the courage to try the new and unfamiliar. In the
name of the Creator, the Redeemer, and the Holy Spirit. Amen.*

Penny B. Ziemer

Who Am I?

(with apologies to Dietrich Bonhoeffer)

*"Come, you that are blessed by my Father,
inherit the kingdom prepared for you from the
foundation of the world; for I was hungry and you gave
me food, I was thirsty and you gave me something to
drink, I was a stranger and you welcomed me."*
—Matthew 25:34b-35

Like many young women of my generation, I grew up with the
expectation that I would someday marry, have children, and live
happily ever after. Dreams of domestic bliss and normalcy eventually crashed and burned within the realities of alcoholism and
depression. Somewhere in the whirl of all that chaos and pain, I
found God in very unexpected circumstances.

I entered into a relationship with the man I would eventually
marry. Like me, he was also alcoholic. But I was soon blessed with
a sobriety that continued to elude him. He died at forty-five from
alcoholic hepatitis and liver failure. I was a widow at thirty-six.

I returned to my childhood church, and found within its walls
the love, friendship, support, and challenge that I needed to make
it through those horrible days of early bereavement. I was still
engaged in Job-like battle with God, but there were also moments
of grace and inklings of peace.

I served my church in a variety of capacities, from baking pies
for the fair to being the finance chairperson and, eventually, the
moderator. I found a joy in all of this that was very lacking
elsewhere in my life. My struggle through the next few years would
be to give up the old dreams and expectations, to come to terms

with the recognition that God's will for me seemed to be mighty different from what I had originally wanted for myself.

At forty, after another bout with depression, I finally listened to the still quiet voice of God and entered Andover Newton Theological School. The five years since then have been times of financial struggle but spiritual blossoming. I have found a joy in living that eluded me for many, many years, and it has occurred to me that it was only when I became willing to let go of my old dreams that God could show me something new. I am born again, in all the pain, struggle, and joy that is a part of such a blessing.

God, grant me the serenity to accept the things I cannot change, courage to change the things I can, and wisdom to know the difference (AA Serenity Prayer). Amen.

Becky Tornblom

Woman of the Future

For it was you who formed my inward parts;
you knit me together in my mother's womb. I praise you,
for I am fearfully and wonderfully made. Wonderful
are your works; that I know very well. My frame
was not hidden from you, when I was being made in
secret, intricately woven in the depths of the earth.
Your eyes beheld my unformed substance. In your book
were written all the days that were formed for me,
when none of them as yet existed. How weighty to me are
your thoughts, O God! How vast is the sum of them!
I try to count them—they are more than the sand;
I come to the end—I am still with you.
—Psalm 139:13-18

I have often heard it said that a baby is God's way of telling the world to go on. Well, we got this message from God in the form of a new precious grandson. When I look at that tiny little body, perfect in every way, I can't comprehend the miracle God has so freely given all humanity. Whether we choose to have children, adopt children, or simply enjoy someone else's child, God has presented us with the biggest miracle of all time.

I don't ever want to take that miracle for granted. I want to tell my new grandson every day that I love him and treasure him and that I will always be here for him. But of course I won't always be here for him. Instead, I will do my best to be an example for him while I am here. I will tell him about another precious baby, Jesus Christ, who came to us as an infant. He lived and died for us so that we could have abundant and eternal life.

I will tell my grandson that we are all equal because of what Jesus did on the cross for each of us. I will tell him that he can make the world a better place by just being here, doing his best day-to-day and living life to the fullest through Jesus. Oh yes, I will tell him many things. And he will show me every day the miracle of life and the miracle of love, which is the greatest miracle of all.

Great God of all children, help us to take care of what you have so graciously given us: the miracle of your children. Give us the patience, wisdom, and understanding to love all your children everywhere in the world. Amen.

Bonnie L. Scherer

In the Wilderness

He was in the wilderness forty days, tempted by Satan... and the angels waited on him.
—Mark 1:13

It was one of those days. I didn't have my keys with me when I left the church, so when the door closed behind me, I was locked out. It was raining outside and my favorite dress was getting wet. And, of course, my car wouldn't start. I had to beg for change twice before finally getting a hold of my boyfriend to explain my situation.

By this time a man who had been trying to sell flowers to passers-by approached me. He offered to help, but smelling the alcohol on his breath, I was skeptical. My boyfriend, thinking I was still at the church, overheard someone offering to help me. He decided he wasn't needed after all, and before I could explain myself, he had hung up the phone. As the rain kept falling, I had little choice but to indulge the vagabond, who told me his name was Gary.

Gary and I walked the two blocks back to my car, and eventually I concluded that at least he wasn't going to harm me. He did genuinely want to help, knowing that there would, no doubt, be money involved if he could provide enough assistance. I was parked a block away from a gas station, and Gary insisted on pushing the car there. Finally protected from the rain by the overhead between the pumps, we had a good look under the hood. "Oh, here's your problem," Gary explained, twisting a few wires. "Right," I thought, but I figured I'd humor the man. I went back to start the ignition once again, and the car immediately revved up. Shocked and amazed, I humbly stumbled over a thank you to the stranger I never fully trusted.

Gary received his financial reward, and insisted upon giving me a bouquet of flowers. God doesn't promise us that there won't be those days; even Jesus endured the wilderness. But there is the promise that we won't be left alone.

Dear God, help us through the wildernesses of life, reminding us that we will, somehow, be tended to by angels. Amen.

Allison J. Tanner

Handing Down the Faith

I am reminded of your sincere faith, a faith that lived first in your grandmother Lois and your mother Eunice and now, I am sure, lives in you.
—2 Timothy 1:5

Chatting with my hostess in her kitchen, I inquired where she would be this weekend. "I am going to my village in Moshi to attend a fundraiser, worship, and visit my family."

I had come to recognize that family was important to Selena, having met many of her family members gathered that night for supper. Selena held a position in government that enabled her to advocate for women and children by targeting various projects that would enable them to become self-supporting and broaden their horizons. Continuing our discussion, I asked her how she came to have faith in Christ.

"It's always been a part of my life," she beamed. "My mother died when I was one and a half years of age. My aunt, who was nursing her own baby, took me as her child. She became my mother. My extended family raised me to know God's love and to show it to others. It's just a natural part of all I do. This weekend I will do one professional act of advocacy and one personal. I will attend a rally to raise money for a computer lab for youth in my village with the First Lady, and I will purchase my 'mother' a dress for my nephew's wedding."

Selena was not boasting about her action. It was a simple manner of faith put into action. Where did her faith come from? It was handed down from her community: family members, church members, friends, co-workers. St. Paul reminds us in Acts 10:1-2 of a certain government worker, Cornelius, who was a devout and God-fearing man. His household also believed. Why? Cornelius was one who gave generously to people and walked close to his God. His example won many to belief in Christ.

Lord, thank you for my family, personal and extended. Help me in my words and deeds to be a faithful witness to them and others. In your holy name. Amen.

Cynthia E. Cowen

Vessels of Justice

He said, "Go outside, borrow vessels
from all your neighbors, empty vessels and not just
a few. Then go in, and shut the door behind you
and your children, and start pouring into all these
vessels; when each is full, set it aside."
—2 Kings 4:3-4

As Coordinator of Church and Community Ministries for American Baptist Women's Ministries, I was able to go three summers to Women's Conference in Green Lake, Wisconsin. There I was blessed as women from throughout the United States and Puerto Rico shared with me about what they were doing in Christ's name.

Over meals, in workshops, between sessions, and even in the gift shop, women told me about the ministries close to their hearts. I heard about a racetrack outreach that prepared and distributed personal care kits. There were soup kitchens, food pantries, and clothing banks. I was stirred by prayer patrols that regularly walked through neighborhoods to pray for those in each home. I learned of puppet ministries done by teens for senior adults and of other ministries done by senior adults for pregnant teens.

Faithful women are involved in domestic violence programs and day care projects. They develop transitional housing and serve on community boards. American Baptist women are making friends with single moms, reaching out through prison ministries, teaching English as a second language, and helping adults learn to read!

Elisha told the woman in our text to gather all the jars she could so that God could work a mighty act. She was only one woman. She had no power to save her children or herself. She didn't even have resources to prepare one meal. But she believed and she opened herself up to the power of God. If she had only collected three or four jars, she wouldn't have ended up with much oil. But she gathered jars from all her neighbors, ready for the great things God would do. And she ran out of oil only when she ran out of vessels.

What we as women of God can accomplish today is limited only by the number of vessels we set out! Won't you be one of those empty vessels that Christ might use you?

God, I bring myself before you for filling. By your mighty power, equip me through the Holy Spirit for works of justice and peace. Amen.

Karen Ann Selig

Together in Unity

*How very good and pleasant it is
when kindred live together in unity!
—Psalm 133:1*

It was a warm evening in June. My husband, David, and I had been invited to a party at the home of Jewish friends. When we arrived, we discovered the party was in my husband's honor: in celebration of his twenty-fifth anniversary of ordination to the ministry of word and sacrament. David and I were the only Christians at the party; it was our Jewish friends who were marking the occasion with festivities.

A card signed by all present quoted the familiar words from Psalm 133 about kindred living together in unity. The gift was a lovely silver chalice, the bowl washed with gold. It was engraved "with love from your universal family."

Fifteen years later, after my husband's death, my son and I celebrated Passover with the children and granddaughter of the friend who had given the ordination party. As the Seder feast began, the college-student granddaughter spoke of the importance of making the Passover celebration enjoyable and meaningful for children. She said her happy childhood memories of Seder were due to David B. McDowell, a Presbyterian minister.

When our sons were young, they attended a preschool at a Young Men's and Young Women's Hebrew Association. After lighting the large Hanukkah candles one year, one son asked, "Are we Jewish or Christian?" I replied, "Jesus was a Jew. One cannot be a good Christian without knowing something of Judaism."

Our sharing with Jewish friends throughout the years has added to our mutual understanding and to our own increased appreciation of our Christian faith. Now when we celebrate Communion, we think of the cup of Elijah and we remember the Passover feast.

In the words of the Jerusalem Bible (1968): "How good, how delightful it is for all to live together like brothers."

God, the parent of all, help us to remember and to celebrate that we are all your children; sisters and brothers who can share understanding and friendship across religions, finding it good and delightful to be together in unity. Amen.

Elizabeth V. McDowell

The Woman at the Well

Jesus said to [the woman]...
"The water that I will give will become in them
a spring of water gushing up to eternal life."
—John 4:13-14

The woman in chapter 4 of John's Gospel must have gone to the well often. Yet it may be that when she met Jesus there on that dry day, she encountered one whose spirit drew her to the wellspring within herself. Through his grace she was startled, refreshed, and renewed.

My friend Lucy and I worked together on many projects. At one point we were working with senior citizens' community meals programs that depended in large part on government funds. Staff, participants, and supporters were working hard to sustain those funds. But when the new federal budget was announced, there were deep cuts to our programs.

It was with a low spirit and a heavy, discouraged heart that I met Lucy the next morning. My feelings didn't last. Lucy wouldn't let them. She was undaunted; the spirit within her was fully alive. Undefeated and confident, she said, "We can't stop now. We can't let them cut a program that's helping so many people. We have to let the budget-makers know whom they're hurting. People can change the budget. We can call all the people we know. Every senior citizen and their helpers can write a note on an empty paper plate and send it to decision-makers in Washington. We'll let them know how many empty plates there'll be because of their budget cuts. What do you think?"

Honestly, my first thoughts were of how few people we really knew and could count on. It wasn't nearly enough to influence the federal government. How could so few people make a difference? But Lucy's spirit startled and convinced me. She didn't even consider being defeated or giving up. She was absolutely clear that there was still something we could do. We were not alone, and together we could yet make a difference.

We got busy and reorganized. We'll never know if any of the notes on paper plates had any effect, but we do know there were some budget changes and the programs continued. What I remember most clearly, however, is how the power and grace of the ever-flowing spirit in Lucy renewed my own spirit.

Oh Lord, I need so many reminders that abundant life and love gush within me. I thank you for people like Lucy, whose spirit is not easily defeated and can convince me to go on. Draw me again and again to the ever-flowing spring of that spirit so that I may be sustained and refreshed in dry times and be able to share that renewing spirit. Amen.

Linda (Schulze) Scherzinger

Message from a Friend

I will sing to the LORD as long as I live;
I will sing praise to my God while I have being.
—Psalm 104:33

As the world picks away at us and wears at our completeness, our Christian friends come and pick up the pieces, put them together, and make us whole again.

Via the wonder of e-mail, my friend who lives miles away helps daily to encourage me and keep me on the right path. Though I haven't seen her for months, Gloria is my best friend. How can we be friends if we see each other only once or twice a year? We share our hopes, frustrations, memories, and, most of all, our faith.

Gloria has an executive job full of responsibilities, but she always finds time to tell me how her day is going, what she had for lunch, her travel and retirement plans, her recommended books and movies. And she'll share with me her trials at work, her concerns for her teenage son, even times of friction in her marriage.

I often feel isolated and alone at work as a woman manager surrounded by men. Gloria is my lifesaver. She's also devoted to the Lord and lives a life full of grace. Today she titled her e-mail "Pray for Joy" and told me how her pastor had prayed that she and her friends would find joy in the Lord. There in the middle of e-mails on new products and deadlines, along with unsolicited sales messages, was the title "Pray for Joy." What a wonderful reminder of God in the midst of work; a Christian friend who cares enough to share a message of love.

Dear God, you speak to me through so many people. Through our relationships with others, we meet Jesus and see you. I praise you for your blessings and thank you for the joy of knowing through messages from dear friends how much you love us. Amen.

Melinda McDonald

When Peace Eludes Me

He woke up and rebuked the wind,
and said to the sea, "Peace! Be still!"
Then the wind ceased, and there was a dead calm.
—Mark 4:39

I don't feel very peaceful today. I have just moved. I am surrounded by boxes. I can't find important papers that I need. I don't have any new friends yet. I don't know where to shop for household supplies. I can't even speak the language very well. You see, I have just moved to Mexico to serve as a missionary.

I feel lonely, overwhelmed and somewhat scared. I find myself thinking about the disciples who started across the lake with Jesus on a calm day, only to find themselves soon caught up in the waves of a storm. And where was Jesus? Asleep in the back of the boat! I can almost hear them thinking, "Wait a minute! Is this what we signed up for today?!"

While I know that Jesus hasn't fallen asleep and abandoned me in my new circumstances, I find it difficult in the midst of transition to remember this fact. I'd rather whine, cry, and wallow in misery than fix my eyes on Jesus, my Lord and my Redeemer. I'm more likely to complain and get frustrated than to take time to pray and stand steadfastly on God's promises. But this is part of being human. This is part of being sinful. This is part of growing in my Christian journey. Many times Jesus asks me to pass through the storm before he rises and says, "Peace, be still."

What I learn from this story is how to have inner peace in the midst of a storm. Jesus is able to sleep because he knows God is watching over him, caring for him, protecting him from harm. And if Jesus is Lord of my life, this is the promise God offers to me as well. I may become afraid, but I have the assurance that God is with me as I traverse this unpredictable "new sea" in my life.

God, I ask for the assurance that you are ever with me, no matter what my circumstances. I exhale the anxiety upon my soul, and then inhale a long, deep breath of your peaceful Spirit. Allow me to rest comfortably in the boat even when the sea is stormy. Amen.

Joyce Anderson Reed

Finding Wholeness

For as in one body we have many members,
and not all the members have the same function,
so we, who are many, are one body in Christ,
and individually we are members one of another.
—Romans 12:4-5

I grew up in a respected church-going family that was affected by alcoholism. Although I had friends throughout grade school, by the time I reached college I had developed a fear of other people, primarily as a result of low self-esteem. I wore a mask of independence, trying to show others how capable I was. I stopped attending church.

Later, therapy and twelve-step groups gradually helped me gain a sense of my own worth. The twelve steps were a gateway back to my earlier faith. I found myself, after many years, drawn back to church. I experienced a profound renewal of faith through conversion and developed a deep desire for closer relationship with Christ.

One of the most important steps I took in my new faith was becoming involved with groups of other believers. I quickly learned how important it is to be in fellowship with others, studying and sharing testimonies. I began developing a greater sense of wholeness as I realized how connected I was to each person. I found myself wanting to spend even more time studying, praying, worshiping, and fellowshiping with others. I found that by being with others I discerned my place in the body of Christ. I learned that I need other people as much as I need food for replenishment and wholeness.

To go from a fear of others to a longing and desire to immerse myself in the body of Christ has been a miracle, as has been my resulting wholeness. I have learned that we are all one in the body of Christ.

Lord, help us to understand how much we need each other. Place in our hearts the courage and compassion to reach out to those who need to feel connected. Only you can make us whole, as we reach out to you in utter dependence. We praise you. In Jesus' name. Amen.

Amy Pearson

Waiting for the Holy Spirit

Gathering them together, He commanded them not to
leave Jerusalem, but to wait for what the Father had
promised, "Which," He said, "you heard of from Me"...
These all with one mind were continually devoting
themselves to prayer, along with the women, and Mary
the mother of Jesus, and with His brothers.
—Acts 1:4,14, NASB

In one of his sermons our pastor challenged the congregation to read the Bible every day. Then he cited the meager statistics regarding Christians who actually do this. Not long after that, I and another person from the church attended a conference on prayer. The conference leaders said to us, "Go back home and pray for your church."

Their challenge made me think: "Am I not reading the Bible? Well, not every day." "Am I not praying? Well, not so much for the church. How does one pray for the church?"

My friend and I took the challenge seriously. We recorded some prayer requests for our church and were amazed at the results of this exercise: there were more than twenty prayer requests that we thought were relevant for the church! My friend said, "But I don't know how to pray." Her honest confession made us realize that not only did we lack knowledge on what to pray for, but we were also unsure about how to pray. But we believed that God would teach us, so we began to pray together every Sunday morning.

In the Scriptures, Jesus commanded those he gathered to stay in Jerusalem until God sent the Holy Spirit. Those who had earlier said to Jesus, "Lord, teach us to pray," obeyed him and met together in a room. What did they do? They prayed. The men and women prayed continually. They prayed to the Lord for discernment in finding another disciple to replace Judas, and they chose Matthias. Jesus had led them to establish his church, his body. And they obeyed him and responded by praying together.

My friend who didn't know how to pray became a prayer warrior—a leader of prayer. We had followed God's call to us through our pastor and the conference leader to be grounded in the Word and to pray. We continued to pray, and soon others began to join us.

Those who asked Jesus to teach them to pray obeyed him and became the catalysts for establishing the church. Christ's challenge to us through all the ages is that prayer is necessary to undergird the working of the Holy Spirit. "These all with one mind were continually devoting themselves to prayer." That prayer meeting continues to this day.

Gracious Savior, call us to change your church in the twenty-first century to be like the one you established. Pour out your Spirit upon us when we pray together as you did in Jerusalem. Give us the courage to obey, to seek your face, to follow the bidding of the Holy Spirit. We ask in the precious name of Jesus. Amen.

Annette L. James

New Life

For as the rain and the snow come down from heaven, and do not return there until they have watered the earth, making it bring forth and sprout, giving seed to the sower and bread to the eater, so shall my word be that goes out from my mouth; it shall not return to me empty, but it shall accomplish that which I purpose, and succeed in the thing for which I sent it.
—Isaiah 55:10-11

Rain and snow bring new life. Rain and snow come down and accomplish what God wants them it to do: water the earth. Water does not return to God without accomplishing the desire and purpose for which it was sent. When the rains water the earth, flowers bud and trees sprout new leaves. When the trees flourish, they give forth fruit, produce shade, provide wood for heat, logs for building houses, wood for furnishing homes and offices. Trees also provide safe havens for birds to build nests.

When the rain waters the earth, vegetable gardens and wheat fields grow and produce an abundance of crops so that human beings and animals have food to eat. So when God waters the earth, it yields back to him, the sower, accomplishing God's desire and purposes.

God's word also goes forth. God speaks a word in the hearts and minds of God's chosen vessels, and the word waters the dry ground of human lives and breaks up places that need fresh new rain. New life brings new opportunities for you to produce whatever God desires and purposes for you.

God's word will yield seed for you as a sower. That seed may be encouraging you to volunteer to help children, to visit the sick, care for the elderly, or show concern for a shut-in neighbor. When you do the things that God tells you to do, God's word will not return to him void, but will accomplish what God desires and purposes for his people. God's promises are real; God will send rain to save God's people and give them new life.

Heavenly Father, thank you for giving us new life. Please strengthen us with nourishing water so that we may always be ready to minister and accomplish the tasks that you have set before us. Amen.

Blanche Clipper Hudson

They Were There

Meanwhile, standing near the cross of Jesus,
were his mother, and his mother's sister,
Mary the wife of Clopas, and Mary Magdalene.
—Matthew 19:25b

They were there.
From the very beginning, they were there.
In the in-between times, they were there.
At the end, they were there.
Always, the women were there.

Often they were nameless, like the one who anointed Jesus and the woman at the well.

Others had names: Mary, his mother; Mary and Martha; Mary Magdalene. In either case, what matters is their presence, their witness, their steadfastness, their faith, and their support. For Jesus, it was invaluable, and possibly meant the difference between his being able and not being able to do his ministry in Galilee. It is impossible, in this time and place, to determine what it would have been like in that time and place without the women.

They were there.

As it was for Jesus, so it is for us. We are no different.
They—the women—are there for us also.
At the beginning, at our birth.
In the middle, during the school days, in marriage, childbearing and rearing, as role models, in the workplace, at church, in sickness, in health, in the bad and good times.
At the end, at our death.
They are there.

Mothers, sisters, friends, mentors, teachers, leaders, heroines, acquaintances, doctors, nurses, directors, therapists. The women are there.

Their presence matters. They make a difference. Our lives would be so much poorer without them. The women are there, and I am grateful. Some are now dead; others continue to surround me with love, affection, and encouragement. I thank God for the many wonderful women who have been part of my life.

Dear God, thank you for the wonderful women of the Bible, named and nameless, who contribute so much to our faith. Thank you, too, for the wonderful women in our lives who enrich and nourish us in our journeys. In Jesus' name. Amen.

Janet K. Hess

One Person Can
Make a Difference!

*...when her father and her mother died,
Mordecai adopted [Esther] as his own daughter.*
—Esther 2:7

*"Who knows? Perhaps you have come
to royal dignity for just such a time as this."*
—Esther 4:14b

At age four, I was orphaned. Since child welfare was not organized as it is today, there was an effort to find someone who would take a child out of generosity. I believe my heavenly father intervened at that point. A neighboring family took me, but I became a medical expense to them during the three years they kept me. When I was seven, they took me to a county orphanage. I was there only three months when I was adopted by a retired physician, seventy-four, and his wife, fifty-four, who was a professional seamstress. Can you imagine authorities today allowing a couple that age to adopt a seven-year-old child? And yet it was the most wonderful experience for me.

Unfortunately, my new mother lived for only five more years, so that by the age of twelve I had lost a second mother. But by sharing the rich experiences that they had lived through, both new parents taught me a great deal about life. And in spite of the huge age difference, my father continued to influence my life after my mother's death.

And I was able to be of help to him, too. I provided care and companionship. I drove him places when he could no longer drive himself. And I defended him in court as competent when his son tried to have him declared incompetent in an effort to gain control of his assets. Perhaps I, like Esther, was placed there by God "for such a time as this."

Probably my father's greatest impact on my life was his devotion to Jesus and the teachings of the church. We attended services every Sunday morning and evening. My father was a lifelong deacon, and ministers were in and out of our house constantly, consulting with him. Those were the days when churches had evangelistic meetings for a week every year. The visiting preachers always stayed at our house. I experienced warmth and energy from discussions my father had with them. There was no radio, no TV—just conversations.

People in our town also loved my father. They told me many stories of how much they appreciated that he prayed with them when he made medical "house calls." When I was eighteen, Dr. Randolph died at the age of eighty-five. The impact he had on my life motivated me to get an education and devote my life to the work of the church.

Our Father, you have shown us time and time again that your love is steadfast and that it endures forever. You have touched us with your love at those times when we were most vulnerable and least in control of our own lives and destinies. And you have touched us through other persons who have been instruments in your hand—channels through which your spirit moved. And for that we give you thanks. Amen.

Delores R. Davis

Finding Our Purpose

We know that all things work together for good for those who love God, who are called according to his purpose.
—Romans 8:28

One evening at a Circle meeting we were discussing how God uses us according to God's purposes. I have always felt there is a purpose for each of us. My fear was that I would not recognize and fulfill my purpose, thus disappointing and failing my Creator.

My husband and I had two small children. One of the women in the Circle suggested it might be that adopting these children was my reason for being. This to me did not seem to be the answer. Had we not adopted them, someone would have and they would have had a good home.

As I was dusting the furniture a few days following that Circle meeting, I was singing and reminiscing about my childhood. My thoughts kept returning to the time when I was five years old. My life was drastically altered that year. I was severely burned over a third of my body—so severely that my neck was burned completely through. At that time, treatment of such extensive burns was minimal, nothing like today's technology. In fact, it was a miracle that I survived.

I have always loved to sing. My voice is not a strong or powerful one, nor is it a "solo" voice. But it's not bad either. With each swish of the dust cloth, as I continued to sing, I dwelt on the discussion at Circle. What was it that God wanted me to do? What was God's plan for me? Then it was as though a quiet voice spoke to me: "You have a voice. Use it, child. Sing for me." Could this be my purpose?

Yes, it was a miracle I survived that tragedy fifty-five years ago. But there was a second miracle also. Despite the extent of my burns, my voice was not damaged. I should not be able to speak, let alone sing. It is only by the grace of God that I do so.

Lord, help all of us to recognize the purposes for which you have made us. Help each of us to know that our purpose may be deceptively simple, straightforward, and part of our everyday lives. Amen.

Rosalyce Grubbs

A Mother's Touch

She girds herself with strength,
and makes her arms strong.
—Proverbs 31:17

How can I forget the gentleness of her touch as she extends her hand in love, the hand that holds, comforts, and protects me from all hurt and harm? That indescribable love that surpasses all of my understanding is expressed as her fingertips reach out to embrace and encourage me when life's perilous journey throws me a curve.

It is her strong arms that hold me close to her bosom and enable me to feel so very secure. When tears roll down my cheeks for reasons I choose not to remember, it is her hand that gently strokes my face and wipes my tears away. It is the gentleness of my mother's touch that caresses me as she tenderly bends her face to mine, as she lovingly receives my goodnight kiss. Then she smiles and hugs me until my breath is almost taken away.

Oh, to hear her laughter and to feel the magnitude and depth of love in just a single touch! What a joy to have this remembrance of a time so long ago. To be able to recall as if it were yesterday—the sweet feel of my own mother's touch. A mother's touch can ease the pressure of life's challenges and encourage you to press on to greater heights. Her touch expresses strength when her child feels weak; her touch expresses hope when doubt is all about. Her touch directs us to someone greater than herself, and that someone is Jesus the Christ.

Oh God, I thank you for the sense of touch. What a marvelous way to express feelings when words are insufficient. God, I thank you for giving to me this beautiful language of touch so that I may through you touch the lives of others. Amen.

Inga O. Green

Why Me, Lord?

But Moses said to God, "Who am I that I should go to Pharaoh, and bring the Israelites out of Egypt?"
—Exodus 3:11

I did not have an undergraduate degree; I felt I was not qualified. Yet I felt called. I took a look at myself and asked, "Why me, Lord? Why seminary?" I felt I would never make it in an academic setting. I was in my late forties, had been out of school for a long time, was divorced, and needed to support myself.

I visited the seminary and met with the academic dean. We had a great conversation. The dean told me I should apply for the Master of Divinity program. I replied, "I do not know how to write academic papers." All I could think about was my lack of preparation.

The dean said to me, "After talking to you, I am sure you can do this program. You are a very smart woman, and you have done all the practical work." I left his office praying and asking God to reveal this to me. I spoke to several people, who all said the same thing as the dean. My family was excited at the prospect of having another minister in the family.

As I continued in prayer, my spirit began to say "yes." So I applied to seminary and was accepted. There were hard times, but God saw me through. I graduated with my Master of Divinity degree and even received the Koinonia award. I am presently continuing my studies.

Many of us hear the call and respond, "Why me, Lord?" I am not capable. Send someone else." But sometimes God answers, "Someone else cannot do the job that you were chosen to do. Everyone has different gifts and talents to offer."

I believe that God does not call those who are already equipped for ministry, but rather equips those whom God calls. I came to realize that God knows the plan for each of our lives, and no amount of questions will keep God from working with us and through us. So instead of asking, "Why me, Lord," ask, "How can I do it, Lord?"

Merciful God, I thank you that you never leave us alone, and I thank you for all the gifts and talents you have given to your children. As we answer your call on our lives, please continue to develop those gifts and talents so we may serve your people with love, wisdom, and understanding. Amen.

Juana L. Francis

A Leap of Faith

"Ask, and it will be given you; search, and you will find; knock, and the door will be opened for you."
—*Matthew 7:7*

Another boring day locked inside my windowless office on a bright July morning in Detroit. Would the Lord really require me to spend the next two years here? My heart yearned to attend seminary full time, but how?

A staff meeting was called for 11 a.m. We would be introduced to the person interested in purchasing our company. If the deal went through we could maintain our jobs if we were willing to move to Kansas City. As I contemplated my family's predicament, the Holy Spirit impressed upon my heart that if we had to move anyway, why not move to Rochester, New York, where I could go to seminary full time? What about our youngest daughter, who was attending an international Baptist conference in Texas and planning to start her junior year in high school? I began to pray with all my heart.

My husband and I talked. I started making calls. My every thought became a prayer. Things began moving very rapidly. The new school year would begin in Rochester in early September. What happened in the next few weeks only the Holy Spirit could have accomplished. Our daughter got off the van from Texas asking, "What major change is going to happen in our lives, Mom?" Two days later we were on the road to Rochester in search of housing and a school for our daughter. I had to give notice at my job before even knowing if our daughter had been accepted in the school we had chosen, before knowing how much financial aid I would be receiving. We had no idea what kind of work my husband would find.

God worked out all the details in wondrous ways. Two years have passed. Our daughter is attending Oberlin College with over two-thirds of her costs paid by scholarships. I graduated from seminary. As I ponder the blessings that the Lord has bestowed upon our family during this journey, I am overwhelmed.

Thank you, Lord for opening the doors to new life. Please guide our footsteps as we continue the journey in your name. Amen.

Sarah Verne de Bourg

Of Resurrection and Revolution

When the sabbath was over, Mary Magdalene,
and Mary the mother of James, and Salome
bought spices, so that they might go and anoint him.
And very early on the first day of the week,
when the sun had risen, they went to the tomb.
—Mark 16:1-2

The very nature of resurrection is revolutionary. The resurrection of Jesus teaches us that that which is dead is not always gone. The resurrection of Jesus teaches us that shrouds and mourning cloths do not always mean the end. The resurrection teaches us that appearance is one thing, but reality is something totally different. Why talk about raising the dead? Because the resurrection of our Savior reminds us that the grave is not always the last stop; tombs are just temporary and stones do not have to stop us. Hope and dreams never die.

Why talk about resurrection in conjunction with revolution? Because something happens from the time of death to the time of new life. Because some 2000 years ago women led a revolution. The resurrection gave believers a new spiritual outlook, for the King of Israel, the new David, had arrived. And women were there. The resurrection engendered a new political outlook, for it mattered not what Pilate, Herod, or Tiberias did anymore. And women were there. The resurrection gave even these women a new social outlook, for they were revolutionaries in the army of Jesus Christ, no longer caring that others considered them second-class citizens. Women at the tomb of Jesus on the first day of the week, early in the morning, catalyzed what would be our model for change.

Yes, they were afraid. Yes, they were scared out of their wits. Yes, the Gospel writer says they were silent. But they still went to the tomb. The Christ they followed is the same risen Lord we follow. The Lord they served is the same ascended Lord we are called to serve. Despite our fears, let us go boldly to the tombs of homelessness and hunger. Regardless of inarticulate moments, let our voices proclaim no more violence or abuse in this new, resurrection day. Where the women at the grave paused, let us pick up the mantle and persevere.

O God of change, use us to be revolutionaries and proclaim new, abundant life to all your people. Amen.

Stephanie Buckhanon Crowder

A Close Call

Whatever your hand finds to do, do with your might...
—Ecclesiastes 9:10a

I can do all things through him who strengthens me.
—Philippians 4:13

It isn't often that one gets to rescue a horse, let alone a Belgian workhorse that weighs more than many cars do. Our horse-shoer rented space in our barn, and there he kept his two Belgians, Smokey and Prince. They were huge animals, gentle in nature and seemingly unaware of their size. Along with the other animals, they became part of the family.

One day I was doing the dishes and heard a terrible thumping noise coming from the barn. I went out to investigate. As I entered the barn, I could hear the heavy breathing of a horse in distress. It was coming from the stall occupied by Prince, the bigger of the two horses. I walked over to see that Prince had somehow gotten the shoe of his left hind leg hooked onto his bridle. How in the world did he do that? Probably trying to swat away some tormenting flies. Coming to his rescue was "man's work." But there were no men around. What to do?

Prince was completely lathered in sweat and I could see the whites of his terrified eyes. I prayed, "Lord, you've got to help us both and show me what to do. I put my hand on Prince's rump to let him know where I was, talking to him gently in an attempt to calm him. I bent my knees just enough to get my shoulder under his giant leg and then, with all my strength, straightened up, lifting his leg enough to unhook his hoof from the bridle. I then quickly stepped aside as he regained his balance, now on all fours. Each of us shaken, I put my arms around his damp neck to comfort us both.

Ron, the blacksmith, later told me that if I hadn't rescued Prince when I did, he could have had a heart attack from the stress and died. From that day on Prince was my buddy. He'd whinny hello and follow me around in the fields or watch me with his big brown eyes. You've just never really been appreciated until you have a half-ton horse show his gratitude to you.

Lord, when situations seem terrifying and the weight seems more than we can naturally bear, help us to "shoulder" the burden, especially when it's to lift someone else out of distress. Thank you for the precious gratefulness of others, which makes the effort so worthwhile. Amen.

Lonnie Lane

A Part of the Family

*For you did not receive a spirit of slavery
to fall back into fear, but you have received
a spirit of adoption. When we cry, "Abba! Father!"
it is that very Spirit bearing witness with our spirit
that we are children of God.
—Romans 8:15-16*

It was our regular monthly luncheon and it also happened to be her birthday. As we sat waiting for our soft drinks, she declared, "I've made up my mind; I'm really going to do it this time. I'm going to locate my natural parents."

In what appeared to be a few seconds, I saw my well-dressed, assertive friend transform into an inquisitive child, a child seeking an adult to provide answers to her simple yet profound questions. Questions like: "Did you give me away because you loved me? Whom do I look like? Did you ever try to find me?" Knowing I could not help much to provide an adequate response, my friend quickly reverted to her normal poise and sophistication.

A few weeks later this same friend called and informed me that she had retrieved all the necessary information: names, phone numbers, and addresses. Her travel plans to South Carolina were finalized. "I will now be able to bring this chapter of my life to a close," she said. "I will be able to move on without ever having to look back again." Our phone conversation was brief, but it was full of excitement.

At the conclusion of our talk, I was reminded that as children of God, we are all adopted and raised as God's own. Adoption though Christ has guaranteed us a place in the kingdom of God. Indeed, the kingdom belongs to us. Our adoption into this family offers us rights and privileges; we are no longer outcasts. We are no longer denied or disowned children. We are joint heirs. We don't just have a room in the mansion, we posses the mansion itself. We are adopted into this family because God loves us. We are a part of this family because we are fearfully and wonderfully made. We are joint heirs because Jesus came to seek and to save those of us who are lost.

God, you took a chance on adopting us, even though you knew our weaknesses. You saw beyond our present realities and knew of our inevitable possibilities. Thank you for allowing us the opportunity to be family. Thank you for allowing us to be your daughters. Amen.

Cherise Valdá Copeland

God in Our Ears

Though the Lord may give you the bread of adversity
and the water of affliction, yet your Teacher will not hide
himself any more, but your eyes shall see your Teacher.
And when you turn to the right or when you turn
to the left, your ears shall hear a word behind you,
saying, "This is the way; walk in it."
—Isaiah 30:20-21

It is wonderful how God gives to us other travelers on life's road. Some of these people may be on the road ahead of us, and some on the road behind. Either way, they are as the voice of God helping to guide our journey.

Years ago I was completing my seminary training and was anticipating that "first call" to pastoral ministry. As a woman, I knew the path to service would not be smooth, but I trusted that as my call was so real, the place of service would eventually open. I knew that God could always make a way.

A little less than a year as interim pastor for my first church had passed when it seemed that God was moving for the congregation to call me as its next pastor. Several of the influential members had been away during the months I had served. They returned just in time for the important congregational vote. Not wanting a woman as their next pastor, they rallied to have the church's call to me voted down.

The day of the congregational vote came. A two-thirds majority was needed for the call to be extended. After the votes were read it appeared that my call as pastor had been denied by one vote. Later that day a young woman in the congregation, a granddaughter of someone who opposed my call to the church, came forward to say she thought her vote had been misinterpreted. She had written "no-vote" meaning an abstention, not a negative vote. That one vote was all I needed!

The "call" as pastor was extended to me. That young woman's action opened the door for my full participation in the life of the church. She became as God's voice in my ears.

In even the smallest of ways, we are called to do and be justice for others along the road. We may be the catalyst who empowers someone else to be the person God would have them be. God puts people on the road ahead and on the road behind. Sometimes it is in the most unlikely of places. Thank God for those who do justice each and every day. Is it today that you are called to be as justice for someone else?

Thank you, God, for others along the road of our journey. Maybe today I am called to act for someone else. Maybe today someone is called to act on my behalf. May we work to be as the voice of God in the ears of another by what we do or say. Amen.

Dawn Nichols Mays

The Darker the Night, the Brighter the Stars

Indeed, you are my lamp, O LORD,
the LORD lightens my darkness.
—2 Samuel 22:29

As a little girl I disliked being alone in the dark and was often frightened upon hearing noises, which actually were just tree limbs brushing against the windows. My childish fear revisited me recently on a dark summer night while I was attending a women's conference.

The evening plenary session lasted longer than expected, so I decided to go back to my room and relax. It was necessary to walk to the guesthouse where I was staying, so during a session break I left to begin my journey. I ignored the night's darkness as the glow of the conference room still surrounded me.

I had a small flashlight that provided limited light, enabling me to walk the narrow road. But finding the guesthouse was a problem since the route was downhill. Then I remembered those childhood years of being alone in the dark, but this time I knew I was not alone: Jesus was with me.

I told Jesus of my situation and felt an immediate calmness come over me. I was able to focus on what I was looking for as I felt his spirit with me. I wasn't alone! Jesus was guiding me, and soon I walked into the guesthouse with heartfelt gratitude.

Through the years I have walked in darkness with burdens too heavy to bear alone. Perhaps you have also, my dear sister. When this happens, I share my concern with Jesus and ask for guidance and patience. Usually I find solutions. Jesus seldom takes the burden away, but he allows me to resolve the problem. My attitude becomes positive, freeing me to activate new ideas that can release the burden. Each one of us, my dear sister, has a loving heavenly parent who is always near and ready to listen, to offer love and guidance, if we but speak to voice our fears, joys, and concerns.

Lord, I thank you for loving me and being near me today, for reminding me of your presence and blessing me with confidence and

calmness to meet the challenges ahead. Use me, Lord, to encour-
age others to do the same: to lose their fear of the darkness. Amen.

Marie Compton

Through the Eyes of Christ

Jesus straightened up and said to her, "Woman, where
are they? Has no one condemned you?" She said,
"No one, sir." And Jesus said, "Neither do I condemn
you. Go your way, and from now on do not sin again."
—John 8:10-11

I was accused of crimes brought against me by the rumor and whisperings of a woman on our staff. Several escalating steps occurred as my supervisor and the system tried to remove me from ministry, culminating in the civilian equivalent of a Grand Jury hearing. During the nine months of investigation, I was publicly humiliated and ostracized. My ministry was stripped from me.

As each stage of punishment was pronounced, I found myself more embarrassed and frightened. I tried to convince myself that the Apostle Paul had a great jail ministry and if that was what I was called to do for the gospel's sake, God would give me the strength and wisdom to persevere. Strangely enough, though still frightened, I experienced a closeness to the Lord and a sense of peace as never before. Somehow I sensed that this battle was the Lord's, if I would only be faithful.

"It's over," said my attorney. "The woman who accused you has been caught stealing from the chapel funds. The only time she didn't steal was the three months when you were the certifying fund official. Her motive is now obvious and the case is over." I wanted to scream, "See, I was innocent! Look what happened and who really was guilty!"

Months later, I was called as a witness at this woman's military trial. As I walked into the courtroom to testify against her, filled with my righteous anger, God struck. How could I hate someone who sat there as frightened and alone as I had been? The fact that she, and not I, was guilty as accused was in some ways irrelevant, for I too was guilty of sin before the Lord—as we all are. I was told that I was the only credible witness and that my colleagues scapegoated their guilt over what they had done unjustly to me onto her. She was sentenced to three years in jail.

I sat in the empty courtroom and watched her being led away in handcuffs. Her husband approached me and said, "Do you hate us?" I told him what God had revealed to me as I entered the court: that she and I were both guilty of sin, though I was not guilty of the lies with which I had been charged. He then asked, "Is it true that there was a thief on the cross next to Jesus who went to heaven?" I replied, "There were two thieves; the choice is still yours to make."

God, and God alone, took my anger and allowed me to see these people as he saw them. I will not chafe if they have experienced the mighty mercy and forgiveness of the Lord. "Neither do I condemn you, go and sin no more."

Heavenly and only true judge, you treat those who approach you with mercy rather than with the justice we deserve. May we see others through your eyes of compassion and forgive as you have forgiven us. Amen.

Janet R. McCormack

Healing and Wholeness

Genuine Self-Worth

You desire truth in the inward being;
therefore teach me wisdom in my secret heart.
—Psalm 51:6

Our views, perception, and understanding of our value and worth depend solely on whether or not we have a personal relationship with God. For centuries, society's view of women has had a detrimental effect. It is a view that assesses our value based on accomplishments, external beauty, and material possessions. Society also says we are complete only once there is a "significant other" in our life. However, these are all false substitutions for obtaining and sustaining inner fulfillment.

How can we determine if these judgments are factual? Let us do some self-examination. Would we feel incomplete if these circumstances were to suddenly change? What if some tragedy were to befall us, changing our outward beauty? If our career were suddenly taken away, would we feel undervalued? What if our "significant other" died or abruptly walked out of our life? How would we then see ourselves?

Do possessions, having a career, or having a man really determine our self worth? Society says it does. But from God's perspective, we are "the apple of His eye" regardless of our circumstances. Our completeness comes from being in Christ. This truth is deepened and nurtured through a faith-filled, abiding, and daily relationship with Christ. We will never see our true worth through our own eyes. Neither can humanity see it or determine it. We desperately need the mind of Christ!

Remember that it was not until the woman with the issue of blood activated her faith by reaching out to touch Jesus that she became whole. He sees each of us as a beautiful, unique creation perfectly designed for a specific purpose, a God-ordained purpose that is sovereignly seen and sovereignly revealed.

The knowledge of God's Word and application of God's principles are life-changing. God's word will give us a new heart, which is a prerequisite for having a new mind, even the mind of Christ.

Father, draw us to you and your Word. Infuse us with a fresh revelation of your inexpressible love for us. Give us hearts yielded to you. Renew our thinking. Show us our inner beauty and worth, and use us to fulfill your purpose in our society today. Amen.

Carmen S. Harris

On Common Ground

There is no longer Jew or Greek, there is no longer slave or free, there is no longer male and female; for all of you are one in Christ Jesus.
—Galatians 3:28

Recently my mother and I attended a prominent Christian women's conference in the Midwest. As we were preparing to shower in the bathroom, a group of women entered. A collective look of shock, possibly fear, was on their faces. "Let's use the other one; it's crowded in here," one woman said, emphasizing the word "crowded." They all looked at us, turned their heads, and walked out briskly. My mother and I looked around and realized there weren't any other people in the room. We two African Americans were the only two people in a room with at least twenty shower stalls.

There is no word to adequately describe being a victim of racism or prejudice. Yet no one has to tell you what it is. You feel it all over. You feel it deep inside. Something cuts into your heart. You feel a combination of anger, sadness, shame, pain, inadequacy, shock, and disbelief, all simultaneously.

Later that day I began to think about the woman at the well who Jesus encountered in Samaria. The other women did not associate with her because of her lifestyle, her social status within the community. Did she attempt to go to the well early in the morning only to be isolated and ignored? Did she find faces that greeted her with fear and contempt? Maybe the Samaritan woman was tired of being "the other," so she strategically planned to go to the well alone. Yet when she encountered Jesus, Jesus offered her living water.

After the incident described above, I knew I needed a fresh taste of the living water. I did not want to become angry or bitter. And so I thought of Jesus coming to give the Samaritan woman this transforming power to live in a cold, dark world. I thought of Jesus coming to heal me from the emotional scars left by prejudice and racism. As women of God, we must proclaim Christ's love within our communities. We must break silence and speak out against the sins of prejudice and racism.

Jesus, use us, your daughters, as instruments of peace to rid the Body of Christ of the evils of prejudice and racism. Help us to take the time to find common ground with our sisters from diverse backgrounds. For we are all one in Christ Jesus. Amen.

Anissa Danielle Gibbs

On Being Real

...I remind you to rekindle the gift of God that is within you...for God did not give us a spirit of cowardice, but rather a spirit of power and of love and of self-discipline.
—2 Timothy 1:6b-7

When I was twenty-seven or so, my chief joy was teaching a three-hour church school class for fifth and sixth graders. My New Jersey Church sent me—a raw "teacher"—to Green Lake, Wisconsin, for a two-week study on teaching. This was in the early 1960s when everyone was learning how to "be real." This poor fledgling had no idea what her instructor meant when he told her that if she wanted to be a good teacher, she "just needed to be real." Thirty years later I think I am finally catching on to what it means to "be real": to be true to who I am and what I think and feel.

One experience I had at Green Lake continues to reverberate in my soul across the miles and years and other experiences. One afternoon we saw a movie filmed by a photographer-artist. He took pictures of tiny fragments of nature and superimposed them on top of each other: a fern leaf in a creek of clear running water and mounds of smooth stones; roses in a snow storm; a dandelion's delicate spores and an orchid's exquisite patterns. There was a medley of classical music as background. The movie lasted for forty-five minutes, and I sobbed all the way through it. It was too much beauty for me to absorb at one sitting. It went so fast! It was over so quickly! Just like life.

I learned to be real by expressing what I felt. I also learned that when I got married at nineteen, I had left my "inner child"—my artist—back in Missouri, and she wanted to come out! Little by little, over the next fifteen years I did let her out of her shell. I learned that keeping a part of myself in a closet was the most damaging thing I had ever done to myself and thus to the people I loved.

When I was forty-nine, I went to college in northern California where the skies are perfect. I would walk into class and ask if anyone else had noticed how beautiful the clouds were. (No one had.) Whenever I see cloud formations and flowers blooming, I want to stop the world and look and smell and touch. It is the deepest hunger I have. It is the way I express my thirst for the Creator, our God, and my awareness of God's closeness.

If you are boxed in, try to find a way out. Find someone to walk with you. Find a church with something like a Stephen ministry, or a reputable pastor who does counseling, or a professional counselor. God is available through the Holy Spirit and through many of his human helpers.

God of open boxes, whose love knows no boundaries, help me to become more aware of the ways I am closed in, especially the ways I deny my gifts and abilities, gifts that you have given me to use for your kingdom. Amen.

Dorothy Larimore Michel

The Burden of a Bent Back

Now he was teaching in one of the synagogues on the sabbath. And just then there appeared a woman with a spirit that had crippled her for eighteen years. She was bent over and was quite unable to stand up straight.
—Luke 13:10-11

In my first year of seminary I was involved in a car accident. A friend and I were traveling in his car and had stopped at a red light. All of a sudden, out of nowhere an old van rear-ended us. Both of us suffered injuries to our backs, requiring six weeks of physical therapy. To this day I have trouble lifting objects over fifteen pounds, and I experience difficulty standing or sitting for a long period of time. All due to a back injury I suffered ten years ago.

Thus I can empathize with the woman in Luke who for eighteen years had been bent over and could not even stand up straight. Can you imagine the stress on her spine? Muscles? Tissue? Cartilage? For eighteen years she stood in an upside-down U position, seeing only the ground. She was physically challenged. She was an invalid. She was crippled. She was lame. There was a spirit that made this woman the way she was.

What makes you lame? What makes you bend over? What makes you physically or spiritually challenged? So many of us are sad and just sitting by the seashore of life wasting away over some past hurt. Over some lost job. Over family issues. What cripples us? A spirit of helplessness? A spirit of hopelessness? Lack of emotional healing?

When Jesus spoke to this woman and laid hands on her, she straightened. What she couldn't do by herself or for herself, Jesus did for her. She needed someone to affirm her. She needed someone to see her and do something about her situation. Jesus did. And this woman did not forget the one who helped her. When she was straightened, she straightway gave praise to God.

God of wholeness, thank you for being so patient with us and straightening us when we need you most. Amen.
Stephanie Buckhanon Crowder

Toddler Justice

She looks well to the ways of her household...
—Proverbs 31:27a

"I need some space! He's bothering me!" my two-year-old son declared, pointing at his eight-month-old brother.

I was hard put not to laugh—or scream—or cry. Is it starting already? I asked myself as I wondered how to handle my toddler's complaint. And where did he learn the word *bother* anyway?

My spouse and I used to be highly articulate, socially minded Christian feminists, passionate about issues of justice and intrigued by questions of theological truth. We are still capable of being those persons. But when surrounded by our two children (as only a fast-growing infant and toddler can surround you), we are swiftly reduced to the kind of person (and parent) we most disdain—impatient, intolerant, and exasperated.

That day I found myself wondering, "God, how can I work for righteousness in your world when the only justice issues that confront me nowadays are how to deal fairly with my toddler's desire for personal space?"

"What better place to teach justice," the Spirit whispered in reply, "than in these early years of childhood? What better place to teach feminist principles than in your own home? What better subjects for such teaching than the boys who will become young men who will teach those lessons to the next generation?"

Suddenly, I no longer want to laugh or cry or scream. Instead, I found it a little easier to draw my son to my knee and explain in quiet understanding about asserting his need for space in a gentle and loving way. And I watched as he fetched a different toy for his brother, gave the baby a solemn kiss, and moved away to create his own space a little distance away.

Precious Lord, thank you for the profound insight that parenting offers the unique opportunity for preventive care in issues of wholeness and justice. By laying strong foundations in my sons' lives, I pray that the world in which they will live will be a better and more just place in which to raise their own sons and daughters. Amen.
Rebecca Irwin-Diehl

"Bearing"

Now Laban had two daughters;
the name of the elder was Leah...
—Genesis 29:16
(For the full context, read 29:16-35 through 30:1-24.)

My best friend in elementary school had long sandy-brown braids and a sun-kissed complexion, which translated into status in the community. In those days I had to bear the "grown folks" who would step in between us to tell her how cute she was. I helped her with her homework, but she was always called on for the answers. I learned "bearing" early.

I loved the stories of Old Testament women, even though they were sketchy and one-dimensional. Reading between the lines, I learned that these women had deep and rich relationships with God. The stories of these "bearing women" helped me make sense of my own bearing. I especially identified with Leah's story because back then I thought it was a story of how to "bear" being second best (as with my friend) and still be loved by God no matter how others treat or view you.

Leah's story fascinated me and revealed something new with every reading. It seemed that Leah's life was doomed to "bearing" from the very beginning: bad eyes, a pretty baby sister, a no-good conniving daddy, an unloving husband, a houseful of boys. and a baby girl to boot! How could she bear so much?

One day after reading Leah's story for the umpteenth time, my tender eyes were opened. I saw a determined woman of great faith who knew and praised God even when it appeared she was bearing one bad situation after another. While many saw Leah as isolated from community, she was spending time with God. When we saw Leah as damaged goods, God saw her as the mother of nations. Leah has taught me that the lesson is not to learn "bearing." but rather to praise and trust God while bearing.

Gracious God, help us to see opportunities in our moments of bearing to be closer to you. Teach us to praise you and trust you at all times. Amen.

Valora Starr Butler

To Whom Should We Listen?

*So they left the tomb quickly with fear and great joy, and
ran to tell his disciples. Suddenly Jesus met them and
said, "Greetings!" And they came to him, took hold of
his feet, and worshiped him. Then Jesus said to them,
"Do not be afraid; go and tell my brothers
to go to Galilee; there they will see me."
—Matthew 28:8-10*

Beginning seminary in the mid 1970s in a class of seventy-six students, I was one of the five women in the Master of Divinity program at my school. In those days ordaining women was still new in my denomination.

The first week of seminary I remember male classmates coming up to me and saying, "What makes you think you can be a pastor?" Only once did I try to respond honestly to the question. But rational thinking and answers did not satisfy the questioner. So after that I simply responded, "Because our church says I can."

Regarding the ordination of women, Paul is often quoted as saying, "Women should be silent in churches" (1 Corinthians 14:34). Or we hear that Paul permitted "no woman to teach or to have authority over a man; she is to keep silent" (1 Timothy 2:12).

One could do serious Bible study focusing on what is or is not authentically Pauline and whether Paul or any other author was addressing a specific concern of the church to which he was writing. We could look at the original Greek and see what nuances certain words had. We could even talk about how the male outlook and upbringing in those days would have affected what authors wrote. Thoughtful study could shed some interesting light on these passages.

But simpler, we can go back to the events of that first Easter morning. It was the women who went to the tomb to find it empty. It was there that the angel told them to go and tell the disciples. Then a few moments later, it was Jesus who urged them to go and tell.

Proclaiming the Good News was a task first given to women to tell the men. If Jesus tells a woman to proclaim the Good News and Paul (or another author) says to keep silent, to whom is she to listen?

God of all creation, help us to look beyond differences to that upon which we can agree: Christ is risen and the world needs to be told. Help all to know that because Christ lives, we too shall live. Amen.

Julia O. Shreve

Managing Anger

Do not let the sun go down on your anger.
—Ephesians 4:26b

What is it that makes you angry? Is it your boss who puts you down? Or your neighbors who are too loud? Or your spouse who embarrasses you? Or your children who do not mind you the way you think they ought to? Or your parents who make unreasonable demands on you? Or the person who cuts in the traffic line in front of you? Perhaps the unfairness life often brings?

What do you do about your anger? Are you like a volcano when it erupts and destroys everything in its path? Are you like the teapot that builds up a head of steam and then sets the whistle to blowing? Anger is without doubt a part of the human condition. Yet our own anger and that of others, especially if expressed in frightening ways, has such power! It can cause an explosive fury like a tornado or flash floods whose destructiveness, though over in a moment, can leave behind significant permanent wreckage, wreckage that can take years to undo.

We have seen relationships destroyed forever by anger. The biblical story of Cain's murder of Abel is a story of explosive anger. Anger can feel like a sinful emotion. There are, however, no sinful emotions. Emotions and feelings come from God. They are not sinful, although how they are expressed may be in violation of God's law.

Anger is an emotion given to us by God. We may be angry as a response to being ignored or injured, or being treated unfairly or disrespectfully. Anger is an appropriate response when we see others treated in dehumanizing ways. There is a place in God's world and in our lives for anger. Paul tells us that we are to be angry, but not to sin, and that the sun is not to go down on our anger. In other words, we are to deal with the authenticity of the feeling, and not abuse its expression sinfully. Anger is to be experienced and released in healthy and constructive ways. And, no, that is not a contradiction.

We do need to control our anger lest it become destructive and out of control. We need to channel it toward constructive ends. We also need to express it, for anger unexpressed, buried within us, is a festering sore that leads us to depression, physical illness, or withdrawal from life and relationships.

Healthy anger, on the other hand, can lead to change. It can fill us with determination to make things better. We must hold our anger in the embracing arms of love. Have you ever felt that God was angry with you? I certainly have! But I also know that God still loves me.

Dear Lord, help us to express anger constructively. Help us to keep our anger from hurting others or, by internalizing it, to harm ourselves. Amen.

Elizabeth Dikkers Killeen

Sacrifice

The sacrifice acceptable to God is a broken spirit; a broken and contrite heart, O God, you will not despise.
—Psalm 51:17

No emotion. Just a blank look as the physician told us of the results of the biopsy. We sat in a cramped room with no windows and no pictures to brighten anyone's day. The physician scanned the room, met my eyes, and declared to my family, as if reporting the local forecast, that the biopsy revealed my mother indeed had lung cancer. "It's inoperable. Maybe radiation and/or chemotherapy will delay it, but nothing will stop its malignancy." Simply put, it was only a matter of time.

I was in my first year of seminary when this happened. I made up my own mind to pack up my belongings and return home to care for my mother. After all, I had only one. After all, she had nurtured me through colds, childhood diseases, and relational heartbreaks. This was the least I could do. I could put my theological studies on hold; my mother came first. No sacrifice was too great!

As I was returning from the hospital one evening, God unexpectedly informed me that I had made a decision without consulting him. I had made plans without God's approval. God asked me a few questions: "Who called you? Who sent you to seminary? And who are you, to put my plans for you on hold?"

God was telling me that I could not sacrifice my studies in order to care for my mother. It seemed to me that God was being cruel, unfair, difficult, and selfish. Yet God revealed to me that when I accepted this call, I had given up my right to control my own life and was required to place all authority in the hands of the Divine.

Sacrifice is giving up what you have no right to keep, or liberating someone you have no power to own. Therefore, I sacrificed my mother to God and myself to my studies. And God sustains us both.

O God, continue to show us how to deny self and pursue your Kingdom first. Give us daring souls to recognize that everything can and will be manifested either in the here and now or in the imminent promise of the future. Amen.

Cherise Valdá Copeland

Lost Treasures

"...she calls together her friends and neighbors, saying, 'Rejoice with me, for I have found the coin that I had lost.'"
—Luke 15:9
(For the full context, read Luke 15:8-10.)

This woman had ten coins and she lost one of them. These coins were drachmas, each worth about a day's wage for a laborer. Losing one of these drachmas meant that she'd lost ten percent of her savings! But she doesn't passively accept her loss. She turns on a lamp to light her way. She gets out a broom and begins sweeping everywhere. And she searches diligently.

This woman engages in several actions that continually guide me in my own personal and spiritual growth. The process of searching, finding, and celebrating the lost parts of myself has been a meaningful part of my own journey. The first step is realizing that something is missing.

Once we become aware of the lost thing, then the real hard work of searching begins. Our own lost coin may be a particular skill or talent. It may take a lot of sweeping and dusting for those parts of ourselves to be revealed, aspects of ourselves to which we have not been attentive.

The most difficult losses to unearth are those that have remained buried within us for a long time. It took many years for me to learn that the numbness I felt inside was not the only way to live. After diligently searching I came to understand that many of my lost feelings could be found buried in my childhood experience of an addictive family. Our loss may be a painful experience, and when it is revealed, we are released from a kind of bondage. We can then live life more fully, abundantly. We all have a treasure within us waiting to be revealed or released.

The process of finding and claiming lost resources has other applications as well. This woman's tenacity in searching is also echoed in the efforts of women who stand up for their rights to a living wage, for health benefits, or for affordable childcare.

Jesus told this story of the lost coin sandwiched between the stories of the lost sheep and the prodigal son. He calls us out of the lost places in our lives. He coaxes us to return to wholeness and justice, into restored relationship with one another, to live life abundantly. And when we find our own lost coin, then we can rejoice and celebrate our discoveries with our friends and neighbors! God wants us to share the beauty we have found within us. Let the woman's tenacious search for her lost coin become a guide for us to find our own hidden treasure. For when we do, "there is joy in the presence of the angels of God."

God of the lost and the found, guide me in my journey to deepen my awareness of those parts of myself that have been lost. Aid me in my search. Open my eyes and ears to be sensitive to the losses of others and help me to search with them for justice. Amen.

Kolya Braun-Greiner

Courage to Find Healing

*Then suddenly a woman who had been suffering from
hemorrhages for twelve years came up behind him and
touched the fringe of his cloak, for she said to herself,
"If I only touch his cloak, I will be made well."*
—Matthew 9:20-21

She lived in a mountain village and had to walk quite a distance to get to the missionary's clinic, which is open one day a week in a village several kilometers outside of Quetzeltenango, Guatemala. Several months before, in the midst of a storm, she had been in her kitchen preparing the family's meal. Lightning struck, shooting down through their thatched room and through her body.

The woman survived, but the skin on the front of one leg had been seared off. In the subsequent months, she tried doctoring it with whatever she had as she suffered through the pain. Asked why she had not come sooner, she told the doctor that her husband wouldn't allow her to do so because it cost one quetzel to see a doctor at the clinic. One quetzel was equal to about twelve cents in U.S. currency. But she finally was overcome with pain, and somehow got a hold of a quetzel to pay the doctor.

I had friends—a husband and wife team—who were missionaries in the area at the time. As Charles told me this story, I could see the expression on his face and hear the tone in his voice. He was angered at the thought of a husband who could love his wife so little as to let her suffer so long.

Years later, I too feel a sense of anger about oppressive circumstances that lead to women's suffering. Then I remember the woman who hemorrhaged for twelve years. She tried a number of things. Then she heard about Jesus and the healings he had performed. Something within her ignited hope and faith. She truly believed if she only touched his cloak, she would be healed. It was enough faith to overcome the taboos in her culture according to which women with her condition should not be in public. She risked a lot to go and find Jesus. With her faith came true courage.

*God of love, in the beginning you created humankind—male and
female you created us. Help our world overcome the attitudes that*

would have women feel unworthy of getting the help they need. At the same time, give women the faith and courage to overcome. Amen.

Julia O. Shreve

Ministry in Shared Pain

...but [the Lord] said to me, "My grace is sufficient for you, for power is made perfect in weakness."
So, I will boast all the more gladly of my weaknesses, so that the power of Christ may dwell in me.
—2 Corinthians 12:9

You know that it was because of a physical infirmity that I first announced the gospel to you.
—Galatians 4:13

When the inflammation first hit my muscles, it settled into my upper back until the swelling restricted the blood flow to my hands and constricted the muscles of my arms. Then the real misery began. Test for Lupus. Try this drug. Test for Multiple Sclerosis. Try that muscle-relaxer. "Bend your fingers. What do you mean you can't bend your fingers?" Fibromyalgia? Chronic Fatigue? Go to this specialist. "Take off your clothes. Put out your arm; we need more blood." Another X-ray. Another test. Inside, I cry, "Excuse me, does anyone realize I've ceased to exist? This isn't me, shivering in my underwear in yet another cold, fluorescent-lighted room! Poke the shell. Prod it. Take more blood. Why not? I'm not even sure you need a needle. I think I can bleed on command by now!" Twisted humor. Tears fall with my clothing.

"The tests came back negative, Ms. Moor. Have you tried a Rheumatologist?" "I'm sorry you hurt." "There's no evidence of arthritis." "Try this drug." Constant pain. Constant fatigue. I'm sick to death of being touched and prodded by strangers. Depression. I want to die.

Months pass. A year. Slowly the inflammation calms down and

the work to regain the use of arms and hands begins. Inch by painful inch I pull on flex bands until my arms begin to straighten. Piano drills work stiff, numb fingers and wrists that refuse to rotate. Every day is a fight for manual dexterity: Drop the cup; clean the floor; drop the plate; clean the floor. Pick up the broken pieces. Of the plate. Of my life. I hate feeling so incompetent!

God, show me something beyond this moment. Give me a reason to keep trying. Then one day I find myself sitting with one of my parishioners, watching the tears stream from her eyes as she grieves the loss of her body's health. "I hurt," she whispers. "I know," my body affirms. Her hands clench into fists: "I am so angry at God!" "I know," my soul responds. "You understand!" she cries. "Yes," my heart answers. She holds my hand and opens her heart, and ministry begins in shared pain.

Lord, let our weaknesses open doors that our strengths never could. Amen.

Kelly S. Moor

Redeeming the Past

*For the grace of God has appeared, bringing salvation
to all,...while we wait for the blessed hope and the
manifestation of the glory of our great God and Savior,
Jesus Christ. He it is who gave himself for us that he
might redeem us from all iniquity and purify for himself
a people of his own who are zealous for good deeds.*
—Titus 2:11,13-14

My husband, Dave, and I had the unique privilege to be in a ten week class with Larry Crabb, who has started a new ministry of spiritual direction called New Way Ministries. We laughed, we pondered, we absorbed like sponges as the Holy Spirit spoke through Larry in powerful ways. One night Larry said a striking thing: "We must find ways to look into the cesspools of our pasts and let God redeem the awful things lurking there, let him use them in some way to bring glory to himself and peace to our spirits. We must look and see if there is anything there that has life in it. And we can ask God to help that life to grow."

It has long been on my lips and heart that God can indeed redeem anything, make it new, change it into something good. I believed it. Unless it applied to my own past experiences. I had found it hard to believe that God could redeem even those things.

My piano teacher sexually abused me practically every week for over ten years. A male babysitter crossed that boundary as well when I was seven years old. And a trusted neighbor exposed himself to me when I was a teenager. A childhood of perfectionism and some of the "cons" about being an only child were easier to recover from than the sexual damage caused by men in my life who had been placed in authority over me. This was the cesspool I immediately thought of when Larry talked about finding ways to redeem our past.

If we read the above Scripture again, it's easy to see that God means that he will redeem us from our own "iniquity." But could he also mean that he can redeem us from the sins others have committed *against us*? I believe the answer is yes. And it's time to apply to my own past the truth that God can take the most horrible things I have lived through and somehow turn them into life for me.

God is all about newness. That includes making *us* new. Where does redemption lie? A renewed love for music? Teaching my kids respect for themselves and for others? Learning those lessons myself?

God's redemption covers more than just our own sin. It can make new the bad things that have happened to us and turn them into something living and holy. We really can believe that.

Living God, redeem my past and turn it into a new, holy, and blessed future, full of hope and anticipation. Help me to find life in even my most painful memories. Please breathe your Spirit into them and grant peace to my soul. Amen.

Martha Palmer Chambers

Wound

He heals the brokenhearted, and binds up their wounds.
—Psalm 147:3

Ten years after the death of my younger son I thought I was as recovered as I could be. But the hurt still came out in various ways, including through quick anger and a need for control. I was diagnosed with depression. In counseling sessions, I dismissed the suggestion that my problems stemmed from unfinished business with Ryan's death. "I have accepted the fact that a piece of my heart will always be missing," I told the counselor.

"You're wrong," he argued. "There is a wound, but nothing is missing. It can heal." While I appreciated him buying into my metaphor, I didn't believe him. My depression grew. My patience became nonexistent, while my angry outbursts increased in frequency and intensity. I was hurting my family and could not seem to stop. I knew I had to do something.

The counselor recommended a personal retreat. I chose a Christian retreat center by a river. I was given a private room and a book on guided meditation. The book included exercises in picturing Jesus physically moving into my heart and discussing my problems. It was worth a try.

I relaxed and mentally cleaned out a place in my heart for Jesus. I even gave him a comfortable rocking chair as the book suggested. I created a mental picture of a snug little room, one with a hole in the roof. But somewhere in the middle of the exercise I lost control. Jesus was sitting in the chair, rocking gently. I pointed out the hole where Ryan's piece of my heart had been. Then Jesus took over and I simply watched. He brought the torn edges of muscle together, and they fit perfectly. He took long, straight thorns and pinned the flaps in place. Then he ran his hand over the seam, and it fused as the thorns fell away. There was a scar, but nothing was missing. I was amazed.

I came away from my retreat with the beginning of healing where I had thought no healing was possible. The scar remains, but scars make a person stronger.

Great Physician, I thank you for the healing that only you can perform. Let us, your children, never doubt your ability to make whole that which has been broken in our lives, for with you all things are possible. Amen.

Julia Miller

Trusting God

"For this child I prayed; and the LORD has granted me the petition that I made to him. Therefore I have lent him to the LORD; as long as he lives, he is given to the LORD."
—1 Samuel 1:27-28

When Hannah took Samuel to the temple and gave him to the Lord, he was very young, perhaps only three. But Hannah remembered that the Lord had given her a child, and she knew that the child belonged first to the Lord. The time was right to surrender Samuel to the Lord.

God hasn't asked me to take my children to a temple days away from my home and leave them to be taught by an old priest. But my children belong first to God, and it's a hard thing to remember when I want to clutch them to myself, to protect them, and sometimes to keep them from others, including God.

I have two daughters. The youngest, who is twelve, prays nightly, reads her Bible, and wants to go to church camp. She also believes that God will help her through whatever trials may come along. Knowing all of this, I can let her go more easily, trusting that her faith will help her make the right choices and will keep her safe. The time hasn't come for her to make her own way, and for that I'm grateful.

My older daughter is sixteen. She does not know what to believe, and she questions everything. Somewhere along the way, maybe because her father and I got divorced; maybe because we switched churches during formative times for her; maybe just because she has an analytical mind and a cautious heart, she has no firm belief.

The time for this daughter to find her own way is drawing ever closer. This child, too, I must give to God. But it is so much more difficult to trust him with her future, her well-being, to know that when the time is right, if she is looking she will find him. Because like this loving mother, he loves her too, though she hasn't met him yet.

Dear God, help me to trust in your goodness and your grace for those I love the very most. Let me be able to turn them over to your loving care when the time is right. Amen.

Melinda McDonald

Christmas Mourning

Thus says the LORD: A voice is heard in Ramah, lamentation and bitter weeping. Rachel is weeping for her children; she refuses to be comforted for her children, because they are no more.
—Jeremiah 31:15

It was shortly after 8 p.m. on Christmas night. I was preparing to leave for home after being on duty as a hospital chaplain. I wanted to spend some time on Christmas night with my husband. I had been in training as a chaplain in Clinical Pastoral Education for several months and had offered to be on duty so another chaplain intern could spend time with his family.

The pager I carried rang and my heart sank. It was the number of the Neuro Intensive Care Unit with "911" after it. I went to the unit to find out why a chaplain was needed. I learned that some family members arrived to see a patient, a fifteen-year-old gunshot victim who had died earlier in the day. The nurse told them they'd come too late and could not see the boy because his kidneys were being harvested. (His mother had agreed to donate them.) The patient representative on duty was checking to find out if their request could be honored.

I was asked to spend time with the family members, four very upset young women who were waiting in a lounge on another floor. One of the women said that the altercation that led to the boy's death had taken place at her house. The patient representative returned and explained that it would not be possible for the family to see their loved one. The women became even more distressed. They wept and pleaded their case. I asked the patient representative if an exception could be made. She said she would try.

The patient representative eventually returned and said that the family could see the victim after all, but would have to wait until the surgery to take out his kidneys was completed. Meanwhile, several other family members arrived. I joined them at the bedside of the young boy as they wept and kissed him. I thanked the patient representative for allowing them to see the patient.

It seemed a sad and terrible irony that what they wanted most that Christmas night was simply one last chance to say goodbye. I felt blessed to have been able to serve as their advocate and to help with this "gift."

Since that night, I cannot experience Christmas in the same way as I did before. Now each Christmas I pray for this family and for the family of the young man who shot him. I also pray for an end to death by guns.

Loving Lord, we pray for an end to violence in our society. Please help us to live in peace with our brothers and sisters. May we fervently work for an end to violence in all forms. Amen.

Sandy Schmidt

Different Treatment

There is no longer Jew or Greek,
there is no longer slave or free, there is no longer male
[or] female; for all of you are one in Christ Jesus.
—Galatians 3:28

In my family of origin I was the oldest child, with a brother four years younger and a sister five years younger. It became evident to me at a very young age that my brother was treated differently from the way my sister and I were treated.

My parents told David that if he got any bad grades in school he couldn't go to the circus. But when it came to town my father said,

"The circus only comes once a year; a boy shouldn't have to miss it." I knew that if my grades fell it would mean I had to stay home. David also didn't have to eat his peas. I did! I had to sit at the table until every last one was gone.

When I questioned why David didn't have to eat his peas or why he got to go to the circus, the answer was always the same, "He's a boy." That never seemed right. Why should he get special favors we girls didn't get?

Although these are simple illustrations, as I look back to my childhood, I understand that my sense of injustice had been aroused early on. Those early experiences of being treated differently and unfairly have been repeated through the years in other, more significant ways. For example, I was devalued by male students in seminary (in the 1950s) and have received less compensation than my male counterparts.

Thankfully, great strides are being made in righting the wrongs of the past and in treating men and women as equals. Paul's statement that "there is no longer male [or] female" was radical for his time, but it reflects the way Jesus related to women and recognized their worth. When we read the many gospel stories that speak of Jesus' interaction with women, and when we read Paul's words, we find hope in God's intention that equality exists between the sexes and that all be treated fairly as children of God.

Loving God, you who value each person as your precious child, help us to see each other through your eyes and to love each one in your spirit. Amen.

Marilyn R. Taylor

The Visitation

*In those days Mary set out and went with haste
to a Judean town in the hill country,
where she entered the house of Zechariah
and greeted Elizabeth. ...
And Mary remained with her about three months
and then returned to her home.*
—Luke 1:39-40,56

The story of Mary's visit to Elizabeth is one of my favorite accounts in the early life of Jesus. Mary was so excited to share her good news with Elizabeth. The angel had just announced to her: "You will conceive in your womb and bear a son, and you shall call his name Jesus" (Luke 1:31). Elizabeth was in "her sixth month" (Luke 1:36). "Mary remained with [Elizabeth] about three months and then returned to her home" (Luke 1:56). Mary helped Elizabeth care for herself and her unborn child, even though she herself was a newly pregnant woman.

My husband and I lost our second baby in the womb at five months. Afterwards, my sister came to visit me. She brought a nice hot meal and tried to comfort me in my pain and sorrow. Although my baby had died and could no longer leap in my womb, my sister Mary's visitation was much appreciated. Just two days before we found out the baby had died I had felt his movement in my womb. This precious life had been given to us and was so quickly taken back. The prayers and visits of my family and friends helped me through this difficult time.

Lord Jesus, thank you for the gift of family and friends. Thank you for visits, visits that help to remind us of your omnipresence. You truly give us the grace and strength we need to come through even our darkest hours. Help me to be Christ to others as they have been to me. Amen.

Joanne T. Mild

Can You Receive the Gift?

*But Ruth said, "Do not press me to leave you or to turn
back from following you! Where you go, I will go; Where
you lodge, I will lodge; your people shall be my people,
and your God my God. Where you die, I will die—there
will I be buried. May the L*ORD *do thus and so to me, and
more as well, if even death parts me from you!" When
Naomi saw that she was determined to go with her, she
said no more to her. So the two of them went on until
they came to Bethlehem. When they came to Bethlehem,
the whole town was stirred because of them; and the
women said, "Is this Naomi?" She said to them, "Call
me no longer Naomi, call me Mara, for the Almighty has
dealt bitterly with me. I went away full, but the L*ORD *has
brought me back empty; why call me Naomi when the
L*ORD *has dealt harshly with me, and the Almighty has
brought calamity upon me?" So Naomi returned
together with Ruth the Moabite, her daughter-in-law,
who came back with her from the country of Moab. They
came to Bethlehem at the beginning of the barley harvest.
—Ruth 1:16-22*

Learning to receive is a challenge for many of us. We have been
taught that it is "better to give than to receive," and so we strive to
be the givers. We find joy in the joy others express when we give
our gifts. But, somehow, to be on the receiving end of a gift seems
hard. When we are the receivers, we can feel weak, out of control.

Recently I did a one-day retreat with a group of women clergy.
We spent the day looking at ways that sisters could minister to other
sisters, putting ourselves in the positions of both giver and receiver.
We saw that there are times when we can stand with a sister in the
places of pain—where there are no happy endings—as the friends
of Jephthah's daughter did for her. We discovered that way that we
could support one another when we were called to work and serve
together as did Shiprah and Puah.

There are times when we show support by being a mentor or a
coach as Ruth and Naomi were for each other. And there are times

when we show mutual support through sharing the dream and vision of another, as Mary and Elizabeth did for one another. Our learning to receive from our sisters helps us also to receive from God, who wants to shower us with love if only we are open to receiving it.

God, help me learn to receive. Help me to remember that I'm not less because I have a need. Remind me that unless there is a receiver the gift cannot be given. Open me up so I can receive the care, nurture, love, and friendship that my sisters want to share and that I have shared with them. Amen.

Marsha Brown Woodard

In Search of Fulfillment

The Lord will fulfill his purpose for me;
your steadfast love, O LORD, endures forever.
Do not forsake the work of your hands.
—Psalm 138:8

Not long ago I was asked to address a group of single Christian women on the subject of dating. The women, ages twenty to forty-five, had come eagerly with pen and paper, expecting some helpful tips. When they learned that I was recently married, their excitement intensified. However, my discussion was radically different from what they expected.

I asked the women to talk about the personal challenges of being single. Their shared common fears included living alone, needing companionship, receiving pressure from co-workers and family members, and of course, being victims of unsuccessful or unpleasant blind dates. I asked them to dig deeper.

Society teaches women that they are made complete by finding a mate, or at least by having a boyfriend. By the age of four, most young girls learn that even Barbie has Ken! Popular magazines provide the "top ten tips to hook your ideal man." Women are socialized to believe that being in a relationship fulfills one's purpose in life. Through the discussion, the women recognized that personal fulfillment and true happiness can be achieved only by developing a relationship with God.

Fulfilling God's purpose in your life is crucial before entering into any relationship. A woman of God should seek to pursue excellence: the highest standards directed by God's Word for her life in every area. For you cannot be in a healthy relationship until you are spiritually and emotionally whole! Seeking God will allow us to become better daughters, mothers, sisters, grandmothers, wives, and friends. True contentment and completeness can come only from our Creator. We can be complete only if we allow God to fulfill God's purpose for our lives. Are you allowing God to accomplish this in every area in your life?

Jesus, I come asking you to fulfill your plan and purpose for my life. Help me to trust the working of your sovereign hands. I pray for women, young and old, who struggle with loneliness. Empower me to encourage them. Amen.

Anissa Danielle Gibbs

Why Is Waiting So Hard?

But those who wait for the Lord shall renew their strength, they shall mount up with wings like eagles, they shall run and not be weary, they shall walk and not faint.
—Isaiah 40:31

One of the greatest challenges to my journey of faith is waiting! When it appears so clear to me that the answers to injustice are obvious, why does it take so long for everyone else to see them? One of the things I don't do well is wait. In fact, I have struggled with this my whole life. Once on a retreat we were invited to spend the entire time concentrating on a problem in our faith journey. Mine was waiting! One of the outcomes was the following poem:

Why is Waiting So Hard?

I wonder if everyone is happy!

If they are glad they came.
I wonder if all the
  things are getting done.
I wonder if lunch will be on time.
  There is so much to do!

Doing is a way to gain
  acceptance in the community.
If I'm doing something,
  I matter. I count.
When I'm busy, everyone is impressed.
  They say, "She is so dedicated!"

When I'm not doing something—
  just being or waiting—
I feel guilty, like
  I'm not earning my keep.

O God! Why is waiting so hard?
  Why do You call me to wait?
Why do I have to wait?
  Why can't I like to wait?
God, can't you work a little faster,
  and maybe a little more obviously!

Why is waiting so hard?

Dear God, teach me what it means to wait upon you, so that my strength can be renewed, so that I, too, might run and not be weary. Amen.

Ellen A. Frost

Woman of Need

You gave me a wide place for my steps under me,
and my feet did not slip.
—Psalm 18:36

Having returned to my hospital room from the recovery room, I was feeling more pain than I'd ever felt before. I was not a rookie in the surgery department. (This was my ninth.) But this spinal surgery had me wondering if life was worth it. Lately various things had gotten me down, but when I was told I needed spinal surgery or I might lose the ability to walk, it seemed too much to take.

Now here I was back in my room feeling more pain than I thought I could take. Little did I know the worst was yet to come! By nightfall I was enclosed in a back brace so tight over the abdomen that I felt I could not breathe. By morning I felt like the end of the world was near. Life was just too tough.

But then the most amazing thing happened. The flowers started coming, the cards started coming, and in due time the visitors started coming. My family had been with me all along. Because someone cared, I started caring again. Because I cared again, I began working hard to overcome the pain and get up and walk. The therapist came and taught me how to get out of bed and on my feet. And then it was on to walking and stair climbing. None of it was easy, but I was determined to do it.

Sometimes it is easy for me to forget what I have accomplished with the help of God, family, and friends. But I was reminded when we had a snowstorm and the snow seemed too deep to navigate. My friend went on before me and made wide steps for me to follow so I would not slip. Isn't that just how life is? Jesus went on before us and made wide steps for us to follow so that we might avoid slipping. And even if we do, he is there to pick us up.

God of all beings, help us to remember the steps that Jesus made on Calvary so that we may learn to follow him during all the phases of our lives. And then help us to make wide steps so someone else can track their way to you. Amen.

Bonnie L. Scherer

143

Fear Versus Love

I sought the LORD, and he answered me,
and delivered me from all my fears.
—Psalm 34:4

I wrestled with some fears this morning. They involved various specifics, but they all boiled down to fear of failure. Such fears come when I am disappointed, or over-tired, or when I surprise myself by not caring about something that usually matters to me very much. I'm sure you know the experience I am describing, and you probably have your own set of indicators.

Take time to cry out to God when you are disappointed, or tired, or uncaring, and you will find fear at the bottom of your cry.

Cry out to God about fears, and the Lord will deliver you from them. For "perfect love casts out fear" (1 John 4:18), and God loves you perfectly.

Rest in that knowledge awhile, and your deeper love for the people or causes that have frustrated you will likewise cast out your fear of failure and enable you to stay committed.

Lord of Love, you know I am afraid of failing. I am tempted to pray that you prevent failure, but I know that sometimes it is unavoidable or even necessary. So I pray for love; a sense of your love protecting me, and a certainty of my love for your people and your work. Amen.

Darla Dee Turlington

Bearing Children

Sing, O barren one who did not bear; burst into song
and shout, you who have not been in labor! For the
children of the desolate woman will be more than
the children of her that is married, says the LORD.
Enlarge the site of your tent, and let the curtains of
your habitations be stretched out; do not hold back;
lengthen your cords and strengthen your stakes....
Do not fear, for you will not be ashamed; do not be
discouraged, for you will not suffer disgrace...
For a brief moment I abandoned you,
but with great compassion I will gather you.
—Isaiah 54:1-2,4,7

As a chaplain intern, I responded to the page by the charge nurse on the maternity ward. Susan's child was stillborn. As I entered the room I saw that Susan was curled up in a fetal position, facing away from the door. Her fist pounded the Bible on her bed. Her sobs shook her body. She was oblivious to my presence in her room.

"Why God? Why now? What have we done wrong to deserve this? Wasn't it enough that our first two babies miscarried? Why did you take our son, our only child? Surely you don't need him more than we did!"

Tears welling up in my own eyes, I gently touched her arm. "Susan, it's Chaplain Jan. Oh Sweetheart, I am so sorry."

Susan literally threw herself across the bed and into my arms. "Oh, Jan, my baby's gone, our little Tony is dead. The doctor said he'd be okay, strong enough to live, not like our other babies. Why again? Why now? Why does God hate us so much to take our little Tony?"

I stumbled for words in my attempt to bring comfort and healing to Susan. I knew God loved her and her child. I knew she wasn't being punished, and I also knew God didn't need to be defended. Somehow I knew words were useless right then. So I just sat on the bed, holding and rocking Susan until she cried herself to sleep.

Another hospital room, but now I'm the patient. The doctor has just removed a tumor from my ovary, as well as the ovary and tube.

He quietly tells me that although the tumor was only pre-cancerous, he has discovered why I could not conceive and would never be able to do so. I am almost relieved to know that there is a medical reason for my barrenness. Then I realize that I have always claimed people, children in particular, as my extended family. I think of all the "spiritual children" I have been blessed to birth as I shared their stories and lives and witnessed to them of the love of Christ. In my hospital room, I smile through my tears. Suddenly, I think of Susan and wonder what spiritual birthings may have come from the labor of her pain and life.

Oh, author of life and of love, hold us desolate women close to your heart and, in your compassion, bring us back to the center of your circle of love for us. Give us the courage and the wisdom to be the mothers of countless children for your vineyard. Amen.

Janet R. McCormack

Praying, All Along...

Then Jesus told them a parable about their need
to pray always and not to lose heart.
—Luke 18:1

Pray without ceasing.
—1 Thessalonians 5:17

O gracious God
There is a hidden prayer list
   of the heart,
That many of us carry,
People we truly care about
   and love,
Whose names we lift
   In thankfulness to you,
Or in petitions for
   Your healing Presence.
We thank you for them,

And we humbly ask
That they might feel
The loving that surrounds
And be refreshed.

Gracious God, we thank you for prayer, for letting us offer our joys and concerns to you at any and all times. Thank you for enfolding us in the caring prayers of others when we are in need. Amen.

                                        Carolyn Hall Felger

Come Unto Me

"Come to me, all you that are weary and are carrying heavy burdens, and I will give you rest. Take my yoke upon you, and learn from me; for I am gentle and humble in heart, and you will find rest for your souls. For my yoke is easy, and my burden is light."
—Matthew 11:28-30

"You can't get tired!" The preacher's words unleashed waves of panic within me. Many need to be urged on to good works, but I was addicted to them. As full-time solo pastor, wife, and mother to three needy adopted children, I was so exhausted I could barely hold my head up.

Years later I again pondered these verses while on retreat. No longer addicted to good deeds, I was still weary from adolescents with countless and complex problems, from divorce, from trying to hold the family together and pay the bills, from church conflict—weary from life.

I realized that if my yoke felt too heavy and my burden too great, the demands heaped upon my overflowing plate could not all be from God. For whatever reason—to be needed, to be seen as good, to prove my value—if my plate was too full, chances were I had done the heaping.

I was learning about spiritual discernment—the quiet listening

to the whisperings of the Spirit and my own authentic heart—
which helps distinguish between those callings and tasks that are
truly mine and those that arise from some disordered part of
myself. Jesus' gentleness is not only for others, but also for me.
Jesus' rest is not only for others, but also for me. When I center
in Jesus, I will know which tasks to pursue and which to release.
I can learn from Jesus, who recognized he was not called to
answer every need, and let go of the rest.

The needs of parents, children, spouses or significant others, our
church communities, our employers or employees can overwhelm
us. Without discernment, we dissipate our energy and ourselves,
dilute our effectiveness, become burned out, angry, resentful, and
bitter. Jesus responds, "Come. I will give you rest. Learn from me
and carry only what is truly yours to bear."

*Jesus, give us courage to let go of some of the many demands upon
us so that we can hear with clarity your whisperings and the wisdom
of our hearts to be free to live and grow and serve with joy. Amen.*
Joy A. Bergfalk

Sinning

*The Pharisee, standing by himself,
was praying thus, "God, I thank you that
I am not like other people: thieves, rogues,
adulterers, or even like this tax collector."
—Luke 18:11*

We are all sinners. We all miss the mark of regard for others; we all
turn away from the divine will, failing to care for and love others
and ourselves as our Creator intended. Words like these have fallen
from my mouth many times: "I am glad that I am not embittered
like that woman!" Criticizing another, putting another down—the
Pharisee did it in Scripture, and I have done it in my life. I must
acknowledge my sin of self-righteousness and the way I exaggerate
my own importance from time to time. This is a place where I
stumble and fall outside God's will.

In whose presence do you regard yourself as superior? Whom do you put down? Short people? People whose skin color is different from yours? Overweight people? Purple haired folk? The tattooed? Non-professionals? Body-pierced people? Jesus gets my attention in this parable and encourages me to think about times when I am in opposition to God's will and purposes, when I move away from being and doing what is right in God's sight.

As a woman I am invited and challenged to rethink ways that I am outside God's will. Feminist theologians and psychologists have increasingly recognized that women's sins tend not so much from an over-exaggeration but rather from an under-exaggeration of self. Too little self results from an underdevelopment of self. Self-negation, frequent diminishment of self, and negative thoughts about self, are other manifestations of too little self-regard and care. Women have tended to rely on others for their own identity, and they often dwell on self-criticism. Under-valuing oneself denies the honor and dignity God gave each and every one of us at creation.

In the verses that follow the Bible passage above, the tax collector prays, "God, be merciful to me, a sinner." Regardless of whether we sin by being self-righteous or by under-valuing ourselves, this ancient prayer helps us to recognize our brokenness, our need for God, and our need to acknowledge our faith.

Holy One of Blessing, we are all so utterly dependent upon you. Guide us in acknowledging and confessing our sins. Help us to amend our ways when we fall outside your will, whether these sins are "too much self" or "too little self." God, be merciful to me, a sinner. Amen.

Nancee Martin-Coffey

We Can't Do Everything

I can do all things through [Christ] who strengthens me.
—Philippians 4:13

Women have learned since the creation story how to do and survive doing. We often find little time to pause and take care of ourselves. We pause to give birth to our children; we pause to take care of our children, our husbands, and others. We seem to always find the strength to do and do over and over again. In the midst of doing, it would be a good thing to realize that at times our deepest fear is that we can't do everything.

When we affirm, "I can do all things through Christ who strengthens me," I wish we would do three primary things during the day. One is to take time to relax before doing. Two is to take time to reflect on what we want to do. And three is to affirm that it is okay not to do everything.

Dear God, please give me the strength to understand the importance of the words "I can do all things through Christ who strengthens me." Amen.

Patricia A. Wilson-Robinson

Invited by God

Many Samaritans from that city believed in
him because of the woman's testimony,
"He told me everything I have ever done."
—John 4:39

For three years during seminary I attended a very conservative Southern church. I did not realize how I was affected by the masculine images in worship. It struck me at a revival service that I had become paralyzed inside by those images. I later wrote:

I looked at the altar and saw
   three men standing there.
Three men, different ages, but all married, all fathers.
They smiled quite the same and said,
   "Won't you come?"
Their faces excited and well pleased with what had proceeded,
They begged,
   "Won't you come?"
It struck me, the power of the sight—
   three men, on stage, above me, smiling, well pleased.
Their invitation became uninviting.
It seemed that they were genuinely calling.
But had I come I would have had to say,
   "I am one of you."
   "I belong with you on the stage, in the pulpit."
   "God has invited me, God has called me."
But the three men did not give that invitation,
   and they did not want that response.
I was paralyzed in my pew, trapped inside,
   and I cried because I could not come forward.

The acknowledgement of that hidden pain was the beginning of healing. The woman at the well has given me a different paradigm for what makes a minister. This woman was called by God. She believed Jesus was the Messiah, and she brought the gospel to her town. She was a preacher! It shocked the disciples. It was a woman, even a Samaritan woman. What is more, she had been known to be a sinful woman. Christ went out of his way to call this sinful Samaritan woman. What wonder, Christ calls women!

It gives me hope to know that my call is from God and not from men. I acknowledge my hurt, but I do not allow it to have power over me. My call is to step into the pulpit, and my hope is that young boys and girls will see in me a new image of what makes a minister. What wonder, Christ has called me.

Lord, give me the courage to see beyond my limited images. Give me a new vision of what your people look like. Amen.

Lesley Walsh Krieger

Mary, Maid of Nazareth

(A Modern Magnificat)

Mary, faithful maid of Nazareth,
    Did your own wonder grow with motherhood
    As life expanded in your novice womb,
    Your body strangely wise in shaping it?

Mary, did you marvel at his birth,
    When nature's forces gathered in yourself?
    You didn't know your body had to thrust
    That helpless, sacred child into the world?

Then, Mary, did you sense your helplessness
    When little Jesus left your sheltering arms
    And what he learned and spoke astounded you
    As in your heart you pondered all of it?

Mary, when in manhood he did deeds
    You surely could not fully comprehend
    Did you not call upon your God in hope
    For wisdom and a faithful clarity?

Mary, when he gave his life in death
    Did you not wail in torment, grieve your loss
    And plead with heaven for an answer
    To your agonizing faith-filled "Why?"

Like you, dear Mary, all we mothers find
    Surprising wisdom in our quiet wombs,
    Feel the urgent miracle of birth,
    Learn the strength and grief of mother-love.

Mary, God had need of womankind
    To enter life like all humanity,
    Chastising those who try to live as gods,
    Exalting those who fear and love the Lord.

Oh, mother-maid of Nazareth,
Remove the halo pressed upon your head;
Exalt your sisters scorned in low degree
And claim all women, like you, truly blessed.

Peggy Shriver

Learning to Be a Friend

Well meant are the wounds a friend inflicts,
but profuse are the kisses of an enemy.
—Proverbs 27:6

Recently the Lord began showing me how our past experiences contribute to the kinds of friends we choose. I often prided myself on being the best friend anyone could ever have. But the Lord began showing me that I was in fact a bad friend. When I met a new person who wanted to be friends, there was always an "initiation period" lasting about four weeks, during which I tested this potential new friend, often in an emotionally grueling way. I weeded out those whom I considered too weak to be my friend.

If the person was fortunate enough to survive the initiation, I then enlisted her or him in a program to help build my trust in them. After all, I knew I was trustworthy. I had to make sure that every friend I had was equally trustworthy. For years this process included subtle verbal abuse and emotional manipulation. In my mind, this was psychological warfare, and at stake were my emotions.

To ensure that I would not be hurt too deeply by any of my friends, I surrounded myself with those who hesitated to be honest. If they were starkly honest, there were consequences; essentially, I encouraged them to lie to me. If their honesty hurt me, I quickly came back with a harsh remark to hurt their feelings.

I recall the last time I did this to a friend. On that occasion, the Holy Spirit for the first time revealed two things to me. The first was that I actually enjoyed hurting people with my words; it brought me satisfaction to be able to hurt. The second thing revealed was the magnitude of the pain I caused others with my words. As I listened to one friend express the pain resulting from my reckless use of words, I began to feel my friend's hurt. For several days I felt the heaviness of the burden I had loaded on that person. For the first time in my life I had to admit that I did not like the person I was. I wanted to change.

I prayed for forgiveness, and the Holy Spirit brought to my mind the many times I had carelessly used words to hurt others. From this time forward I began to be more conscientious about the words I spoke to others. Proverbs 17:22 states that a cheerful heart is good medicine, but a crushed spirit dries up the bones.

I realized that my words could either make another person's heart cheerful or break that person's spirit. My focus and desire shifted from tearing people down to encouraging them. I further acknowledged that true friendship allows people to express their thoughts and opinions honestly, without fear of being hurt in return.

Lord, teach me to be a true friend. Help me to grow in faithfulness and integrity. Give me an open heart and sincere spirit that freely gives and shares with every person I meet. Show me how to let go and let you be in control, and when I feel slighted, let it be your throne of grace that I seek. Amen.

Tawanda N. Tucker

A Garment of Praise

Let all who take refuge in you rejoice;
let them ever sing for joy.
—Psalm 5:11

Having been a Christian for only five months, much had changed. For the first time, my life made sense. I was at peace with God and with myself. My husband's first response to my becoming a Christian was, "I envy your faith." As weeks went on he seemed distant, but I looked confidently forward to the time when we would share the Lord together. I was not prepared for another change when he announced he was leaving me and walked out.

As the front door closed behind him, I collapsed on the floor in shock. I lay there in unimaginable pain. "I cannot go on," I told myself. A small, quiet but firm voice inside of me said, "Yes, you can." I knew it was the Lord's voice, but I had no experience yet of God being sufficient for me in weakness or crisis. "I cannot go on," I repeated. "Yes, you can," echoed the voice.

The pain of rejection was accompanied by the fears roaring within me: "I can't raise three children alone. I can't make enough money. I can't take care of this big house by myself. I can't endure the pain." With each new thought the reassuring voice whispered, "Yes, you can."

As the days wore on, a little song I'd recently learned in my women's Bible study group continually floated into my mind. The song spoke of Jesus offering beauty for ashes and giving a garment of praise for a spirit of heaviness. I began to sing this song, and I found that each time it lifted the heaviness just a little more. I continued to sing it daily until one day I realized I believed every word! Sorrow and joy, I found, can exist side by side. People actually told me that the beauty of Jesus was on my face.

That was twenty years ago. Each of those problems has long since been resolved. When sorrow or troubles arrive, which they periodically do, I know they will pass. Jesus will bring the oil of joy, and I will be able to go on.

Lord, no matter what comes, help us to exchange the garments of heaviness for one of praise, knowing that with you we can go on. We choose to make room for your joy. Let the beauty of Jesus always be seen in us. Amen.

Hannah Leafshoots

Grace and Dementia

And now, O Lord, what do I wait for?
My hope is in you.
—Psalm 39:7

My mother has Alzheimer's disease. This formidable and ferociously intelligent woman has become like a child. This woman who knew the name of every plant in her garden, in Latin, cannot now tell a flower from a weed. She, a nurse who wrote policies, led meetings, and helped to run a hospital, can no longer dress herself or write her name. She who used to paint pictures can no longer draw.

Yet even in the midst of such desolation, there is still grace. She has rediscovered the simple pleasures of patting the dogs and sneaking them tidbits from the table. She sticks her tongue out at you when you catch her, delighted in her own naughtiness. She greets me at the door with a hug and laughter, so visibly overjoyed. As the dementia continues its progression, I see glimpses of the child she must have been, the little girl who laughed and cuddled and was spoiled by her family. I am saving these moments in my memory, for I know all too well that this jolly little girl, too, will soon be lost to the sweeping tides of advancing disease.

Another instance of grace in the midst of this tragedy is my father, who cares for her with the love rooted in fifty-two years of marriage. She no longer realizes he is her husband, but the bond is still there—an almost instinctive realization that this "nice guy" is somehow very dear to her. Love may forget the details, but the embers from that long-burning fire linger. Dear God, let them stay a little while longer.

Because of my mother's illness, our family has become much more aware of both our strengths and our weaknesses. We care for each other very carefully, somehow finding the strength and fortitude to cope with this long, slow dying. These are bittersweet times, beauty amidst the ruins. We have been blessed with the simple realization that God is there amidst both the flowers and the weeds. We are graced by a love that also knows grief.

O God of endless love, reach out to us, your children, for we are all afflicted. Help us live, help us see the beauty of your creation in all its seasons, in all its lives. Amen.

Becky Tornblom

Getting It Done

I can do all things through him who strengthens me.
—Philippians 4:13

Even in these "enlightened" times, women bear much of the work and often all of the responsibility. We are so overwhelmed that we often can't take time to consider how to ease our burdens. We just need to "get it done," and this constant mantra drives us onward and often drives us crazy.

Ironically, one way to manage everything we must do is to not consider *everything* we must do. To understand what I mean, think about all the food you've ever eaten: the collard greens, yams, fried chicken, sweet potato pie, carrot cake, chocolate anything—all of it. Then visualize all this food in a pile in the room. That's right, make a great pile in the center of the room of all the food you've ever eaten. Now eat it! Go ahead! Eat it! I can imagine many of you getting sick at the mere idea of consuming all that food. But be reminded that the pile consists only of food you've *already* eaten. And how did you consume it all? One forkful at a time!

The idea of dividing a task into more manageable components— or "partializing"—is not new. It is an important concept in the field of social work, it undergirds the familiar saying that a journey of a thousand miles begins with one step. We have heard this concept many different times and in many different ways. Yet we are continually stressed because we fail to remember that in reality the way to get something done is bit by bit, piece by piece.

We cannot become overwhelmed, or it leads to a sense of helplessness and hopelessness, neither of which is of God. Nor should we limit ourselves because the journey is long or the "pile" is large. If the task is something we need, want, or, more importantly, are called to do, we must get it done. One forkful at a time. One step at a time.

Dear Lord, you alone can see all and do all. Remind us of this as we attempt to do your work and your will. Help us as we take on the awesome task of leading, guiding, and encouraging your people. Slow us down so that we can lean on your strength and not our own. Encourage us so that we demonstrate that with you and in you, all things are indeed possible. We pray this in the name of your precious son. Amen.

Rhonda Rhône

Caregivers: Giving and Receiving

*After leaving the synagogue he entered Simon's house.
Now Simon's mother-in-law was suffering from a high
fever, and they asked him about her. Then he stood
over her and rebuked the fever, and it left her.
Immediately she got up and began to serve them.*
—Luke 4:38-39

Who knows where the tasteless genre of mother-in-law jokes got started, but it certainly wasn't with Simon Peter. His mother-in-law was a gem.

You wonder if Peter doesn't have an ulterior motive when he invites the Lord to his home. Ordinarily, you wouldn't ask someone to dinner with one of the chief cook-and-bottle-washers ill. Perhaps Peter is hoping Jesus will relieve his mother-in-law of her dangerously high fever.

When Jesus heals her, the mother-in-law gracefully demonstrates that there is no boundary between receiving care and giving it. For her to alight from her sick bed and begin serving guests is as natural as breathing in, breathing out.

For eight years I have been caregiver for my husband, who was totally paralyzed by a stroke. He is no longer able to give me the care he once provided so effortlessly: fix my computer, replace the leaky faucet, drive us safely through the winter snowstorms, hold and caress me.

Yet I am breathless at the many ways he does care for me. I am humbled when he struggles through his barriers of wordlessness to tell me he loves me. I am grateful beyond measure for his patience when I cannot meet his needs immediately. I am awed by the beauty of Christ that radiates from his helpless body.

My life as a caregiver has taught me the truth in the Prayer of St. Francis: "For it is in giving that we receive." As I reflect on these eight years, I know I have received far more care than I have given.

I pray that even in times of anxiety and weariness, I will give thanks that I have been called to serve, for my rewards are beyond measure. Amen.

Mary Koch

Grace

For by grace you have been saved through faith,
and this is not your own doing; it is the gift of God—
not the result of works, so that no one may boast.
—Ephesians 2:8-9

I've known these verses for as long as I've been a Christian. One of my teachers told me that this was one passage I absolutely needed to memorize. I learned to explain it to others, in the context of our salvation: that grace is a free gift from God, and that there's nothing we can do to earn eternal life. Over the years, I went on to share this message with many people as part of witnessing to my faith. I thought I understood what this verse is about. Little did I know I had only scratched the surface.

Years after I first encountered this verse, I found myself in distress over the increasing volume of the critical voice within me saying, "Why did you do that?" or "What you said was so stupid!" In all my years of knowledge of the concept of grace, I had never truly embraced its reality for my own life. I had made the mistake of labeling it as only an initial salvation issue, when in fact grace is a lifestyle. Grace is present in every aspect of our lives. In a world that seeks to define me as "incompetent" or "unworthy," God's grace enters in and calls me "special," "beloved," and "adequate." This sense has nothing to do with what I do, but everything to do with who I am and the grace I claim by faith.

Oh God, help us to remember that we do not "earn" our way into your presence. You have given us your presence through your enduring grace. Help us also to recognize and reject the false judgments society sometimes makes of us. And those we make of ourselves. Amen.

Carolyn Iga

An Adventure

Even though I walk through the darkest valley,
I fear no evil; for you are with me.
—Psalm 23:4a

In the first volume of *Women at the Well*, I wrote about instances in which I did not experience the fear that I had expected. Since then, I have had major surgery for a rare form of breast cancer known as Paget's disease. The telltale lesion had been with me on and off for two years while the surgeon attempted a diagnosis. I was anxious at times, although mammograms had been negative and I was assured it was not cancer.

When a biopsy revealed the truth, and surgery was imminent, I expected to be scared to death. I had always assumed that impending surgery would turn me into a basket case.

I told friends in the neighborhood and at church, and of course I told my scattered family. All promised to pray. I am convinced that the assurance of all these prayers played a large part in carrying me through. God was with me. I felt strong and went through the days before surgery finishing up chores for Christmas so I could take it easy afterwards.

Even on the day of surgery, I was calm. (I can't believe this even as I tell it.) I woke up in mid-afternoon asking for my glasses and my book. I read and dozed, read and dozed, visited and walked during my four-day hospital stay. I was sent home with no restrictions, so I was up and around at once.

A week after surgery, on our way to the doctor's office to have drains removed, my husband and I went to a movie at the mall. Friends rallied around and brought meals in for two weeks. I felt so good that I suffered from guilt while accepting this help. But these friends made the difference—they and the True Friend to whom we all turn. Six chemo treatments later, I still felt fine. My hair thinned slightly, but I experienced no nausea or other effects. We were able to take our mid-winter vacation as planned. Then I was dismissed by the oncologist for three months, and the whole experience has taken on the feeling of an adventure, even a test that I passed with flying colors.

I'm not taking credit for my good fortune. God was with me, and so were my friends—more of them than I ever suspected I had. Perhaps we all need experiences like this to realize how fortunate we are, how blessed.

Healing and caring God, thank you for every healthful day. Be with those who suffer, give them strength, and shower your blessings upon them. Amen.

Cathie Burdick

Tackle and Conquer

The LORD is my light and my salvation; whom shall I fear? The LORD is the stronghold of my life; of whom shall I be afraid?
—Psalm 27:1

When it looks like what it is,
turn away and listen to what the Father instructs.
Don't let the eyes bring you down.
In turning away and listening,
find strength in the instruction to go back,
tackle, and conquer.
When it feels like what it is, there must be a knowing that
feelings are not
all encompassing

and nerve endings are not where life lies.
Feelings are not included in the call.
When it tastes like the taste it is,
the head knows it's the same stuff
that gives you that familiar sick feeling as always,
forcing your face to frown
in the same direction
that makes you want to cry the same tears
as any constant force-feeding would.
It's during such dinners that one must remember
not to talk with the mouth full because
there is a container being passed around
in which to drop more tears for the processing of joy
for your future ownership
and life-sustaining dessert.
When it is, what it is, going on and on,
and you truly cannot take it anymore,
know that "He" surpasses "it" and is lifting you out
    from under,
that you may live in spite of "it,"
in the midst of "it,"
while seeing "it,"
feeling "it," and
consistently eating "it."
Just remember not to swallow.

Dear God, remind me when I need to be reminded that you are
bigger than all the trials that threaten to defeat me. Amen.
                                                    Natalie Jones

162

Who Is My Neighbor?

*Which of these three, do you think, was a neighbor
to the man who fell into the hands of the robbers?
[The expert in the law] said, "The one who showed
him mercy." Jesus said to him. "Go and do likewise."*
—Luke 10:36-37

My week of sermon preparation kept being interrupted by thoughts that went back to my mother's death. Because of increasing dementia, she lived at a wonderful nursing home during the last year and a half of her life. My father had died four years before she entered the home, leaving me to be responsible for her care.

As I relived those years sitting at my desk trying to write a sermon, the Holy Spirit suddenly connected the thoughts of my past with the sermon text. Jesus taught in the parable that there is no difference in God's eyes between people whom society or the church decides are "insiders" and those deemed "outsiders." It is those who show mercy who find favor in God's sight.

In the relationship with my mom, I was the victim. I was also the Priest and the Levite. I was the "insider": an obedient, respectful daughter who was innocently caught in the web of care taking, and who did not always respond to this task with the greatest patience. Who was the Samaritan? My mom, of course! She was the "outsider." She had forgotten how to cook and asked the same questions over and over again, having lost most of her connection with reality.

Our family was never very demonstrative with the love we had for one another. However, while at the nursing home one evening as I was about to leave, she hugged me hard and said, "I love you!" I was shocked! From then on, that gesture became our goodbye ritual, and all the hugs and "I love yous" became grace-filled moments for both of us. I cherish the fact that the last words we spoke to each other the night before she died of a massive heart attack were, "I love you!" My mother, like the Samaritan in the parable, was an "outsider" who showed mercy. Thanks, Mom!

Open our eyes, O God, to see all people as neighbors, even those society or the church considers outsiders. In Jesus' name. Amen.
                                                                    Naomi Hawkins

Finding Freedom

About midnight Paul and Silas were praying and singing
hymns to God, and the prisoners were listening to them.
Suddenly there was an earthquake, so violent that the
foundations of the prison were shaken; and immediately
all the doors were opened and everyone's chains were
unfastened. When the jailer woke up and saw the prison
doors wide open, he drew his sword and was about to
kill himself, since he supposed that the prisoners
had escaped. But Paul shouted in a loud voice,
"Do not harm yourself, for we are all here."
—Acts 16:25-28

Before starting my prison ministry I, like most of you, knew very little about the prisons and jails of America. My first ministry was with the women inmates in minimum security. I soon found out that I was not dealing with a statistic, a number or an inanimate object, but with women who had desperate spiritual and emotional needs that were not being met by the criminal justice system.

As the women began to share their stories—and they were quite candid—I began to realize that some of their stories were my stories too. And consequently they took me to places I did not want to go, to places I had left buried and hidden away. They made me face the "stuff" in my own life that I had no desire to deal with. They were bringing to the surface all the feelings I thought I had packed away about my own experiences of being molested and raped, my own rejections by the men in my life, my own failures as a wife, mother, and daughter. As the women worked through their struggles, I worked through mine, and I too found my freedom behind prison walls.

And now before I begin a session in prison, I pray,

Dear Lord, we are all here. Tear down the walls in our lives, open the closed doors, loose the chains that bind us, and set us all free. Amen.

Janice I. Thompson

Something, Surely

Surely there is a future, and your hope will not be cut off.
—Proverbs 23:18

Two years ago, a diabetic condition caused a mental fogginess that threatened my hope of continuing to write books. By then I was well-acquainted with the disruption of life goals. Once again, I took stock: "What do you most want to do?"

From the experience of progressive blindness, I had learned ways other than sight to manage my life as a parish minister. I had been stymied temporarily when jaw arthritis allowed no more singing or preaching. Then a computer equipped with screen-reading programs entered the market. It read audibly as I typed. I could give voice to my ministry by writing worship resources for other pastors.

But the diabetes problem stymied me. I could not sustain thinking or concentration. "If you are going to lose your mind, too, then what do you most want to do?" I asked myself.

My two "home-sicknesses" are ministry and poetry, I answered. I am a minister by calling and ordination. I am a writer by gift. Could I still manage a short poem? A plan emerged. Who else, I asked, is closed in by life conditions? One answer was obvious: care center residents.

I made a phone call to the activity director at a local nursing home. "How about an oral history and poetry writing group?"

"Perfect."

"When is a slow time for residents?"

"Saturday morning, from 10 to 11."

"Is a hand-held microphone available?"

"Yes, and a quiet place. We will set up tables in the chapel."

An average of sixteen men and women in their late eighties and nineties, the eldest a ninety-nine-year-old former schoolteacher, have been meeting now for two years of Saturdays. I tape their work, transcribe it to my computer, and print it in the large type several can still read. They read aloud their work as well as poetry I download from web sites. They find voice and legacy through the town newspaper that shares their group poems. In one corner of town, two injustices, isolation and homesickness, have melted into hope.

Dear God, where hope and a future seem cut off, teach us to look again at possibility. Through your love. Amen.

Dallas Dee A. Brauninger

The Power of Language

For it was you who formed my inward parts; you knit me together in my mother's womb. I praise you, for I am fearfully and wonderfully made. Wonderful are your works; that I know very well. My frame was not hidden from you, when I was being made in secret, intricately woven in the depths of the earth.
—Psalm 139:13-15

I remember the saying from my childhood, "Sticks and stone may break my bones, but words will never hurt me." How wrong that is! In language resides great power. Language conveys a persuasive message, sometimes oppressive, sometimes liberating.

I am a person with a mobility impairment, i.e., a person with a disability. In our society I experience negative perceptions of persons with disabilities. This happens in the language that is used, in words that exclude rather than include, deny rather than affirm the humanity of persons with disabilities. And negative language hurts.

When I and others are labeled negatively with words such as "crippled," "handicapped," "less than," we are seen only in the context of our functional limitations. Our personhood is disregarded. We are perceived as diminished human beings, perhaps perceived just as wheelchairs, hearing aids, white canes.

But we know we are treasured by God. We know it from Scriptures such as Psalm 139. The psalmist declares each person to be "fearfully and wonderfully made." These words assure me of my value and I respond, "Wonderful are your works, O God."

And of how much value am I? Jesus teaches that even the hairs of our heads are counted. Such reassurance affirms and supports me. I resist being drawn into the language of our world, a language

by which I may be belittled. Being cherished and valued by God
redeems me from society's often degrading messages.

*Gracious and Holy One, I praise you with great joy because you
affirm me for who I am, not for what I lack. I am beloved by you.
Having received and accepted your affirmation and loving-kind-
ness, grant me the gift of compassion to receive others into my life
as you receive me. Amen.*

Gay Holthaus McCormick

Discovering Community

*Indeed, the body does not consist of one member
but of many....Now you are the body of Christ
and individually members of it.*
—*1 Corinthians 12:14,27*

During my time in seminary, I experienced two "book-end events"
through which God allowed me to see beyond what I had imagined.
The first took place during my first semester. I was working on my
first sermon for the church that my husband and I were serving as
co-pastors. As I prayerfully considered the "word" for the congregation, I sensed that the members needed to be assured that their
actions, individually and collectively, mattered.

So, I went to the Scriptures. But I couldn't find a verse that fit.
In desperation, and since I was a seminarian, I went to my homilet-
ics professor and explained my problem. He wisely counseled,
"Maybe you can't find it because it isn't there." Oh.

Then we spent time talking about the biblical culture, and he
helped me remember that the concept of an individual was at that
time nonexistent. Community was the determining factor in
peoples' lives. Maybe, he suggested, I would want to look at 1
Corinthians 12. That wasn't the direction I had planned, but that's
the direction in which the Scriptures took me. My first sermon
became one of the most powerful learning experiences throughout seminary.

The other "book-end" took place my last semester, as I participated in a class on the trinity. I became deeply impressed with the necessity of relating to God as Trinity—the *perichoresis* of God as community. God's self-community of a three-in-one relationship began to represent for me the community that God wants for all of us. This knowledge strengthened what I had learned earlier from 1 Corinthians 12, and I fully realized that one of God's strongest desires is for community among God's people.

This has been a difficult truth for God to impress on me. As a woman in ministry, I have experienced rejection by God's people, and I have sometimes told God that there has to be a better way than the church. But these two "book-end" experiences continue to sustain and enliven me as I minister as a part of God's community.

Gracious Three-in-One, show us your ways of relationship as we work, with your strength and guidance, to build your community. Amen.

Cheryl Gale Harader

Treasure Your Tears

You have kept count of my tossings; put my tears in your bottle. Are they not in your record?
—Psalm 56:8

I love tears. That does not mean I love the things that cause them. I do not love pain, or sadness, or frustration, or fear. But I love the fact that, for me at least, tears bring genuine relief to my suffering. I wish more people appreciated tears rather than seeing them as something to be dried up or stopped up. Holding them in seems terribly painful to me, and I don't even attempt it. If I need to cry, I cry.

I love this verse from the Psalms, because it seems to imply that God values our tears—treasuring them, and even saving them in a bottle. I don't think it's purely coincidental that tears are made of the same substance that is used to cleanse open wounds: saline (salty) water. If God finds our tears of value and worth counting, who are we to look upon them with shame and revulsion?

I use this verse a great deal when I'm offering pastoral care to the bereaved. Tears are a wonderful, natural way for the body and soul to release tension and fear. But somehow, this culture doesn't place a very high value on them. Pain and sadness are feelings to be ignored and anesthetized, not honored and weathered. Those who are grieving are made to feel that there is something wrong with them if they "can't stop crying." Certainly grief has the potential to trigger other griefs and even depression. But stanching our tears is rarely the solution. Stymied tears will eventually spill out one way or another, perhaps in the form of anger or depression.

In the process of training chaplains through Clinical Pastoral Education, I spend a lot of time urging my students to get to know and to treasure their own tears. The more they know about and honor their own experiences of grief, the more available they'll be to persons in crisis and the less likely they are to become overwhelmed and useless to someone in pain.

Loving God, thank you for the gift of tears. Help us to honor our griefs and losses, so that we can bring healing to others who suffer. Amen.

Amy Greene

Secure in the Pulpit

I [Paul] commend to you our sister Phoebe, a deacon of the church in Cenchreae, so that you may welcome her in the Lord as is fitting for the saints, and help her in whatever she may require from you, for she has been a benefactor of many and of myself as well
—Romans 16:1-2

I was another reluctant "Moses" when God called me into ministry. It wasn't that I believed theologically that women should not be in ministry, but I had just never seen a woman pastor before. It took my church and friends to convince me that they recognized my spiritual gifts and call as legitimate. By the time I graduated from seminary, I had settled "the woman in ministry issue" for myself.

Still, I often found that I had to explain and defend my calling to parishioners, colleagues, and supervisors alike. As difficult and hurtful as that was, it helped me even more to internalize the legitimacy of my calling with no apologies. As I progressed in ministry positions and there were more women in ministry, others got more comfortable with the idea of female chaplains, and the challenges to my ministry were fewer. Yet just when I would feel safe in my ministerial role, I'd get blindsided.

My husband was an Air Force security police officer commander. He and I would often get late-night emergency calls. Sometimes they were for him, sometimes for me, and sometimes for both of us. He is not a night person, and although he was quite coherent when he spoke to others, he was often still half-asleep. So I was not surprised to hear him answer the phone and say, "Let me get my wife. That's right, she's the chaplain, I'm a cop... No, *I'm* a cop, she's the minister." At this point he began to wake up and got louder. That was not a good thing. "Yes that's right, my wife's the chaplain, I'm a cop."

When the caller again questioned him about what I presume was the right of a woman to be a minister, he got even louder and angrier. Now fully awake, he said, "Look I have loaded guns and nukes (nuclear weapons); she has prayer. Which one of us do you want!" Very quietly and with a smile he handed me the phone and said, "Honey, it's for you." I don't remember the details of that case, but I will always remember the unconditional support of my husband, who has never once wavered in believing in me and my call to ministry.

Heavenly Potter, thank you for the persons you send into our lives who believe in us and our call to ministry—those who strengthen, support, and help us go back into that pulpit yet one more time. We are especially grateful for the courage of men of credibility who are not afraid to commend us and our ministry to others. Amen.

Janet R. McCormack

Name Calling

They said to her, "Woman, why are you weeping?"
She said to them, "They have taken away my Lord
and I do not know where they have laid him."
—John 20:13

"They have taken away my Lord, and I do not know where they have laid him," Mary cried to the angels sitting in the tomb. "They have taken away my father, and I don't know how to help him," I whispered to no one in the dim light of the hospital foyer.

I was waiting for a security escort to my car in the minutes just before midnight. I had sat for hours beside my father's bedside that evening. The medical professionals had come into the room every hour or so, checking the tubes that fed chemotherapy drugs into his veins and presenting in tiny paper cups the pills for fending off both the nausea and the anxiety that filled his eyes. With only a cool washcloth held to his forehead, I could not touch the pain, the fear, the cancer.

As I waited by the door, I thought of Mary Magdalene at the tomb. Her Lord had been taken, arrested, beaten, and killed. She had watched helplessly. And now she had come to complete the last act of love due him, the anointing. But he was gone, taken out of the tomb, out of her reach. Distraught and desperate, she had turned to the gardener, continuing her whimpering complaint: "If you have carried him away...."

There by the door, I was not alone. In the hospital foyer, as close as my own breath, stood an alabaster statue of Jesus. The pose drew me closer. He might have sat this way as he invited the little children into his embrace. The eyes were kind, but filled with pain. The outstretched hands gleamed white in the dim light, and in the palms I saw scars of the nails that had held him on the cross.

The next moment unfolded for me just as it must have for Mary there in the garden, standing next to a man she did not recognize. In a sound like music, he had spoken her name: "Mary." With that one word he loved her and owned her. I, too, heard my name as surely as if I had felt his arms around me. Despite all the technology my father had to bear, still the loving strength of Jesus held me fast.

The doctors, nurses, and technicians wielded the power of drugs and skill at administering them, but they did not have his power to take my father's pain—and my pain—and soothe it.

Human beings, no matter who they are, have no power like the power of Jesus. Mary Magdalene knew it the moment she heard him call her name. I knew it, too, in a hushed space empty enough to be filled with him. In your own moments of helplessness, find that quiet space where you can listen for Jesus' voice. There it will claim you, strengthen you, and hold you fast.

Lord Jesus, when life's impersonal forces overwhelm me, open my ears to hear you call my name and claim me as your own. Amen.

Jennifer M. Ginn

Hold Your Head Up!

Now he was teaching in one of the synagogues on the sabbath. And just then there appeared a woman with a spirit that had crippled her for eighteen years. She was bent over and was quite unable to stand up straight. When Jesus saw her, he called her over and said, "Woman, you are set free from your ailment." When he laid his hands on her, immediately she stood up straight and began praising God.
—Luke 13:10-13

It was a late December evening. My students were unusually quiet as I lectured. I was discussing verbal abuse. Suddenly a young woman who appeared to be in her early twenties raised her hand. She disclosed that her boyfriend would insult her in front of his friends on a daily basis. He would hurl insults at her, devalue her accomplishments and abilities, call her derogatory names. Each day she would cry, hoping to please him. My student was broken, and she did not realize she could be made whole.

Verbal abuse is an attack on someone else's self-esteem; it is devaluing someone's self-worth. When Jesus was teaching in the Synagogue, the Scripture states that he saw the woman who was bent over, the helpless woman who could not raise herself up. How many of us as women have felt bent over with ridicule, harsh criticism from our mothers, fathers, family members, boyfriends, or husbands? How many of us have experienced the feeling of being stripped bare of our self-dignity and respect? Discouraging words bruise and cut and wound, tearing us down until we cannot raise ourselves up.

But when Jesus sees the bent-over woman, he immediately recognizes her and calls her woman, a precious gift of God. Jesus speaks healing, and immediately she is able to stand up straight. She is free of her past, and she is made completely whole. She can hold her head up, both literally and figuratively. Like the crippled woman, if we have been discouraged or bruised, we, too, because we belong to Christ, can hold up our heads.

Dear Jesus, because I belong to you, I know that I am fearfully and wonderfully made. Empower me now to recognize the needs of others who are hurting from verbal abuse. Help me to use my words to encourage and heal. Amen.

Anissa Danielle Gibbs

The Laughter of God

Now Sarah said, "God has brought laughter for me; everyone who hears will laugh with me."
—Genesis 21:6

Recently a friend gave me a picture of Jesus laughing. "That's more like it," I said. For years I have been sure that one of the least understood aspects of God is God's laughter. According to my concordance, the Bible mentions laughter only three times.

Growing up, most of us didn't hear about Jesus laughing in the temple. Don't you bet that he did? I imagine that he used humor just as he used parables: to enliven the spirits of the disciples, to make cogent points, and to empower through imagination the creativity of his followers. If he were here with us today, don't you think he would e-mail a few pertinent jokes to his group? There are several books out with "holy humor" in the titles, revealing the humor that surrounds church life. We need more! Humor that lifts one's eyes to the love of God truly is holy.

I once attended a workshop titled, "Your Health Is a Laughing Matter!" The young presenter had used humor in recovering from cancer. I not only learned facts about the effects of humor on physical healing, but I laughed for two hours. My laughter was accompanied by tears of disbelief and gratitude. He had spent his time and energy giving the workshop just to me, since I was the only one who came! I thought, "This is something Jesus might have done for someone like the woman at the well." My life, too, was changed.

Divine Holy Spirit of love and laughter, spark us to touch others through our humor so that they may see you and heal their souls as well as their bodies. Amen.

Judith Northen Eastman

Occupying My Space

There is no longer Jew or Greek, there is no longer slave or free, there is no longer male and female; for all of you are one in Christ Jesus. And if you belong to Christ, then you are Abraham's offspring, heirs according to the promise.
—Galatians 3:28,29

After my having dragged luggage through rainy streets up and down the London underground and over half of the English countryside, the clumps of people standing directly in my path at the airport irritated me as I made the long trek to the gate. I was exhausted. My body hurt. I thought if my suitcase flipped from one more evasive action, I'd scream. Immediately feelings of shame engulfed me. "How unloving, how un-Christian!" But the irritation lingered, nudging me to pay attention. On the flight home I reflected on my experiences.

In London, I had found myself dodging empty-handed pedestrians as I pulled my topsy-turvy luggage behind me. I recognized the same pattern in my daily journey—getting out of the way of others, temporarily irritated, then feeling ashamed and adapting my course to accommodate them.

After living apologetically for "taking up space," a new metaphor presented itself: occupying *my* space. As a lifelong accommodator—or, when push came to shove, a defensive person "standing her ground"—the idea of unapologetically occupying my space was revolutionary.

I realized I often cede my territory and path in the name of being loving, humble, and Christlike. But it is an abdication of the space God has given me and of the path to which God has called me. There is nothing Christian about dodging others and giving up my calling. I not only have the right to my space and path, but I have the responsibility to occupy my space and walk my path. I need not be belligerent or rude, just firm.

I arrived home empowered. I will no longer cede my path and space but will occupy them and attend to my calling.

"Let no one despise your youth" might be paraphrased for us: "Let no one despise your gender." Since all are offspring and heirs, we have the right and responsibility as women to unapologetically occupy our space, walk our journeys, fulfill our callings. Anything less would be a failure of stewardship of who we are and the ministry entrusted to us.

O God, who calls and gifts us, empower us to occupy the space, the journey, the call you have given us. Amen.

Joy A. Bergfalk

Loving One's Self

*"...You shall love the Lord your God with all your heart,
and with all your soul, and with all your strength, and
with all your mind; and your neighbor as yourself."*
—Luke 10:27

I have been living with metastatic breast cancer for ten years. When it was first diagnosed, I set out to fight and beat the cancer. Cancer was an enemy to be destroyed. The battle has taken its toll. I am no longer able to do the things I used to. In fact, a good day is just being able to get out of bed and spend a little quality time with my family, not doing anything in particular.

The treatments have totally changed my appearance to the point that people do not recognize me. Much has been taken from me. The losses, along with this exhausting image of battle and "the enemy," became too much. Mentally, physically, spiritually I found I could not fight it any more.

I discovered I needed a new image. Instead of doing battle with an enemy, I needed to befriend my cancer. Cancer develops when, for whatever reason, normal cells begin to grow abnormally. I needed to learn to embrace these cells and love them into health. This process involved continuing with the chosen treatment but with a new attitude of peace. I had to learn how to love and accept the physical and lifestyle changes I was experiencing. I needed to learn to love myself in a different way.

We all have things about ourselves that challenge us: our faults, weaknesses, those things we try to hide. Yet we are told that we need to love ourselves. We are instructed to love our neighbors but we cannot fully love our neighbors until we can fully love ourselves. It is not an easy task to accept, let alone to love, certain parts of ourselves. Yet God loves us—every tiny speck of our being—blemishes and all. Further, God is willing to teach us how to love ourselves if we willingly open ourselves to God's unfathomable love. Perhaps today is the day to embrace that part of ourselves we thought was unlovable and to be opened to the possibility of receiving and giving love in a greater way.

Loving Lord, open me to your love. Help me see through your eyes and show me how to love myself so that I may love others as you do. Amen.

Debbie H. Deane

Drink from the Living Waters

Ho, everyone who thirsts, come to the waters...
—Isaiah 55:1

It is one thing to hear a good sermon or meditation about the Samaritan woman at the well, and it is another, much bolder, move to be like her and drink of the living waters. Many times we think we can get by on a little bit of religion and that we'll kick into overdrive when trouble comes our way. We regard our bodies the same way. Everyone knows that we are supposed to drink a certain amount of water every day in order to maintain proper fluid levels in our bodies. And yet many of us struggle to do so.

What we forget is that by the time we feel physical evidence of thirst, dehydration has already progressed. Dry mouth, sallow skin, feeling tired and weak, and other symptoms are the physical manifestations of a lack of fluid that started hours and sometimes days prior to feeling it. As in the physical body, spiritual thirst starts before symptoms appear.

Praise God for the example of the Samaritan woman. As soon as she heard the powerful message from Jesus of the thirst-quenching waters, she wanted to drink. She drank first, and then she went out to exhort others to drink. It was important for the Samaritan woman to drink first before she could tell others. In other words, you can't give what you don't have. You can't give love if you don't have love. And just as thirst shows in the body, spiritual thirst robs the soul of the living waters.

As women, it is easy for us to neglect ourselves for the sake of others. Friends and relatives can see that not all is well, but as long as we can get out of bed in the morning, we take it as a sign to keep going.

On an airplane the flight attendants always instruct parents traveling with children to use their own oxygen mask before attending to the child. As caretakers, we women often have to be reminded to take care of ourselves. The living waters are for all to drink. Everyone is exhorted to drink from the waters of everlasting life. The Samaritan woman is powerful because she heard the message, and she wanted the living water for herself. She was not selfish, nor was she ashamed to ask. She was a woman, and she knew that if you want to help others, you have to be helped first. Praise God the help is available for all.

Thank you, God. Thank you for the Living Waters that flow for all to be blessed. Thank you for showing me how to drink. Guide me that I may show others. Amen.

Weptanomah B. C. Davis

The Power of Bread-breaking

Jesus said…, "I am the way, and the truth, and the life."
—John 14:6a

Our circle of eagerly expectant women snaked around the small chapel, moving down the altar steps past the open door, in front of the piano, and back up again to the table and the weaving where it had begun. It was nearly time for the closing Eucharist. We leaned forward to hear the short reflection that preceded it. Part lament, part confession, and part celebration, it hushed us and made us absolutely still. Benedikte, the teller of the story, held her text in both hands and read slowly and deliberately. On less than a four-inch square of rumpled paper she had printed the most painful experience of her life.

"When I arrived in this retreat center nearly five days ago, I put a stone in our weaving, our collage of 'life-stories' on the altar. On it, I wrote, 'LIAR.' This I wrote because deep inside of me was a little girl who still believed that she had lied about incest. And I had not been able to free her of that lie. One morning, though, here in our place of worship, in a conversation with Monica, I realized that the real liar was my father."

She continued, "In a few moments, I will sing the words of preparation for the Eucharist. To me the Eucharist means everything because it represents the opposite of lies. It is the truth. To celebrate the Eucharist here means everything to me, for I am not ordained. My bishop did not think he needed a pastor who wanted to work with people who had been hurt by incest. I thought for a long time that I had done something wrong in the ordination conversation with him, and that I was not 'good enough' to serve. But I have come to see that the opposite is true. I was too strong and dangerous for him."

Shortly thereafter Benedikte began the words of institution. With her back to those of us in the circle, she poured the wine and broke the bread and sang from the depths of her soul. It was as though a long-held sob had been set free; liberating words of promise came from deep within her—low, clear, loud, and strong. Primal. Not many of those present understood Norwegian, her mother tongue. But we all knew the words of preparation and sang them silently in our own languages with her. Blessed by the truth she had entrusted to us, we responded to this courageous pastor with love and thanksgiving.

Benedikte offered no explanations of the concept of forgiveness, nor did she give us any prescriptions to follow. There was nothing we could write in our theological journals. Instead she simply told us a story of what happens when God stays with us on our rugged, painful, and often lonely journeys; when God, in unexpected places, sends us sensitive listeners who help us hear ourselves—without judgment or counsel—in freeing ways; when God gives members of the beloved community the authority to acknowledge and affirm those who have answered the call to serve as clergy. Believing in the power of the "priesthood of all believers," the women assembled in that circle saw Benedikte as pastor and prophet, healer and truth-teller.

Something significant that had long been denied Benedikte was restored in that evening Eucharist. The little girl so unfairly labeled "liar" was left in that small stone in the weaving-collage on the altar. And the pastor who broke bread for women who had gathered that week "to break the silence and stop the violence" against women worldwide emerged as a gift. Benedikte's stubborn search for truth had enlarged our own understanding of truth and our own experience of God's love. In the liturgy that was sung we heard the ringing promise of justice. In the bread and wine we offered one another, the healing power of God spilled once more into our lives.

Loving God, I have no other place to go. Give me the strength I need to trust you, and you alone. And when the night is at its darkest, help me to remember that you will pray for me, if I am not able to pray myself. Amen.

Jean Martensen

Working and Waiting

The farmer waits for the precious crop from the earth, being patient with it until it receives the early and the late rains.
—James 5:7b

One Sunday I had the opportunity to hear a well-known college chancellor speak at our church. Commenting on the above Scripture passage, he said, "Now here we have a farmer, planting a seed in a field. The seed goes in the ground, the farmer covers it with soil and waters it. Then what does he do? Does he sit there on the ground and watch the seed? No! There is plenty for the farmer to do while the seed is growing! *He works while he waits.*"

That last phrase really stuck in my mind. I have been praying for years and years for the opportunity to answer the call that, I believe, God has placed on my life: to go to seminary and to open a center for Christian women's studies. But God has continuously told me, "Wait." I have worked hard to put my husband through seminary so that he could become a pastor. When is my chance for rest and refreshment, for growth and challenge, out of the secular world where I have a job that is not my vocation? God keeps saying, "Wait."

Being told to wait is not always comforting, especially if it happens over the course of many years. This picture of the farmer working while he was waiting was helpful to me. It showed me that God can still work in my life, changing me, growing me up into his image, while he waits for the right time to direct me. God can work even in the circumstances that I feel are not optimal. And not only can God work, but I can choose to work, too. I can trust and accept grace and work while I wait for God either to fulfill my dreams or change them.

I realize that God is always working while we're waiting. And I can work, too, while I'm waiting.

God, thank you that you are not just sitting and waiting for the seed of your Spirit to grow in my life. Thank you that you are always working in me, working in my life, changing circumstances as you see fit, and using them for your glory. Help me, too, to work while I wait. Help me to see, every day, that all work is your work. Amen.

Martha Palmer Chambers

My Hope Is in the Lord

O Israel, hope in the LORD!
For with the LORD there is steadfast love,
and with [the LORD] is great power to redeem.
—Psalm 130:7

Three weeks before my trip to El Salvador, I was told I would be laid off from my chaplain position due to downsizing. While I understood the need to cut costs, I was still dealing with my sense of loss. Other feelings were also swirling through my being as I boarded the plane for San Salvador, the capital city. But the trip had already been planned and my tickets purchased well before the news about my employment. So I went.

With each day, encountering wonderful people in another culture, the cloud above my head slowly lifted. Then we had a trip to Santa Ana. Not having made the connection between the name of the town and the fact that we were visiting a church there, I was excited to see the "Christo Rey Iglesia Luterana," a sister parish to a congregation I had belonged to in Madison, Wisconsin. Having heard so much about this church, I was thrilled.

There were three women with whom I had a conversation in Spanish. One was a deaconess serving a congregation in a nearby village. The other two were laity, familial sisters who served a congregation and clinic in another village a few miles away. As we sat there, they shared with me the plight of women in their community. They said that it was typical for women, after bearing three or four children, to have their husbands leave them to raise the children on their own.

Being in my forties, I was even more shocked by what they shared next. They said that it wasn't a problem for young women to get employment. However, once they turned thirty the factory or other employer would let them go in order to hire someone who was younger and could be paid less. A woman could be left with four children, no job, and no source of income.

I asked, "Where is your hope?"

"*No hay,*" came the answer. They feel there is none for them, at least not in this world. Their only hope is in Christ to abide with them in the midst of it all.

All shadows of sadness about my loss of employment disappeared that day. In the midst of everything I, at least, had hope. I knew I would be returning to job interviews. With each interview would come the hope that God would bring me one step closer to a new ministry.

God of life, let the light of Christ shine throughout your world, bringing hope and promise into the lives of all your people. Help each of us to be messengers of your love and hope. Amen.

Julia D. Shreve

Come and Drink from the Well

Jesus answered her, "If you knew the gift of God, and who it is that is saying to you, 'Give me a drink,' you would have asked him, and he would have given you living water."
—John 4:10

Love, money, security, and fame. These are just a few of the countless springs at which women have stooped to drink, only to rise from them to find that they offered no lasting fulfillment, no personal satisfaction.

A lonely woman, considered to be indiscriminate with the men, comes to the town's well to draw water at a time when she could avoid the rejection of the crowd. Needless to say, she had to endure the brazen sun during the hottest part of the day. For she thought, "If I go when all the other women are at the well, surely they will ridicule me." From her front porch she could see the other women as they passed by with their water pots on their heads. She could hear them laughing and exchanging monotonous pleasantries. We can imagine one woman saying, "It's a beautiful day," while another exclaims, "It is so good to enjoy the fresh morning air."

Shortly thereafter, in the heat of the brazen sun, the lonely woman approaches the well. She comes face-to-face with a strange man, who asks her for a drink. The woman responds defensively, "Why ask me for a drink?" However, the stranger does not take offense. Instead, he offers to give her more than water. For he knows that her needs are greater than filling her empty pots.

The stranger says, "Come and drink from a spring that flows so freely and so full." There are no restrictions as to who can come. An invitation is extended to all those who are imperfect, who are failures, who are guilty of wrong doing, burdened with guilt and shame. "Come and drink. This ever-flowing spring can quench the thirst of your soul and give hope beyond the present."

Father, you are the God of acceptance, and in your presence there is enough love to mend the brokenness in our lives. In your presence there is peace to calm our troubled spirits. For only you can quench the thirst of our souls. Amen.

Betty H. Long

Second Goodbye

But we do not want you to be uninformed, brothers and sisters, about those who have died, so that you may not grieve as others do who have no hope. For since we believe that Jesus died and rose again, even so, through Jesus, God will bring with him those who have died.
—1 Thessalonians 4:13-14

It was time. He was affecting my life—my judgment, my relationships, my work.

He stood between me and fulfillment, got in the way of my productivity, blocked me from happiness. As long as he was with me, I was not free.

I went down to the river, after praying and crying and listening. I knew he had to be sent away for good. My good. So I sat on a bench and I told him I loved him. I told him I would see him again when it was time. I told him to go. And he went.

I watched him cross the grassy place across the river, enter the stand of trees. I saw him rise as he left the far side of the trees and get smaller and smaller until he was gone. I was alone for the first time in ten years.

The fact that I had held his hand and said goodbye ten years before as his breathing slowed, as he left his ravaged little body behind in the hospital bed, had not mattered. I hadn't meant it then. And so I had taken him with me everywhere, and had allowed him to come between me and healing, between me and life. He had gone when he was called. I was the one who held on. Ten years.

He is healed. He is happy and loved. He has been since his first leaving. Now I can allow healing to come to me, too.

Holy and healing God, grant us the faith to let go of the hurtful past and to walk with you in the present. Amen.

Julia Miller

Justice

Exercising the Call

*For this reason I remind you to rekindle the gift of God
that is within you through the laying on of my hands; for
God did not give us a spirit of cowardice, but rather a
spirit of power and of love and of self-discipline.*
—*2 Timothy 1:6-7*

Recently I was with a group of ministerial leaders discussing the future of the church. One woman, advocating for women in ministry, yearned for the day when the church would more fully recognize women's gifts for ministry and "allow" them to exercise those gifts more completely.

As I listened to her speak, I thought of Paul. I wonder if Paul would have waited for someone to give him permission to exercise his God-given call to ministry. Whenever Paul saw a place to minister, he did not hesitate to step into the breach and to exercise his call. The only call he ever needed was God's call.

Whether lay or ordained, all of God's people who hear the call are commissioned by God to answer that call wherever it takes us. There are many places of injustice in our world that are waiting for the Good News of the gospel. It is not necessary to have anyone's permission for any of us to address these needs.

When a daughter was killed by a drunk driver with a suspended license, her mother did not wait for permission, but began immediately to organize Mothers Against Drunk Drivers (MADD).

When Anna, a volunteer in mission, realized that women were being released from prison without proper food or housing, she did not wait for permission to begin addressing those needs. Today she ministers to scores of women in her prison-release ministry.

Whenever God places before us an injustice that touches our hearts, we need to remember that we have been given a spirit of power and love and that we are commissioned by God to minister to that need. It will be a great day if and when the church fully recognizes women's gifts for ministry. But until then, we do not have to wait for permission. We need only to begin ministry when and where it is needed. The recognition will come from our Creator.

God of justice, you have called all of us to be your ministers. Let us never forget that we have been given the spirit of power and love to minister in your name. Give us the courage today to minister wherever the need is greatest. Amen.

Mary L. Mild

The Hebrew Midwives

The LORD saw it, and it displeased him that there was no justice.
—Isaiah 59:15b

According to Exodus 1, ancient Egyptian rulers, like elites through the ages, feared upstarts who appeared to threaten their power. Ignoring what the Hebrew people had done to help preserve Egypt, the pharaoh imposed forced labor on them, including brick-making and working in the fields. Since these measures didn't have the desired effect of decreasing the Hebrew people's numbers, the taskmasters became increasingly strict. Finally Pharaoh went to the Hebrew midwives, Shiphrah and Puah. "Listen," he ordered, "when you act as midwife to these Hebrew women, kill the male babies." The midwives listened, but they did not obey.

When the ruler discovered that Hebrew baby boys were being allowed to live, he demanded an explanation. "It's like this," Shiphrah and Puah responded, "Hebrew women are strong! The babies are born before we get there."

Whenever I use this story in a Bible study, I am amazed at how many people are primarily concerned with two questions: "Were the Hebrew women telling the truth?" and "Did the midwives sin by lying?"

By reducing the issue to the truthfulness of the midwives, we avoid dealing with institutional evil. Oppression was imbedded in the culture. Pharaoh, his officers, and all the Egyptians who went along with the oppression of the Hebrews were accountable. Instead of realizing this, we blame the victims for lying, though they were doing it to save the lives of innocent infants! It is the same response we often give to contemporary forms of oppression.

Why are we more concerned about the theft of a coat than with an economic system that deprives people of the income to buy the clothing they need? When a homeless woman sleeps on a park bench, why do we focus on the fact that she has violated a local ordinance rather than doing something about a system that produces thousands of homeless men, women, and children. Why do many of us remain silent when children live surrounded by drugs and violence, and react only when these problems hit our own neighborhoods?

God of justice, you know we cannot be fully just in an unjust world, but help us to try. Help us work together, confronting evil systems that keep all of us from being what you have called us to be. Amen.

Wilda K.W. (Wendy) Morris

Healing the Rich

Then, opening their treasure chests, they offered him gifts of gold, frankincense, and myrrh.
—Matthew 2:11b

Between Nativity and Epiphany the magi sit on the organ console with their camels, regal robes, and crowns, waiting to be moved into the humble crèche scene where they look like a bunch of misfits! Are these treasure-laden, wealthy trespassers truly welcome at this new "inn," this new messianic banquet?

The gospel is not friendly to the rich. They are sent away empty, perceived as servers of mammon, and it is harder for them to get into the kingdom of heaven than for a camel to go through a needle's eye. Does God love the poor best? I feel uncomfortable, guilty. I wonder if I should really give it all away, live in poverty.

Women with lots of money often feel squeamish, maybe as out of place as the wise men at the stable. I know wealthy women who hide, afraid of their wealth, worried that it isn't natural, that they won't be seen except for their riches. And here is Jesus saying over and over that rich is just plain not good! I'm not one of those rich, but I am rich to have what I need and then some. So how can I be healed of these uneasy feelings? How can I have money and be a follower of Christ?

This year, when the wise men were placed next to the Christ child, I had a funny new thought: "Well, well, here come the rich!" Then when I envisioned them opening their "treasure chests," I knew who the backers of the new kingdom project would be. I chuckled at this realization and felt the grace of a healed connection.

The three kings are symbols. They represent royalty, wealth, and power. In Matthew's Gospel they are an essential part of the messianic scene. They are the rich, in fact the filthy rich—humble, generous and wise, men and women. There is room for the rich at this new inn. There is an invitation to this banquet table for rich and poor alike.

O God, make me rich, rich with inner and outer wealth, that I may pour out my riches for all to have enough. Help me discern wisely, as the Magi did, the very best use of my material and spiritual riches to further your beloved community of love, justice, and peace. Amen.

Lyn G. Brakeman

Doing Justice

He has told you, O mortal, what is good; and what does the LORD require of you but to do justice, and to love kindness, and to walk humbly with your God?
—Micah 6:8

The prophet Micah calls us to do justice, love mercy, and walk humbly with our God. I believe God particularizes that call for each of us. For me this call comes presently in the form of advocating for persons with serious brain illnesses, or "mental" illnesses.

Persons suffering with these illnesses are also suffering injustice on every hand—in our families, in our health care system, in our society, and, unfortunately, in our churches. It is the "leprosy" of our day, and the result is a conspiracy of silence that often negates the possibility of persons getting the treatment they need and deserve. One in five is affected by these illnesses. Thus it is likely that you know someone who is struggling with schizophrenia, manic depression, depression, anxiety, or obsessive-compulsive disorder.

The dictionary defines justice as "the principle or ideal of just dealing or right action." What is the right action to which we are called relative to justice for people with brain illness? We are called to love one another as Christ has loved us. This means reaching out to persons and families in our circles of influence and demonstrating our love. It means talking about these illnesses and educating people that these are biological brain disorders for which treatment is available. It means advocating for health insurance coverage in treating these illnesses as being comparable to every other medical illness. It means providing adequate support services, including access to housing and jobs.

I believe God is calling all of us to forsake ignorance, stigma, and denial and to work for justice for persons so afflicted, whether the illness be in ourselves, our family, our co-workers, or our church family. We are all made in God's image and are God's beloved. We are called to live like we really believe that.

Dear God, open our hearts to those who suffer from debilitating stigma and discrimination. We know you understand, for even your son was accused of "being out of his mind." When we have such an illness, give us the strength and courage to seek treatment, to talk about it, to become workers for justice. You came to give us life abundant—a life of wholeness and health. Let us claim that, as we continually praise you for creating us in your image. Amen.

Norma S. Mengel

Justice, Small Scale

Execute justice in the morning.
—Jeremiah 21:12

When my husband and I relocated, I was still smarting from having lost my eyesight. Within our new church family, however, I soon had an opportunity to bring a small bit of justice and hope first to one and then to another child. Mark's mom phoned first. Mark was in trouble with reading. Both parents worked. Neither had extra energy or enough patience to add reading work. Mark failed to respond to the efforts of reading teachers. He had lost heart.

I had time to tutor. I would be no reading-over-his-shoulder threat. In fact, my own inability to read printed books would turn him around. My curiosity became his reason to read. He caught my love of books. My blindness became an instrument of justice.

Mark began to trust his ability to sound out words. He found his capacity for patience. Into our midway snack break, he sandwiched ten, then fifteen and twenty minutes of free flowing conversation. He enjoyed the trust and friendship of an adult.

After five years, much work, and several classics, Mark was a high school junior and honor student. Our reading times have become more occasional. We spring as quickly into catch-up talk as our latest book.

Last week, Kyle's mom and I talked. Kyle's parents have little time to sit with a boy or a book. Kyle is a fifth grader with a reading problem. His hesitation is keen. He needs someone to cheer his confidence.

Gracious God, show us how to meet injustice by doing something just. Let us see that a modest remedy can turn around sprouting injury so early that even at first light, justice announces its clear presence. Keep open the eyes of our heart so we might interrupt injustice in the morning before it frustrates a child's life. Hone the ears of our hearts so we might hear the first note of hope meeting hope. Amen.

Dallas Dee A. Brauninger

Righteous Anger

*Making a whip of cords, he drove all of them out of the
temple, both the sheep and the cattle.... He told those
who were selling the doves, "Take these things out of
here! Stop making my Father's house a marketplace!"*
—*John 2:15-16*

Anger can be a negative and destructive emotion, but it is sometimes an appropriate reaction to injustice. Jesus was remarkably
slow to anger, but when provoked he took whips and cleared the
temple of the moneychangers.

The value of anger in dealing with injustice was made clear to
me during a public speaking class I took a few years ago. While I
have always been an anxious speaker, there was one in the class
who was even more timid than I. She was the only black woman in
the class. But although she was nervous, she was motivated, perhaps because she was footing the bill for her education rather than
attending at company expense, as was the case with most of those
in the class.

One evening our assignment was to give a speech about a
personal incident. One of the first students to speak was the instructor's wife. She gave a short, emotional speech on the birth of her
first child, concluding with the punch line, "And then I looked down
and thought, 'Oh my God, the baby's black!'" While she may have
meant this to be funny, the class sat in stunned silence, which was
slowly followed by a bit of nervous laughter. The black woman got
up and left without a word. She never came back.

She was angry, and she took immediate action. I too was angry.
But at first I did nothing, even though it was clear to me that the
incident had offended the woman deeply. Finally, after having
dinner with the woman, I decided to e-mail the national chairman
of the training group about how wrong I felt the incident had been.

My action got results. After receiving several phone calls from
various organizational officials, the instructor made a public apology. Still, I regret not listening to my anger at the moment. Had I
not delayed action, maybe the woman would have been in class to
hear the apology.

Dear God, let me remember Jesus and to be in such a close relationship with him that I will act as he would act and do what he would do to help those whom no one else will help. Amen.

Melinda McDonald

The Prayer Commonly Attributed to Jabez

"...keep me from evil, that I may not cause pain!"
—1 Chronicles 4:10, NKJV

Is there anyone left in the American church who has not heard of the book *The Prayer of Jabez*, by Bruce Wilkinson? The little volume has acquired a cult-like following, but I must confess that what most resonated in my spirit as I read it was the Scripture text itself.

However, the phrase that most captivated me is not even explored in Wilkinson's book. Moreover, when I looked up the text in my own favored translation, the rendering was completely different. Not particularly fazed, I checked every one of the two dozen Bible versions on my shelf. Not a single translation or paraphrase seconded the New King James Version's rendering of the text.

In every other English version, Jabez's prayer is as typically self-centered as any other petition, whether ancient or modern: "Oh, that you would bless me and enlarge my territory! Let your hand be with me, and keep me from harm so that I will be free from pain" (NIV). Biblical scholars would undoubtedly reject the NKJV as inaccurate.

I'm usually on the side of biblical scholars. But in this case, I think the New King James Version of Jabez's prayer is more honorable than Jabez himself was.

What if Jabez really had concluded his prayer with words spilling over from a heart throbbing with empathy? What if Jabez (and we) were intimately conscious of how one person's gain is often another's loss, and how power and influence may be used for good *and* evil? If we all possessed hearts anxious never to cause hurt in someone else, what transforming effect would the compassionate prayers of such hearts have on the world in which we seek to expand our influence and establish God's reign?

God of compassion, make us sensitive to how even our pursuit of justice causes pain in the lives of others. As we seek to enlarge your territory, keep us from committing evil in your name, that we might not cause unnecessary pain. Amen.

Rebecca Irwin-Diehl

All God's Creatures

They will not hurt or destroy on all my holy mountain;
for the earth will be full of the knowledge
of the LORD as the waters cover the sea.
—Isaiah 11:9

Curry, my yellow Lab, lay her head on my chest as I slept on the couch. I awakened to see her black eyes staring into mine, plaintively asking, "Are you okay?" I had just returned from the infusion of a toxic chemotherapy drug administered in hopes of controlling my fourth-stage breast cancer. I petted her. She licked my hand. She understood something. Exactly what, I couldn't tell.

Curry wasn't the only non-human animal involved in my healing. I am alive because other animals died in gruesome medical experiments. Because my cancer was so advanced, it didn't seem that I had a choice but to follow my oncologist's suggestions for chemotherapy and radiation. Even so, I constantly thought about the animal poisonings and deaths that led to the chemotherapy drugs and therapies that put me in remission.

Isaiah talks of a paradise, a messianic age when nothing will be hurt or destroyed again, not even for "good" reasons. "The cow and the bear shall graze, their young shall lie down together; and the lion shall eat straw like the ox" (Isaiah 11:7). No animal—human or non-human—will die because some other creature deemed it necessary. There will be no cancer-causing chemicals and poisons in the air we breathe, the water we drink, and the food we eat. All creation will rejoice.

I know that where non-human animals are abused, eaten, worn, used experimentally, and seen as disposable property, women and children are also likely to be treated unfairly. An intrinsic interconnection underlies all relationships. How we treat one group usually reflects how we will treat another.

To strive for women's rights, to care for voiceless and impoverished children, and to protect animals who cannot speak for themselves is all one work. Justice comes only when we understand that oppression of one creature is oppression of all.

Curry's tail thumps exuberantly as I toss a ball for her to retrieve. I have been given the gift of life. I give thanks for that. I return the gift when I work for those who cannot work for themselves.

Thank you, God, for the gift of all creation celebrating life together. Amen.

Adele Wilcox

How to Walk in Justice

Therefore walk in the way of the good, and keep to the paths of the just. For the upright will abide in the land, and the innocent will remain in it...
—Proverbs 2:20-21

On a bus trip home from our quadrennial assembly of Christian women, I was engaged in a discussion with a woman minister of my denomination. The topic was the injustice women have faced over the eons and especially in ministry. Women ministers do not have it easy if they choose to minister from the pulpit. They meet resistance from all areas, including and perhaps ironically, from women in churches seeking pastors.

My friend said that if women were given preference for the next fifty years, it wouldn't make up for everything that has been done in the past. I had no argument. That was a true statement. This statement is also true in the context of black-white race relations and as it pertains to the many ethnic and religious conflicts in the Middle East, Ireland, Africa, and elsewhere.

I could not get this statement of frustration and despair out of my mind. I would not say I am a visionary, but shortly afterward, I saw in my mind a solution: I was standing shoulder-to-shoulder holding hands with my sisters and brothers. We were all races, all shades of colors. We were looking forward and stepping out—together. No one was looking back.

Webster defines "just" as "upright." We must be upright: looking ahead and not twisted and straining to look back at the past. We cannot erase the past. We cannot apologize enough. We cannot make it better. We can only move forward—together.

Holy God, give us courage to walk in an upright manner in your sight. Help us in our search to be just and holy as you are just and holy. Through the power of the Holy Spirit and in the name of Jesus we pray. Amen.

Ethel A. Ragland

A Human Concern

" 'You shall love the Lord your God with all your heart,
and with all your soul, and with all your mind.' This is
the greatest and first commandment. And a second is like
it: 'You shall love your neighbor as yourself.' On these
two commandments hang all the law and the prophets."
—Matthew 22:37-40

Sandy was a tall, lanky young woman and an exceptionally diligent student. Toward the end of the fall semester, I noticed that Sandy looked somewhat different. One day after class, she approached me. She disclosed that she was seven months pregnant, but assured me she would finish the course. However, during finals week, Sandy disappeared.

I made arrangements for her to take the exam after the Christmas vacation. Upon returning from vacation, however, I learned that Sandy had died during delivery. She was only eighteen years old.

At the beginning of a new century, how could this young woman die? Sandy had been diagnosed with toxemia weeks earlier, but the hospital, one of the poorest hospitals in our state, did not inquire about her medical history until it was too late.

When Jesus is questioned by the lawyer, he explains that as we love and faithfully serve God, we are also called to love others. Jesus challenges us to love others as we would love ourselves. True love for God is not complete without true love and compassion for others. A woman's body—whether black, white, Asian, Latino, young or old, poor or financially stable—should be treated with dignity and respect. How can God use us to recognize the need for all women to have quality medical care? Women's health is a human concern. It is loving our neighbors as we would ourselves.

Jesus, we humbly acknowledge that in the busyness of our days we sometimes fail to recognize the needs of others. We pray for our sisters everywhere who need quality health care. Empower us to show compassion and concern right where we are, and then let it spread throughout the world. Amen.

Anissa Danielle Gibbs

Moving Stones

When the sabbath was over, Mary Magdalene, and Mary the mother of James, and Salome bought spices, so that they might go and anoint him. And very early on the first day of the week, when the sun had risen, they went to the tomb. They had been saying to one another, "Who will roll away the stone for us from the entrance to the tomb?" When they looked up, they saw that the stone, which was very large, had already been rolled back.
—Mark 16:1-4

When I first met Billie C., she was seventy-five years old and a veteran social activist. Through her church and local ecumenical groups, she had been involved in working for civil rights and in protesting the Vietnam war. She had been arrested outside the South

African embassy in a demonstration against apartheid. Now she was delivering a protest speech at the annual meeting of a local utility company that was proposing to build a nuclear power plant near an elementary school. Over lunch after the meeting, she told me how upset her politically conservative son was with her for this latest "misguided" campaign.

About five years later, I saw Billie again at an event focused on opposition to capital punishment. With glee, she told me that her son had assumed that old age would put a crimp in her social activism. When he learned of her new anti-death penalty work, he said in total disgust, "Mother, do you know what I am going to have put on your tombstone? Here lies Billie C., under the only stone she ever left unturned!" Billie said, "I know he meant it as an insult, but I really hope he does it. Can you imagine a better way to be remembered?"

When Mary Magdalene and the other Mary and Salome wondered who would roll the stone away, I imagine they expected to have to do it themselves. After all, they were the only ones out so early, the only ones who seemed concerned that Jesus' body receive the traditional ritual ministrations. The women, both historical and contemporary, whom I admire and after whom I hope to model myself are those who know that the social and religious landscape is littered with enormous barriers to justice and wholeness, but are unafraid to name the barriers, to confront them, and try to move them.

O God of unlimited possibilities, thank you for sisters who teach us how to speak truth to power. When we are daunted by seemingly immoveable obstacles to justice, give us courage. And make us grateful for those rare and wonderful times when we find that the stone has already been rolled away. Amen.

Peggy Halsey

Nightmares and the Good News

While he was sitting on the judgment seat,
his wife sent word to him, "Have nothing to do with
that innocent man, for today I have suffered a great
deal because of a dream about him."
—Matthew 27:19

Pilate's wife had a very troubling dream. It was so vivid and painful that she actually sent a message warning her husband to keep away from Jesus. She had knowledge and fear but no power to change anything. All she could hope was that her words might influence another human being. So she spoke, and then she waited to see what would happen.

As a young woman I worked with a battered women's program, back before people began to call it "domestic violence." Listening to the women who came to our support groups, I heard living nightmares. I discovered that there was nothing *domesticated* about the violence that was occurring. In one group, women actually accused me of lying when I said that my husband of fifteen years had never hit me. They didn't believe any woman could live with a man without being hit!

I had troubled dreams during those years. I knew I had to speak out, to unveil some of the myths about abuse. Many people wouldn't listen. One minister said, "She must have done something to deserve it." Other people told me, "That happens only to poor, uneducated people." I encountered racist stereotypes and lots of denial, but I couldn't stop speaking.

I wasn't alone in this experience. As the months went by, I met other women who were working to educate people about the realities of abuse. My words alone had little impact. But the voices of many women and men, speaking together, speaking insistently, speaking the truth, resulted in significant changes in our country's response to such abuse. We still have a long way to go, but we have progressed.

Do you have troubled dreams? Do you see things that need to be done, innocence that needs to be declared, injustice that needs to be addressed? Speak out. Your voice is vital, for Christ is revealed to the world in you!

*Lord, you are the way, the truth, and the life. Trouble our
dreams. Teach us your way. Give us your truth and the courage to
declare it. We pray this by the power of your resurrected Life.
Amen.*

Karen Ann Selig

Abigail the Mediator

*David said to Abigail, "Blessed be the LORD,
the God of Israel, who sent you to meet me today!
Blessed be your good sense, and blessed be you, who
have kept me today from bloodguilt and from avenging
myself by my own hand!... Then David received from
her hand what she had brought him; he said to her,
"Go up to your house in peace; see, I have heeded
your voice, and I have granted your petition."
—1 Samuel 25:32-35*

Abigail was married to a very wealthy owner of sheep and goats.
His name was Nabal, which means "fool." Before David became a
leader, his men were camped near where Nabal's flocks pastured.
In the season of shearing, when Nabal was collecting his wealth,
David sent a message that his men had not harmed but had protected
Nabal's property. At the time of the shearing festival, David asked
that Nabal share some of his abundant food. Nabal insultingly
refused to consider the request. When David got the response, his
temper flared, and he told his men to prepare to take vengeance by
killing Nabal and all the men associated with him.

When Abigail heard about this, she quickly prepared bread,
wine, sheep, grain, raisin cakes, and fig cakes, putting them on
asses. She courageously went to David in the mountains of Carmel
and begged him not to focus on the foolishness of her husband and
not to kill their people.

At the fiftieth anniversary gathering of the World Council of
Churches in Zimbabwe closing the "Decade of Churches in Soli-
darity with Women," we sat at round tables with women from all

over the world. How should Christians respond in the face of the pride, greed, and foolishness? Abigail can give us some hints. God's creation provides an abundance for all, and God's love reaches out to all.

God of all peoples, Abigail, who courageously mediated, points to Christ our mediator and reconciler. Abigail, who shared food, points to Christ, who has enough bread for all if we will only work with him. Give us Abigail's humility, wisdom, and courage that your realm of peace may prevail. Amen.

Martha Ann Kirk

Revenge

> *When his disciples James and John saw it, they said,*
> *"Lord, do you want us to command fire*
> *to come down from heaven and consume them?"*
> *—Luke 9:54*

The female country band the Dixie Chicks performs a ballad called "Earl." This song swirls to mind when I meditate on this piece of Luke's Gospel.

Revenge is the prominent theme in this passage. James and John ask Jesus if they can bring harm to the people of Samaria because they have rejected Jesus. He turns and rebukes the disciples. No revenge here, no doing damage, injury, or punishment in return. We see Jesus forbidding violent actions as a response.

In the Dixie Chicks song, Earl is a scoundrel guilty of repeated physical spousal abuse. The ballad tells of one friend coming to the aid of the victim; the story cleverly and humorously depicts the women's revenge: Earl's death. I must admit that I like to sing along boldly with this ballad, laughing wildly while dancing in the kitchen, deriving vicarious satisfaction on behalf of women who have been physically abused. The pain and destruction of domestic violence are huge and vicious and evil.

But I am caught up short singing with the Dixie Chicks as I think of this Gospel passage. The ballad's cry is for retaliation, suggesting that it equals justice. But revenge is not justice. Revenge is biting and devouring and life-consuming and self-indulgent. Instead of being seduced into supposedly getting back at that person, however temporarily satisfying that might feel, we are better off examining the deeper issues and causes of spousal abuse, fervently seeking to be a part of God's redemption and healing.

The cross is a message to us about not taking revenge. Who better deserves to have revenge cast upon them than we do for taking the life of Jesus, our advocate, whom we so poorly used and abused. Jesus was condemned to death unjustly, a victim of human sinfulness and rejection. Jesus does not take revenge, but loves us all.

Creator God, as Jesus did not allow a violent response to rejection in Samaria, he would not use violence at his death. Indeed, the cross is a message about non-violence and not seeking revenge. Direct us in understanding the deeper issues that underlie cruelty and abuse. Inspire us to get caught up in the dance of healing and reconciliation. In Jesus' name. Amen.

Nancee Martin-Coffey

Drying Eyes

Again I saw all the oppressions that are practiced under the sun. Look, the tears of the oppressed—with no one to comfort them! On the side of their oppressors there was power—with no one to comfort them.
—Ecclesiastes 4:1

He has told you, O mortal, what is good; and what does the LORD require of you but to do justice, and to love kindness, and to walk humbly with your God?
—Micah 6:8

When conscience and compassion are compromised, humanity weeps. Do you want to retard the crying of the innocent? Then do the right thing.

God, grant that we will be conscientiously Christian regardless of how sacred or secular what is before us may appear. Amen.
Bernadette Glover-Williams

Response to a Mugger

"Blessed are the merciful, for they will receive mercy."
—Matthew 5:7

As an "on-call" chaplain, I was often paged in the middle of the night. When this happened, I was always especially careful. I was aware of my surroundings and took other precautions so that both I and my personal effects would be safe.

And so I found it bitterly ironic that I was mugged in broad daylight on a warm sunny afternoon in the parking lot of the local library as I was on my way to return some books. It happened so fast I was stunned. A man came running toward me and yanked my purse off my shoulder. Fortunately I was not physically injured. He was arrested a few days later and confessed.

A woman from the victim witness program guided me through the process and maze of details. I was given the chance to write a victim impact statement, which I did, and to appear at the sentencing hearing to present a statement to the court about the effects of the crime on me. Although it was one of the most difficult things I have ever done, I was in court that day. I felt that it was necessary for my healing.

In my written statement I was allowed to make suggestions the judge could consider in sentencing the offender. After much reflection I suggested community service, a letter of apology, drug treatment if needed, literacy training, and restitution. I was seeking restorative justice, not retribution.

The offender, I learned, was nineteen years old and this was his first felony conviction. I thought this incident might serve as a "wake-up call" for him and that he could turn his life around. I knew I was not responsible for this; it was not my place to be counselor this time. There were other professionals who could help him. At the same time I wanted him to know how his actions had harmed me, especially emotionally. I was hoping he would accept responsibility for his actions.

I was satisfied with the terms of the sentence. The judge had used some of my suggestions. The young man was also sentenced to serve ninety days in a house of corrections. In addition, his attorney suggested a face-to-face meeting between the offender and me under terms of "victim reconciliation."

I could not seek retribution; it would not undo the mugging or its aftermath. And it seemed contrary to who I am as a person and as a pastoral minister. I strive to follow the model of Christ in my encounters with other people.

All I can do is pray that the offender will use this experience as a means to change his life. And I pray for healing for all crime victims and their loved ones.

Loving Lord, when someone harms us, help us to seek justice, not retribution—restorative justice tempered with mercy. Let us learn to persist in following the example of Christ. Amen.

Sandy Schmidt

Standing against the Crowd

*When he heard that it was Jesus of Nazareth,
he began to shout out and say, "Jesus, Son of David,
have mercy on me!" Many sternly ordered him to be
quiet, but he cried out even more loudly,
"Son of David, have mercy on me!"*
—*Mark 10:47-48*

Blind Bartimaeus hears that Jesus is coming and begins to call out. The crowd surrounding him doesn't just tell him to be quiet; they sternly order him to be quiet. Bartimaeus can do as the crowd orders, or he can continue calling out. He chooses to call out louder to Jesus. Bartimaeus wanted to be heard. Knowing that Jesus could heal him, he was not going to let the crowd stop him. He used what faculties he had—mainly his voice—to call out and be heard.

We too are given those moments of choice. Our communities bear witness to the wounding effects of racism, prejudice, intolerance, evil, and injustice of all sorts. We are called to see with God's eyes and be awakened to the reality of the world around us. We are also called to be God's presence in this world, to be a part of the answer to its problems. We are not to be silent but are called, in some way, to take a stand. So often the world tries to silence us: "Don't rock the boat; don't initiate change." Yet as Christians we are called to stand up for truth and justice. We are called to bear God's love to all of God's creation. When the world tries to silence us, we are called like Bartimaeus to use whatever faculties and talents we have to call out even louder until our voices are heard and God's will is done.

Loving Lord, help me to see the world through your eyes. And help me to be a vehicle of your truth and love to a world broken and yearning for you. Amen.

Debbie H. Deane

The Persistent Woman

"In a certain city there was a judge who neither
feared God nor had respect for people.
In that city there was a widow who kept coming to him
and saying, 'Grant me justice against my opponent.' ...
And the Lord said, "Listen to what the unjust judge says.
And will not God grant justice to his chosen ones
who cry to him day and night?"
—Luke 18:2-3,6-7

In 1990, after the war in Mozambique, children were roaming the streets of Maputo, scavenging from garbage dumps, stealing from passers-by, surviving by any means they could. They learned their skills from being homeless and orphaned.

After seeing the street children day after day on her way to work as a treasurer for the Mozambique Council of Churches, Amelinda Pedro left her job to find a way to care for the children. When city officials refused to help—in fact, they threatened her with harm if she persisted—she went to people in the community. But neither were they interested in helping these "dangerous" children.

A persistent woman, Amelinda found a woman who was willing to invite children into her home. Amelinda prepared food, donated by her husband, to attract the children. On the first day, twenty-five children came to the house. Others heard there was free food available; and on the second day there were fifty-eight children. Once word spread that Amelinda was trying to take care of the children, a Baptist missionary brought her clothing and blankets.

When it became known that Amelinda was teaching the children, as they were not attending school, an injured victim of the civil war came and offered to help her teach. Amelinda told him she could not pay him. But he told her he was willing to suffer with her and showed her his credentials as a licensed teacher. She later appointed him director of the school.

In 1993 a man from Denmark generously offered Amelinda money to build a school. She went to a Presbyterian church to ask if the pastor would manage the money for materials and construction. He agreed to help, and construction began. She named the school "Escola Comunidade Deus Todo Poderoso," which means "God is Powerful Community School."

When I visited in 1998, the building had four rooms to hold five hundred twenty-seven children. They sat in orderly rows on the dirt floor since there were no desks. Nine teachers, also without desks, received $16 a month pay from contributions given to the school. Classes were held in shifts to accommodate the children, ages four to seventeen, in seven grade levels. All the students were passing national tests.

The United Methodist bishop of Mozambique found support among colleague bishops from the U.S., one of whom returned home from a visit and raised over $200,000 from American congregations. This was enough to build and completely furnish a new, larger building in 1999 for the more than eight hundred children in the community.

The persistence and faith of this one woman—who saw the need to feed the children, in more ways than one—eventually led to justice after rejection and struggle, and faith.

Loving God, may we be persistent in our struggle for justice when we see those in need of our help. Let us remember Jesus' words assuring us that God grants justice to those who seek it without giving up. Amen.

Elizabeth Okayama

A Light on the Way

"No one after lighting a lamp hides it under a jar, or
puts it under a bed, but puts it on a lamp stand, so that
those who enter may see the light. For nothing is hidden
that will not be disclosed, nor is anything secret that will
not become known and come to light. Then pay attention
to how you listen; for to those who have, more will be
given; and from those who do not have, even what
they seem to have will be taken away."
—Luke 8:16-18

Over the last few months, three women I've known have died. Each lived freely and assuredly, showing hospitality to many. There's no doubt that each, at various stages of her life, knew the generosity required of the faithful. Each intercepted my life at times and in ways that enhanced it.

One woman was the mother of a good friend and colleague. Her death came a year or two short of 100 years of age. At her sixty-fifth birthday celebration she answered a news reporter's query: "Oh, this year's college degree was my gift to myself." I marvel, yet am not surprised. She was a sensible woman and knew that one's concern for personal development is not a selfish act. Goals are worth setting. To achieve them is good for the soul.

Another of these women was a distant relative whom I knew only in adulthood. We enjoyed an evolving commitment to one another and to our families. She lived on the west coast and I on the east coast, but we were far from strangers. If our needs were great, calls went out at midnight or very early in the morning. Friendships and family were precious to each of us, just as was sharing the value of some action in a variety of situations. Her faithfulness never wavered.

The third woman was my paternal aunt, who embodied the supreme idea of being, teaching, and guiding. I was recently gifted with a box of notepaper that pictures a large apple with the words, "To teach is to change lives forever." Her life confirmed that message during thirty-eight years of teaching in a small Texas town. I remember her as a caring relative who, in the 1940s and '50s, took some twenty eighth- and ninth-grade boys and girls from my hometown to live with her at different times so they could finish high school. Just think of attending to teaching chores AND living with three or more teenagers at a time.

She knew personally the unjust situations black families faced: the separate and unequal schools for their children or no schools for them beyond a certain grade level with no public plan for providing an alternative. And so she offered this godsend to their parents. She survived those years with the help of the children's parents, who admonished their sons and daughters to behave and to learn. Where there was no justice, she worked faithfully to liberate in society a vulnerable and marginalized group of people. May we do the same.

Creator, redeemer, provider of all our needs, we're grateful for your generosity. We pray that peoples and nations learn to gather at the wells of this world and to drink your fresh water and discover your light. Amen.

Theressa Hoover

A Heritage to Treasure

On the sabbath day we went outside the gate by the
river, where we supposed there was a place of prayer;
and we sat down and spoke to the women
who had gathered there. A certain woman named Lydia,
a worshipper of God, was listening to us...
The Lord opened her heart to listen eagerly
to what was said by Paul.
—Acts 16:13-14

Dreams can come true, but they aren't always as you might have expected. I discovered this fact when my husband and I took a tour to Greece and Turkey, following in the footsteps of Paul on his second missionary journey.

I had thought that I would find some tangible evidence of Paul's journey. I didn't know what it might be, but I expected something more than a lot of antiquity. In Veria (Berea of the Bible), there were tiled pictures of Paul speaking on the "bema." Otherwise, the journey was one for the imagination as we beheld the variety of ancient ruins.

In Phillipi, we visited the river where Paul baptized Lydia. I'd never given Lydia much conscious thought before, but this experience led me to appreciate her boldness in responding to a stranger and his gospel. She has inspired women in succeeding centuries to believe that we are precious in the eyes of God.

Lydia was also a woman who, as a seller of purple cloth, pioneered for women who make their way in this world by their own labors. We aren't given insight into any prejudices she might have experienced, but we know it was a man's world and that the role of women was to provide service and pleasure.

Paul has much to say about the spiritual needs of the people in these ancient days. They worshipped beauty and a variety of gods and goddesses. But Lydia presented herself as a believer in the one true God. Her later witness would surely have helped in founding the church in her area.

At the same river where Lydia was baptized, I renewed my baptism and commitment as a believer in and follower of the Good

News that Paul proclaimed. I gave thanks for women who have always been at the forefront of the church and its establishment. The same is true today, even though there are still those who deny that a woman can know the call of God to ministry. We are still walking on precarious paths when as women we seek to make our voices heard.

Thank you, God, for granting me this journey into the past. It provided new meaning and understanding of the early church and the difficulties it encountered. May I remain as true to the gospel as did those early believers and the generations that have followed. Amen.

Mary Jo Ferreira

Where Is My Rest?

He makes me lie down in green pastures;
he leads me beside still waters; he restores my soul.
—Psalm 23:2-3a

My world, and probably yours, is full. Full of tasks, work, schedules, to-do lists, and many other things. The on/off switch is always on. Society and culture impose burdens on women that are not imposed on the other half of human kind. As if that were not enough we impose additional burdens on ourselves.

So what should we do when we see injustices and other ills in our society? As women of faith we feel compelled to work for justice, to stand with the marginalized. We are overworked as it is. What should I do? Where is my rest?

As women of faith we are called to seek justice, not to burn out seeking it. I am not going to fix the world by myself. I have to realize the fact that sometimes I try to do too much and end up doing nothing.

I have found my rest with the realization that my part can be small. One letter to the government, an organization, a company can add to the effort of others. Some volunteer hours for a worthy cause. Such efforts grow larger when we find partners to share the load. It can be anybody, even a child.

I have found that God can indeed use my help to make the pastures greener. Every day I can contribute a handful of seeds, water, and soil to the pasture. Others will, too. Through advocating for justice, speaking against stereotypes, contributing my resources (tangible or intangible), and in many other ways, I can contribute to making still waters.

My soul will be restored every time my efforts toward environmental, social, or economic justice are put into action, one step at a time. This restoration is also my rest. We must work to sustain the rhythm God has built into life. God worked and rested. We must do the same. Jesus taught and healed, then retreated. We can follow his example.

God, help me to be honest with myself and to weigh every action according to my ultimate goals. Help me to rejoice and find satisfaction with every step of the quest. By adding my efforts to those of others, we may all enjoy the green pastures and still waters you have give us to restore our souls. Amen.

Diana Rodríguez

A Righteous Adulteress

*Then Judah acknowledged [his pledge] and said,
"She is more in the right than I, since I did not
give her to my son Shelah."*
—Genesis 38:26

The biblical story of Tamar and Judah revolves around the ancient tradition of Levirate marriage, developed to protect the inheritance of a man who died without male heirs by marrying his widow to his surviving brother.

Under the Levirate code, the woman was a pawn: merely a vessel to receive the male's seed and to bear the male heir. But how the tradition played out in Tamar's life involves twists and turns befitting a modern soap opera. A mediocre first husband died young, leaving Tamar to "inherit" an even worse second spouse, one who was so dishonorable and deceitful that Scripture says "the LORD...put him to death." The only son left in the family was just a boy, so the childless Tamar, unjustly labeled "barren," was sent back to her family.

After two bad marriages and the prospect of a child groom for the third, one might assume Tamar would be content to forget the whole patriarchal tradition that passed her from one man to the next. But Tamar was no passive pawn. She went right to the patriarch of the family in her pursuit of justice—for herself and for her first husband. Whether she *intended* to "seduce" Judah into fathering her child or not—reciprocal deceit *does* seem to be a theme running throughout the larger Jacob narrative—the means certainly attained the desired end: a pregnancy that nearly cost Tamar her life when she was accused of adultery.

When she presented proof concerning the paternity of her unborn child, Judah's cheeks must surely have burned with shame. "She is more in the right than I," he acknowledged before those who witnessed Tamar's judgment. Other translations render that text "She is more righteous than I." In Hebrew, *righteousness* was synonymous with *justice*. Thus Judah affirmed that justice had been served, however unorthodox and even apparently immoral the means. God seemed to agree, for after suffering two husbands for the Levirate cause, Tamar was blessed with two sons, twins, one of whom became the ancestor of Jesus, the Messiah.

Righteous God, thank you for the reminder that issues of justice often transcend legal codes and traditional morality. Help me to be a daughter of Tamar as I take action to set right the wrongs that tradition and law have perpetuated or overlooked. Amen.

Rebecca Irwin-Diehl

On Not Losing Heart

So we do not lose heart.
Even though our outer nature is wasting away,
our inner nature is being renewed day by day.
—2 Corinthians 4:16

I was returning home after a brief vacation, driving through the heart of the small town where I had recently accepted a call as a pastor. My mind was on the stacks of mail that awaited me, the phone messages needing immediate attention, the sermon that would have to materialize before Sunday morning.

I was also wondering how—and if—the three small churches I served would be able to move beyond their nostalgia, their attachment to what had "always" been done. Nor was I clear about my own journey. In the previous eighteen months, my mother had died, a long-time personal relationship had ended hurtfully, and I had job-searched and moved twice. Was I in the right place, doing the right thing?

Something about the vehicle ahead of me penetrated this haze; something wasn't right. Then I realized what it was. Even at 35 mph, the car's brake lights were constantly flashing. The driver was keeping one foot on the brake. Not quite stopping, but not inclined to move forward, either.

This lurching movement reminded me of the way the church typically seems to move. One foot on the gas and one foot on the brake. Faith in the past but extreme caution about the future. Over the past half century, gender roles in our society have changed enormously, giving way to diversity and flexibility—except in the church, where women are routinely presumed to be less fit for leadership. Even in my tradition, which has been ordaining women for almost fifty years, many churches are slow to elect women as lay leaders and to hire women as ministers. It's discouraging.

How do we keep going? Paul says that our faith and hope are a priceless gift from God. "This treasure," he says, is held in the clay jars of human frailty and fallibility. Only by God's grace can we hold on to our calling—in spite of difficulties and doubts.

"Therefore, since it is by God's mercy that we are engaged in this ministry, we do not lose heart" (2 Corinthians 4:1).

God of our deepest reality, move within both our caution and our impatience as we seek to be faithful. Open to us the treasure of kingdom living, the freedom of your love. Amen.

Cathy Carpenter

The Timbre of Love

Steadfast love and faithfulness will meet;
righteousness and peace will kiss each other.
—Psalm 85:10

We stood on the street corner singing. The voices that mingled with the noise of the passing traffic were not those of a trained choir. Some in our group were young children. Some were senior adults. The rest of us were a scattering of ages in between. The light reflecting off our faces revealed several hues of skin color and varying degrees of wrinkles. Our music was not professional, but it was beautiful, for our songs were songs of faith and trust in our God.

Standing there with my family at that city intersection was one of the pivotal experiences of my life. Born in 1953, I had never expected to find myself at the site of a cross burning in the mid-1980s. Yet there I was with my husband and two young daughters and some of my friends, re-consecrating a site that had been desecrated by hate—hate that had set fire to the symbol of ultimate love.

It wasn't the first time our "choir" had come together. Several crosses had been burned in our city; each time a group of us from the NAACP, along with other Christians, had gathered to pray and sing and reclaim the site. As a mother, I was both sad and glad that day. I grieved that Jenny and Cali had to learn so early that hate is strong and ugly and ever-present in our world. But I also rejoiced that they could learn at a young age the blessing of Psalm 85:10. I was glad they could experience the joy that comes when people of love and faithfulness meet together to work for righteousness and peace.

Hate may be strong by human standards, but it is a pale thing when confronted with the rich hues and timbre of God's amazing, enduring love. The steadfast love of the Lord never ceases. It cannot be burned away, sneered away, or scared away. But it can be given away, even to people driven by hate and fear.

Lord, thank you for your amazing love. By the power of that love, bind us together as a community of faith. Give us the strength to work and pray and speak and act for your righteousness and justice among all people. May your kiss of peace and righteousness bless our world today. Amen.

Karen Ann Selig

Serving Others

Making Room

Jesus said, "Let the little children come to me,
and do not stop them; for it is to such as these that
the kingdom of heaven belongs."
—Matthew 19:14

I was in grade school when the new neighbors moved in next door. My bedroom window looked out over the carport and driveway of their house. And every Sunday morning I watched the ritual as they moved in and out of the house wearing suits and fancy dresses and carrying books. The family would all get into their car. Often somebody would get out and go back inside. Sometimes another would follow. Sometimes the car would start out of the driveway, stop and come back. And after a brief trip inside, they would take off again. A few hours later they would come back home. Week by week, I sat at my window watching them and thinking that one day, I, too, would go to church.

My mother was with us one afternoon as my brother, sister, and I played in the backyard. Our neighbor ventured over. She asked if we might want to go to Sunday school with her family the next week. It was finally decided that my sister and I could go. (My brother was too young.) On Sunday morning we were dressed in our best dresses and shoes and reminded of our manners. We were given a coin or two to take along. I was delivered to the Junior Department, where I joined the other children as they worked on a craft project and then broke into small groups.

In my group, they gave me a Bible so I could join in reading the story. The books I usually read were borrowed from the library, so I was sure they would want me to return this one. But they told me it was my very own to keep. It was a fine book with a soft cover and black and gold letters outside. Inside it had parchment pages, and some of the letters were red. They told me it was all the stories about how God loves people. And, especially, about Jesus. They told me that Jesus takes care of God's people like the shepherd takes care of sheep.

They won my heart and soul that day. My life was changed forever. I often remember that family and their concern for a neighbor child. I think also of others who have been teachers and preachers, counselors and coaches, friends and fellow servants on my journey of faith.

I am reminded that we are a people with a mission. There are still boys and girls, men and women looking up from desks and counters across the aisle, in offices and classrooms, through windows and doors down the street—watching, wondering, and waiting for us to notice them.

Lord God, direct our vision outward to the many places and many people in our world who watch and wait and wonder when and if we will notice. Help us to take time, opportunity, and initiative to reach out with an invitation. And may they find in our congregations warmth, welcome, and hope. Amen.

Linda G. Frost

A Taste of Agape

"But I say to you that listen, Love your enemies, do good to those who hate you, bless those who curse you...
Be merciful, just as your Father is merciful."
—Luke 6:27-28a;36

"Mama Dansanit" was a spunky local prostitute my husband and I came to know during our years as missionaries in north Kenya. She was infamous in the local community for her persistence as a beggar, cheat, drunkard, and liar. She made no effort to pretend to be worthy of the food and money she asked for; her usual routine was to shamelessly curse and insult the people from whom she begged.

She visited our door regularly for a couple of years, then disappeared for several months. When she reappeared, she was dying of AIDS and carrying a skeletal newborn. Though the disease rendered her physically unrecognizable, her obnoxious personality was intact. Because she was despised by the local community, she had nowhere to turn in her desperation. She chose to live out her dying weeks under the lemon tree outside our front door.

Mama Dansanit (which means "The Bad or Unwell Woman" in the Borana language) was my ultimate test of compassion. I battled daily with the conflicting desires to do good for her and to get rid of her. Her loud, demanding presence was an overwhelming strain on my time and emotions. It served as a constant reminder of how far I had left to go down the road of unconditional love.

But I am ever grateful to her and for her. As she and her baby continued to appear in our yard each morning, looking to us to provide the few things they needed to survive, an uncontrollable, painful yearning and affection began to well up within me.

Though there was a part of me that always wanted to escape her, Mama Dansanit and I somehow connected. Once we touched one another with our common humanity and womanhood, I caught sight of God's image hidden deep beneath her brokenness. I couldn't help but feel blessed by her presence in my life. She taught me a kind of love that I had never known before. She gave me a sip from the cup of *agape*.

Oh God, thank you for bringing into my life people who stretch the limits of my love. Teach me to love the "unlovable," as you have loved me. Amen.

Christie A. Eastman

Forgotten Child

"Can a mother forget the baby at her breast and
have no compassion on the child she has borne?
Though she may forget, I will not forget you!
See, I have engraved you on the palms of my hands."
—Isaiah 49:15-16, NIV

I went with Pon, the director of children's ministries at our Thai church, to visit a little girl from the surrounding slums. We found the girl. She was with an older girl we did not know. They were playing with bottle caps, pretending they were dishes of food. The mother told us that the older child was from a previous marriage and that the girl lived with her father. But since he entertained a lot of drinking buddies, the mother told us, he didn't have time to look after her.

The younger child had been wandering the streets. The mother's present husband would not allow the girl to stay with them, but she could come during the day to help with the housework. "How old is she?" Pon asked. The mother looked puzzled and said she couldn't quite remember. It was either nine or ten. I asked the little girl how old she was, but she looked shyly away and didn't answer as she played with the bottle caps.

What is her real name, we asked? (Her nickname was "Bia.") Again the mother looked puzzled and said she couldn't remember for sure. Was it this or that? She couldn't remember. The little girl "Bia" sat there overhearing her mother say that no one wanted to care for her, that no one had time for her, that no one could remember her age or even her name. As we left, my heart ached for this little girl, and I wondered what the future held for her.

Later, as I reflected on this experience, I was reminded of the passage in Isaiah 49:15. Bia's mother might have forgotten her name and her age, but God has not forgotten her. It is my prayer that Bia will come to know the God who has her engraved on his palm and knows her by name.

We pray, Lord, for all the little ones who have been forgotten and discarded. You know them by name and you long for them. Give us the passion to find justice for these little ones and to bring them into your loving arms. We pray in your name, Jesus. Amen.

Annie Dieselberg

The Father at Work

Jesus answered them, "My Father is still working,
and I also am working."
—John 5:17

It is amazing how the Lord breaks in on your life when you are minding your own business. Take, for instance, that Saturday morning when I was intent on making my way to Wal-Mart to purchase some vacuum cleaner bags on sale. As I entered the store for the first time, I could not have imagined how big this place was, and I had no idea where the vacuum cleaner bags were located.

As I started to walk past the first cashier I saw, with my flyer in hand, I thought, "I should ask her about the location of these items. Otherwise, I could be wandering around this store forever." As I approached her, I asked, "Would you please tell me where the vacuum cleaner bags are? I have no idea where to look." She started to direct me, but then she appeared unsure, so she responded, "I'm not sure where to find them, so I'll go with you."

As we started walking, she asked, "You go to church, don't you?" I was a little surprised at the question, and I responded, "Yes, how did you know?" She replied, "I saw the name of the church on your T-shirt." This was even more intriguing since I was not wearing a shirt with the name of my church imprinted on it. I explained that what she saw was actually the name of a family reunion I had attended. Her next question was even more surprising: "Would you please pray for me?" As surprised as I was, I responded, "Yes, of course, I'll pray for you." She then went on to request that I pray her children would not be taken from her. She explained that she had four children, three in foster care and one with his father. The state was pursuing putting the children up for adoption.

As we walked down one of the aisles, I sensed a strong urging from the Holy Spirit to stop and pray for this young woman right then and there. I said to her, "I want to pray for you now. What is your name? And also, please give me the names of your children." She gave all of the names to me. I reached in my purse for one of my business cards and asked her to write the names on the card. I don't know how she did it, but she recorded her name, the names of each of her four children, and the specific illnesses of two of the children, along with a request for prayer for her to find a husband and also to get a house. All on the back of my little business card!

As we bowed our heads, she took my hand in hers. As I lifted up her concerns to almighty God, she affirmed my requests in gratitude by responding with, "Thank you, Jesus, Thank you." It didn't matter that people were passing by—we were communing with the Lord, who deserved our full attention! In the midst of shoppers, merchandise, and cash registers, we had entered into the Heavenly domain.

At the end of the prayer, I looked at her. Her countenance had changed from one of hopelessness to one of thankfulness and relief. Amid anxiety and hopelessness, the Lord had intervened to bring about thankfulness and reassurance.

Father, help us to be aware of where you are working each day so that you can use us to minister in Jesus' name. Amen.

Eleanor James Edwards

From Death to Life

The last enemy to be destroyed is death.
—1 Corinthians 15:26

We are visiting the city of Khartoum in the Sudan during a drought. A civil war rages in the south. African Christians are being slaughtered and starved out by Muslim Arabs in the north. It is a religious, cultural, and racial conflict set up long ago by European nations that divvied up the Middle East and the African continent. We are riding through mustard-colored sands swirling up around the windshield. Our destination is a refugee camp just outside the city. It is Khartoum's garbage dump. Exhausted and often ill, refugees stream into this field of garbage where they make shelters out of rusty tin, old and mottled canvas sacks, cardboard—whatever is thrown out.

We get out of the car, the dry heat searing our faces and the odor of the garbage overwhelming us. A group of ragged children, faces breaking into smiles, run over to us chanting, "Welcome uncle, welcome sister." My colleague and I stare at them, amazed at their energy and hospitality amid such desolation. My colleague starts talking to an official of some sort. I find a ball and start playing with the children. *Yes,* I think to myself, *we shall play in the midst of hell, these children and I.*

Out of the corner of my eye I see an old woman lying half outside her tent. She is dying, and there's nothing to be done for her. I also see a young woman leaning against a wall, eyes blank, body slack, and am told that she has just walked one hundred seventy-five miles from the war-torn south with her baby. The child was being fed and examined by church workers belonging to several Christian relief agencies. (Right in the middle of the garbage there is a clinic and a school and thus doctors, nurses, and teachers.)

Some of the flimsy shelters resemble the village huts from which so many fled. On the makeshift roofs tiny flags made from rags wave in the wind: *We are alive, we are alive.* Crosses are everywhere—on relief trucks, worn around people's necks, on people's clothes. But the emphasis here is not on crucifixion; it is on resurrection.

After several hours, my colleague and I regroup to confer. We are getting used to the garbage and don't notice it anymore. We see life and hope. We get back into the car. Neither of us smiles or has much to say. It is not necessary to say anything really. God is working very hard here. God is among us, indeed.

Hear me, O Lord! Let me find you where death reigns so that I may know life, where injustice profits from parents' ever-giving love, where the weak fall to the ground by the boot of the strong. Let me find you and work with you to deny death its kingdom, injustice its mockery and the mighty their victory. Take my hand and guide me to your life, your justice and your strength among us all. Amen.

Jill Schaeffer

In the Silence

*The women of my people you drive out
from their pleasant houses; from their young children
you take away my glory forever.*
—Micah 2:9

In the silence of the night I heard a cry
    from a child who asked the question *why?*
    she was beaten with a strap,
    she was tossed or kicked or slapped.
In the silence of the night she's asking *why?*

In the pinking of the dawn I heard a moan
from a girl who feels she's almost on her own.
    no one looks into her eyes
    with love, joy, and surprise
so she feels that she is very much alone.

In the bustle of the day I heard a prayer
from a hungry boy whose home is anywhere.
    He's living on the street
    where guns, drugs, and children meet.
Midst the hustlers and the gangs has he a prayer?

In the flashing of the storm she's feeling blame
for the actions of the man who often came
    told her not to ever tell
    why she feels like she's in hell.
In the flashing inner storm she's feeling shame.

We should ask ourselves the questions *who?* and *when?*
will we find the will to help and nurture them.
    We have stolen children's dreams,
    left them hopeless, so it seems.
        Will we change our ways and give our love to them?

*Loving God, give us the determination to protect all children,
and to help them get a good start in life. Take from each of us our*

*reluctance to speak out for children, and give our nation the
resolve to provide for their needs. Amen.*

Wilda K. W. (Wendy) Morris

You Were with Her

"Comfort, O comfort my people," says your God.
—Isaiah 40:1

*Jesus answered him, "Those who love me will keep
my word, and my Father will love them,
and we will come... and make our home with them."*
—John 14:23

I had spent the night consoling a woman who had been through an
abusive experience. Arriving home around 4:00 a.m., I crawled into
bed but could not sleep. Anger constricted my chest, robbing my lungs
of air, until I leapt from bed and ran from the house into the yard.

"Oh God," I cried, "be with her." But the words tasted bitter in
my mouth. I screamed into the night sky, "God be with her, my foot!
Where were You? All this rhetoric about You being our 'refuge and
strength,' our 'shield and defender,' the One who is 'always with
us.' What difference did that make for her tonight?"

Never had the sky appeared so dark to me, the stars so tiny
and distant. I felt God was somewhere among those stars, safe and
distant from this mess. I wanted to shake apart that tranquility.
I flung my accusations into the sky, "Why weren't You with
her, Lord?"

The faintest whisper returned, "You, my child, were with her."

I was astonished. I was with her? So what! I felt so inadequate!
She cried on my shoulder, and I felt helpless to ease her pain or fear.
What happened to all that stuff about "I am in Christ and Christ is
in me"? "I didn't see You there!"

Under the quiet of the sky, my spirit began to calm. I thought
about Jesus telling the disciples, "You won't be alone. I'll make my
home in you." I thought of the prophet of Isaiah, who proclaimed

hope to a defeated people. He had no proof, no army, nothing but his vision. Still, he walked into the middle of despair and said, "God is here with you." How did he know? Because God sent him.

An abused woman and I sought hope together. Unlike me, however, she didn't feel she was screaming into silence. Her faith was greater than mine. When she needed reassurance of God's presence, she called me. While I was looking for Christ somewhere else, she saw Christ in me.

Lord, give us courage to trust Your voice of hope in us. Amen.
Kelly S. Moor

Open Our Eyes

"If you continue in my word, you are truly
my disciples; and you will know the truth,
and the truth will make you free."
—John 8:31b-32

I met Helen in September of 1989. She was the first person I'd ever met who used a battery-powered wheelchair and drove a van with hand controls. Helen could go anywhere she wanted to go. Well, almost anywhere.

One day Helen and I went shopping together at a local department store. The first obstacle we encountered was the doors into the store. Helen could not open the heavy glass doors easily, and there was no power-assist plate for her to push to open them. The second obstacle we encountered in the store was the escalators. Using an escalator was not an option for Helen. We found the elevators and took one down to the first floor. We made our way from the elevator to the housewares department along the wide, main pathway that ran through the store. At housewares, we encountered our third obstacle. The display fixtures were not placed far enough apart for Helen's wheelchair. She could not enter the area to shop. She told me this was the usual situation in any department store: she needed a friend or a store employee to bring her the items she wanted to look at. Nor could she get her wheelchair to the cashier's station.

Sometimes the glimpses of truth that God has for us are painful. Through Helen, I learned that people in the United States labeled "disabled" are disabled more by the obstacles they encounter than by their "disabilities." Through lack of awareness, and sometimes through sheer rudeness, those of us who are considered "able-bodied" disable the "disabled." People who use wheelchairs, people who cannot see with their eyes or hear with their ears are marginalized in our society because "able-bodied" people place obstacles in their way.

Jesus Christ calls those of us who would be his disciples to notice, to reach out to, and to find ways to include people who are excluded and marginalized in our society. If we do not, we are not continuing or remaining in the Word. Christians also need to work toward making our church buildings and our worship services accessible. Even though churches have been legally exempted from complying with the Americans with Disabilities Act, we are called to find ways to comply with the gospel of Jesus Christ.

Can a pastor who uses a wheelchair get to your pulpit area? Does your building need ramps or an elevator? Can someone who uses a wheelchair get to a bathroom and maneuver the wheelchair into the toilet stall? Can someone who does not hear well or hear at all follow the worship service? Are the words to hymns or a printed order of service available in Braille? What unnecessary obstacles can we remove?

God of all people, you call us to remain in your Word so that we can see the truth and be set free. Open our eyes to the ways in which we block the freedom of people to move about with ease in our world. Show us how we create disability where there is none. Help us to change the ways we think about disability and to take action toward removing the obstacles that can be removed. Amen.

Margie Ann Patterson Latham

To Whom Do You Belong?

*So we, who are many, are one body in Christ,
and individually we are members one of another.*
—Romans 12:5

As we followed Margareth up the dirt path, I noticed a hen with her brood of chicks scratching the dirt around a clump of trees. This wasn't the first time I'd seen chickens roaming so freely. "Margareth, do the chickens know to whom they belong?" I inquired.

"Oh, yes. They always return home when it gets dark," she replied. I knew this was also true for this faithful servant of God. Margareth knew she belonged to God. God had given her a vision to make a home for African children on a plot of land in a remote village in order for them to obtain an education. In 1992 she began with three buildings and forty-two youth. Ten years later, after much sacrifice and hard work, three hundred Tanzanians were now receiving quality education.

Entering each classroom, Margareth, the headmistress, greeted her students. They rose in respect to greet their guests. As visitors to this facility, we felt the excitement of children being given the opportunity to learn.

Education is a light for a path that will enable women and children living in poverty to find their way to a better existence. All over the world there are faithful servants of God working hard for others. Funds are raised, libraries built, text books purchased, dormitories refurbished, medical needs met. Those who have the means know that as they share their money, they are investing in God's kingdom. Those who are called to use their gifts in teaching and administration know that they are laying a foundation for others to build on. As we work in global partnership with one another, we realize that we all belong to God. And so does all we have.

Lord, thank you for helping us see that we belong to a greater body. Stir us to use what we have to benefit those in need, enriching lives with a faith lived out in action. Amen.

Cynthia E. Cowen

Gloves without the Fingers

"...and everyone who lives
and believes in me will never die."
—*John 11:26*

My brother Michael spent time in the worst part of town in abandoned "crack houses" preaching the gospel. He continually asked me to join him. For a long time, fear kept me away, but one day I knew I had to go.

Michael took me to meet "a friend." This friend hobbled toward me on one crutch, crippled from using up the veins in his legs. Even through his raggedy coat I could tell it had been many months since he'd had a bath. Such deprivation frightened me terribly. But my fear subsided as we began to talk. About God—he wanted to talk about God!

He didn't have the courage or strength to go "cold turkey" or to commit himself to a program. (He'd done it before and it was so painful that it drove him back into the streets.) He, who once sang in the church choir, was now terrified that he was going to hell.

"What do you believe about Jesus?" I asked him. "He's the son of God and he died for my sins," he immediately responded, "but I can't get free of my sin. Look what I'm doing!" It was suddenly so clear to me that he and I were no different. We both desperately need Jesus. My sins were more socially acceptable, but equally in need of a savoir. His heart wanted to please the Lord; doesn't God judge us by our hearts?

"My understanding of the Bible," I told him, "is that we go to hell because we reject Jesus, not because of what we do or don't do. It's about our hearts. Do we want him or don't we?"

A look of relief began to spread across his face. He was silent for a moment. Then he reached out and took my hand in his—his filthy hand with the fingers missing from the gloves—and raised my hand to his lips and kissed my finger tips. "Thank you," he whispered. "No one's ever told me that before." When we left him he was hobbling back into his "house" singing a hymn. No other kiss will ever be as meaningful.

Thank you, Lord, for letting me see that there is no fear in love and that the ground is always level before your cross. Amen.

Lonnie Lane

Caregivers: Out of Bondage

The king of Egypt said to the Hebrew midwives,
one of whom was named Shiphrah and the other Puah,
"When you act as midwives to the Hebrew women,
and see them on the birthstool, if it is a boy, kill him;
but if it is a girl, she shall live." But the midwives
feared God; they did not do as the king of Egypt
commanded them, but they let the boys live.
—Exodus 1:15-17

We tend to think in Cinemascope when we recall the Israelites escaping captivity in Egypt. We remember the giant, dramatic events: Moses' and Aaron's daring confrontations with Pharaoh, the plagues, the parting of the Red Sea.

The first chapter of Exodus reminds us that the seeds of liberation were quietly given life and nurtured by women—women in the business of health care.

People dealing with serious illness or injury today can easily feel as if they are captives of our health care system, the penurious HMOs and confusing bureaucracy of Medicare.

The United States has the most expensive health care system in the world, yet the World Health Organization ranks it thirty-seventh in its effectiveness. The poor in this country suffer health conditions as bad as those in Third World countries, says the WHO.

Health care professionals, too, can feel as if they're in bondage when economic pressures demand that they do more in less time. Some leave their professions; some, like Shiphrah and Puah, find clever and creative ways to provide care.

"Hebrew women are not like the Egyptian women," the midwives told the king when he asked why they weren't obeying his command; "they are vigorous and give birth before the midwife comes to them."

Anyone who spends even a little time in a nursing home, clinic, or hospital will inevitably meet a Shiphrah, a Puah. There are still people working in health care because they do care. They are doing God's work and quietly nurturing the seeds of change.

I pray in thanksgiving for those who keep alive the seeds of

hope and faith through their care. May I as clearly hear and follow
God's directions for caring. Amen.

Mary Koch

Leaving the Many for the One

"Which one of you, having a hundred sheep and losing
one of them, does not leave the ninety-nine in the
wilderness and go after the one that is lost until he finds
it? When he has found it, he lays it on his shoulders and
rejoices. And when he comes home, he calls together his
friends and neighbors, saying to them, 'Rejoice with me,
for I have found my sheep that was lost.' Just so,
I tell you, there will be more joy in heaven over one
sinner who repents than over ninety-nine
righteous persons who need no repentance."
—Luke 15:4-7

I am a pastor's wife. I am also an introvert. I'm really not the type of person who is drawn to large groups of people. My husband, on the other hand—the extrovert, the shepherd, the pastor—sees a group of people and sets out to meet and talk to every single one. He enters with a big grin and his hand outstretched, and proceeds to win over everyone in the room. It's his job, but more than that it's also his personality.

How does my tendency to be drawn to quiet and solitude reconcile with my role as the wife of a man in the public eye? I read the above passage and find great comfort in it. A shepherd, knowing that his flock is safe, leaves them to find the one little lamb who has strayed too far. He leaves the many to find the one. When he finds it, he puts it on his shoulders and, rejoicing, brings it home.

Often when I am in a large group of people, a person will come up to me needing my attention. I like to take her aside, away from the group, away from the noise, and really talk, really listen. It's in my nature to leave the crowd in order to focus on the one. I like it that way. And apparently, sometimes God works that way, too.

We often look at the gospel stories of Jesus as snapshots: we picture him, surrounded by a few people, out in the middle of nowhere, having intimate conversations. What we easily forget is that he was probably surrounded by crowds of humanity: mothers, prostitutes, beggars, merchants, farmers, children. He was good at focusing on the few while life went on around him. He didn't forget the crowds: He just "left" them for a moment while he spoke to someone who needed him.

It is good and right to do the same thing ourselves.

Lord God, help me not to feel guilty when I leave a crowd to focus on the one. You send each of these people to me. Help me to concentrate, to encourage, to listen. Put away distraction; make the background around me fuzzy while I focus on a friend. Amen.

Martha Palmer Chambers

Helping Restore Those Who Suffer

And after you have suffered for a little while, the God of all grace, who has called you to his eternal glory in Christ, will himself restore, support, strengthen, and establish you.
—1 Peter 5:10

Even though the walls were made of mud, everything in Rekha's house looked clean. There were a few vegetable plants growing in her tiny garden. Her hair was neatly braided and her faded cotton sari appeared freshly washed. Rekha, a woman married at thirteen, lives in a small village in Bangladesh. Her husband was thirty years older than Rekha, but he worked hard and owned several hectares of land. At fifteen, Rekha was proud when she pleased him by giving birth to a boy.

Two years later her husband died, and Rekha, at seventeen, found herself in a terrible dilemma as a worthless widow. Even her parents wouldn't take her back into their home in a nearby village. For years she earned extra money by weeding other people's fields, with her small son always near her. Eventually one of her neighbors took pity on Rekha and taught her how to farm. To everyone's surprise, she became an excellent farmer, and people started asking her advice about crops and cultivating the land. At twenty-five, she was already a leader in her village.

Now at age forty, Rekha still farms and is respected as an elder by both men and women in the community. With some crucial help, her suffering has turned into strength. "I'm not afraid anymore," she told me. "Now women come to my home to talk and learn from each other. I think women should help one another become strong. It takes time for things to get better. But I think about myself, and I'd say, 'Nothing is impossible.' "

Jesus' life on earth was a perfect model of loving and caring for those who suffered. He turned people's pain and afflictions into strength. What about us? Do we reach out to support those who are in need? Or do we turn our heads and look away?

God of strength, Jesus showed us how to love those who are poor and distressed. Help us to mirror the Christ and to have compassion for those who are suffering everywhere. May we also help them to be restored and strengthened. Amen.

Joy Haupt Carol

While We Were Still Sinners

But God proves his love for us in that while we still were sinners Christ died for us.
—Romans 5:8

At an urban church nestled between low-income houses, voices can be heard through an open window, mingling with the sounds of car stereos, traffic, and kids playing football. The voices are discussing finances; more specifically, the church deacons are considering requests for various kinds of financial help from church members and neighbors. There seems to be a critical theme echoed in many of the comments. "We helped with his rent last month," and "She still needs a rides to the Laundromat?" With a tired sigh, a voice asks, "Why should we help buy her glasses when we don't approve of the way she spends the money she does have?"

Then amidst the critical comments, one voice rises, wavering with age, yet clearer and stronger than the others. "I, for one, am glad that God did not wait until he approved of me before he helped me out!" Now only silence can be heard coming from the church. The sound of a mariachi band rolls down the street through the open windows of a low-rider car. The sound drifts away, leaving the thrum of the vibrating bass to linger in the thoughts of each deacon.

Christ showed his love for us while we were still sinners. Today our board of deacons voted to help those whom we can—not on the condition that they meet some standards we have set, but simply for the joy of reflecting the character of God.

Forgive me, Jesus, for holding back when it comes to reaching out to others. I remember how your love in the midst of my sin and rebellion drew me to you. I felt your love through your people, as they loved me unconditionally. Help me to be an instrument of that love to those around me. Help me to love those in need with the love that brought you to the cross. Show me, Lord, who I can love today. Amen.

Jeanne L. Williams

Love One Another

For thus says the LORD..."As a mother comforts her child, so I will comfort you."
—*Isaiah 66:12-13*

"Love one another as I have loved you."
—*John 15:12*

The sermon at my church one Sunday was on opportunities to put love into action. Examples cited included familiar stories from the mass media about families affected by flooding in Western Canada. We also heard about less publicized stories of families slowly dying from famine in North Korea. It was difficult to know how to relate to and help people in such a distant, politically isolated setting.

One woman spoke afterwards. Lynn had read a small newspaper that told of a mother in North Korea who had watched her child die of hunger. Another of her children was punished for crossing the border into China to get food. Lynn said, "I've been a single mother struggling to feed and take care of my little boys. But I always had the help of family and friends. What if that mother were me? What if I had to watch my son go hungry, get sick, and die. Or be punished for getting food without permission? What if there was no way I could help or comfort my child?" Lynn concluded, "I'm going to do something for those mothers and children."

Lynn had musical gifts and musical friends. Her idea was to put together a benefit concert for the North Korean famine victims. We agreed that it would be most helpful to involve as many people as possible in order to raise public awareness of the famine and ways people could help. We eagerly started organizing.

People listened politely and commended our interest. But almost everyone had reasons for not getting involved: "It's bad timing." "I have plans." "I'm too busy." "Try someone else." Busy, tired, and frustrated, I too began to wonder if our timing was wrong or if our effort was unrealistic. But every time my spirit sagged, there was Lynn. She was only one mother who kept repeating the story of another mother who was unable to comfort her child. But soon it was not only the image of incredible human suffering in North Korea, but also the depth and determination of a mother's compassion that kept urging me on.

Eventually others did join the effort, which became a successful community event. It drew out gifts and built on the strengths and concern of many neighbors in one part of the world on behalf of distant, unknown neighbors in another part of the world.

Thanks be to God for love that does not give up; for love that knows no borders or limits! Thank you, God, for comforting us as a mother comforts her child. May we have the strength, determination, and compassion to comfort your children as you love and comfort us. Amen.

Linda (Schulze) Scherzinger

237

Learning to Receive

*"...if you offer your food to the hungry and satisfy
the needs of the afflicted, then your light shall rise in
the darkness and your gloom be like the noonday.
The LORD will guide you continually and satisfy your
needs in parched places, and make your bones strong;
and you shall be like a watered garden,
like a spring of water, whose waters never fail."*
—Isaiah 58:10-11

We had so much to give,
    and our hearts were so ready for giving.
We—
    well fed, well dressed, laden-down with things
        North American women—
   had arrived...

"Here we are! What can we give you?"

      ...had arrived in Nicaragua,
        (the war recently ended,
        Sandinistas and Contras, enemies drawn together
        by their common enemies—scarcity, hunger, need.)

    —a hospital where patients direct from surgery were carried
    from floor to floor (no elevator) and cared for by
      medical personnel
    who had almost no medicines available

    —a starving baby, the mother with no milk in her breasts,
    cans of infant formula an impossibly expensive alternative.

And then we sat down with our Christian sisters in that country.
    They poured for us cups of juice,
      fed us sweet bananas and warm tortillas,
    and we learned that receiving simple gifts with grateful hearts
      is so difficult when we believe that we should be the givers.
And we learned that accepting another person's gift prepares
    us to give,

not from our sense of being the bountiful, privileged ones,
but from our mutual sense of being family.

We pray together: God, we your children share the need to
receive
                    and the need to give—
                        from you and to you,
                        from and to each other.
May we both give and receive graciously and generously. Amen.
Carol Q. Cosby

Trapped

*When they kept on questioning him, he straightened
up and said to them, "Let anyone among you who
is without sin be the first to throw a stone at her."*
—John 8:7
(For the full context, read John 8:1-12.)

Visiting prostitutes in the bars of Patpong, in Bangkok, Thailand,
has been an eye-opening but significant ministry. I have discovered
many tender and beautiful women whose hearts have been trampled
in the gutters of human greed. My weekly visits have allowed me
to get to know these women and to hear their stories. Most of the
young women I meet are married. Typically, after these women
have children, their husbands leave them for other women.

Left with the responsibility of caring for their children as well as
for their aging parents, these young women end up in the city to try
to find work. Having a limited education, they have been convinced
that the only thing they can do is sell themselves to strangers. As these
women tell me about the children they've left behind, tears well up in
their eyes. They turn to call for the men with tears still glistening on
their lashes. We go to the bars to offer them alternatives and to tell
them of a love that doesn't leave them in the morning.

After they've been living this kind of life for a while, they are
both numbed and addicted to the money. They want out, but money

has trapped them. If we catch them early on, however, their hearts are still tender and they crave escape from the hell they are in. We try to help them see that the money and the one-night stands leave them empty, but the love of God offers them wholeness, self-worth, and a whole new identity. Some of the women have believed, and now they, too, are telling of God's redemption to their sisters who are still in bondage. Most have yet to believe, but God is breaking down the walls. And the promise of his faithful love is a light of hope in their darkness.

Lord, forgive us for the prejudice and judgment that come so quickly. Open our eyes to see that behind the wayward lifestyle is a heart of pain longing for healing and redemption. Help us to be vessels of your love and healing for these women. Help us, Lord, to seek justice and mercy that frees women from this bondage of self-hate. And, Lord, change the hearts of the men who take a part in devaluing these children of God. Amen.

Annie Dieselberg

Not Me, Lord

"I was in prison and you visited me."
—Matthew 25:36c

In 1973, as my mother lay in the hospital dying, Sister Rosemary came often to pray for Mother and me. We became good friends, and she asked me to join in her new ministry at the Johnson County Jail, presenting weekly Bible studies. I had no desire to engage in such a ministry, but Sister was persistent, even after Mother died. I finally gave in, mainly out of my feeling of debt to her.

I was literally "shaking in my boots" as I climbed those steps to the jail and entered the gloomy library. They locked us in. Not even thinking what good it would do without a key, I sat as close to that door as possible. Sister provided the lesson. I continued to go weekly, still frightened. Gradually, I moved away from the door and began, little by little, to participate. After the lesson, we had time to chat with the inmates.

Eddie, the most obnoxious, vile-mouthed man I had ever known, was one who made these visits frightening. As we walked into the jail every week, we could hear him screaming obscenities. He would come to the Bible study, quiet down for the lesson, but then begin screaming as soon as he left.

One day, after Bible study, Eddie and I walked to the window together. "Woodye, why do you come here every week, anyway?" he asked. I knew I was coming to repay Sister for her kindnesses, but without a moment's thought or hesitation, I said, "Because I love you, Eddie." I was shocked. Only God could have put those words in my mouth. Then I realized that I did love Eddie and all the other inmates. Only God could have put that love in my heart! I heard God calling me to become invested in this ministry with all my being. I was to love the inmates. I was not to condone their misdeeds, but neither was I to condemn the doers. Rather I was to tell them of God's unconditional love for them and of God's call to repentance and service.

This was the beginning of a jail and prison ministry that I have continued weekly for twenty-seven years. After Sister Rosemary retired, I continued and eventually expanded the ministry to include writing letters to inmates, visiting prisoners in four other states, advocating for prisoners' rights, and giving them yearly Christmas gifts and parties.

This was not originally a ministry of my choosing, but it has truly blessed me.

God of mysterious ways, thank you for the call to love the unlovable and for the blessings you've given me as I have striven to respond to this call. Amen.

Woodye Webber Kessler

Bringing Living Water

"Let anyone who is thirsty come to me, and let the one who believes in me drink. As the scripture has said, 'Out of the believer's heart shall flow rivers of living water.'"
—John 7:37-38

I watched the little children carry large plastic jugs down the hill to the river. They returned in a few moments, laboring to carry the heavy jugs now filled with river water. A mother carried a large jug on her head as water splashed out over the sides.

I was sitting on a bamboo porch in a Lahu village in the northern hills of Thailand. We had come here to work with the villagers to install a gravity-fed water system. There was a spring at the top of the hill. We ran pipe from the source down to the village and through a concrete filter system into a 17,000-gallon holding tank. For nine days we had labored side-by-side with the villagers.

This was a Christian village, and the people invited us to worship with them. I was the only pastor in the group of American volunteers, so I was asked to preach. "What, me Lord?" I felt like Moses with all the excuses running through my head. We were the first white people to be in this village. I was the first woman to ever preach in their church. I shared with them how we had come to help them have clean, fresh, life-giving water. But the true living water comes from Jesus Christ.

I knew that the only way I could speak to these dear people was through the living water within me. The living water, Christ's Holy Spirit, empowers us to do what we are incapable of doing as ordinary human beings. That week, I had to step out in faith many times and rely on the Lord and His Spirit as I directed an outdoor Bible school and led our mission team meetings each evening.

On the completed water tank, we wrote in Lahu, "Jesus Christ is the living water."

The villagers were very excited to have the project completed. They made us gifts and thanked me for sharing about the living water. They gathered round, waving and blessing us as we climbed in the back of the pickup truck to leave. Christ had been the bond between Americans and Lahu. His life-giving water had enabled us to serve him and these wonderful people. The women and children would no longer have to carry heavy jugs of water from the river to their houses.

Lord, may we remember to draw from the spring of water within us to do your will and to serve others. And may the streams of living water flow out of us and make others thirsty for you. Amen.

Donna Buckles

The Heart of a Child

"Truly I tell you, unless you change and become like children, you will never enter the kingdom of heaven."
—Matthew 18:3

Recently, I made my first trip to Europe to visit my sister-in-law. Early one Sunday morning we visited the grand Notre Dame Cathedral in Paris. As we waited in line, I saw the figure of an old, decrepit woman seated by the front entrance. Just beyond her was the sign: "Watch out for pick-pockets." She looked down at the tin plate in her lap. "Your purse can be snatched away in an instant," the woman behind me whispered. From my pocket I retrieved only Swiss francs. (We had not yet converted our money to French currency.)

I allowed myself to be swept along by the skeptical sentiments. Then I saw another poor woman, who had a baby and boy about six. The boy was eating ravenously one of those wonderful French pastries. Even so, when he saw the old woman, he did not hesitate for a moment to wrap up the remaining roll and deposit it in the old woman's tin plate. His eyes did not contain all the questions I had seen in the glances around me and in my own heart: "Is she planted here by someone trying to milk tourists?" "How will this help her?" "Will I be hungry later if I give this away?" No. In his eyes were none of those adult rationalizations that harden the heart and destroy compassion. He simply did what water does when the vessel is full: it flows from fullness to emptiness. He poured out what he had to someone who had less.

Inside, when the Eucharist was lifted up from a gold vessel, all I could see was that piece of pastry in the tin plate. When I went outside, the woman was gone. Suddenly I wanted to be purged of all that hindered me from skipping up to that woman and putting in whatever I had. It was I, not the money, that needed to be converted. A little child taught me that.

Lord, help us to understand with a simple heart and to be converted. Amen.

Penny B. Ziemer

Mourning the Loss of Holy Ground

Bless the LORD, O my soul.

O LORD, my God, you are very great.
You cause the grass to grow for the cattle,
    and plants for people to use,
    to bring forth food from the earth,
    and wine to gladden the human heart,
    oil to make the face shine,
    and bread to strengthen the human heart.
The trees of the LORD are watered abundantly,
    the cedars of Lebanon that he planted.
In them the birds build their nests;
    the stork has its home in the fir trees.

O LORD, how manifold are your works!
    In wisdom you have made them all.

May the glory of the LORD endure forever.

I will sing to the LORD as long as I live;
    I will sing praise to my God while I have being.
May my meditation be pleasing to him,
    for I rejoice in the LORD.
        —Psalm 104:1,14-17,24,31,33-34

Reflection on a Prayer Landscape Being Turned into a Parking Lot

Window Sanctuary
Setting of seasons' beauty of the Holy
Healing Presence in times of pain
Refreshing Presence in times of weariness
Spirited Presence in inner renewal
Sacred Presence of communion

Morning dawned upon this Holy Ground
In stillness I breathed in the goodness of a new day
To this Window Sanctuary I came to be
    in the silence . . .
    in solitude with the Life surrounding me.

Bird song was broken by machines' mighty roar.
Voices of destruction could be heard. Tears fell as I felt the
pain of Mother Earth
    being stripped of the Life she held in her embrace.
My inner spirit cried within as I saw
    her being encased in darkness
        hard and cold . . .
life unable now to spring forth from her.

Gone this window Sanctuary of the seasons' beauty of the
Holy.

My entire being grieves the loss of this sacred ground.

*Creator God, you gave us the gift of Mother Earth to sustain
us and care for us. So often we abuse her by our desire for
progress and by our greed. In your great mercy, forgive us. Help
us to be good stewards of your gift of Creation and reverently
hold Mother Earth in gratitude for the life she so abundantly
shares with us. Amen.*

Mary Kemen

Abundance for All

*"Look at the birds of the air; they neither sow nor reap
nor gather into barns, and yet your heavenly Father
feeds them. Are you not of more value than they?"*
—Matthew 6:26

The church group engages in a familiar social justice exercise. A
list of people stranded in a life raft is distributed to the group
members. Among those in the group are a forty-two-year-old male
physician, a Chinese immigrant woman, an eighty-nine-year-old
gay philosopher, a pregnant teenage girl, a recovering twenty-five-
year-old male drug king, and so on. The life raft can't hold all of
them. The group must decide who is expendable.

Karen, a new member, stands up. "I refuse to play this game,"
she exclaims. "It may be a Sunday evening exercise to you, but for
me it's real. When I worked for a mission group during an African
famine, we made such decisions. We had to look at people and
decide if they had a chance of surviving before we could give them
some of our limited food. Only those we thought strong enough to
survive ate. We made life-and-death decisions. The faces haunt me
to this day. I will never do it again."

The world operates on the scarcity model according to which
there is not enough to go around: not enough food, clean water,
shelter, money, and medicine. It says that we have to make choices.
It implies that suffering is normal.

God's kingdom does not operate on scarcity. God's kingdom
flows with abundance. Enough food, clean water, shelter, money,
and medicine exist. It is the inequitable distribution of wealth that
leaves starving people in lines where sometimes they cannot receive even a few grains of rice.

Jesus tells us that God's providence is sufficient. Yet, how can
we carry that message to the poor and destitute of the world when
we hoard more than our share? When can we stop saying to the
40,000 children of the world who will die each day from starvation,
"Sorry, there's not enough room on the life raft for you?"

Working for social justice means doing more than writing a
check to a favorite hunger organization. It means changing social

structures that allow the rich to get richer and the poor to fall off the life raft unnoticed.

God of all creatures, thank you for the abundance of food. Help us to ensure its distribution to everyone. Amen.

Adele Wilcox

A Knock at the Door

"Do not store up for yourselves treasures on earth, where moth and rust consume and where thieves break in and steal; but store up for yourselves treasures in heaven, where neither moth nor rust consumes and where thieves do not break in and steal. For where your treasure is, there your heart will be also."
—*Matthew 6:19-21*

It was a quiet Saturday morning. My husband and I were moving about our home doing our weekly chores. Earlier that morning we had been lamenting our small living area as we were renting our cozy duplex waiting to build or find just the right spacious place to call home. There was a knock at the door. Being new to town, we were both curious as to who it could be. My husband opened the door. Standing in front of us was a mother with two young children. Each was unkempt, with dirty hair, unmatched clothing, hunger in their eyes.

"Well, ask them!" the mother told the little girl. I knew right away they were selling something. The little girl looked up at us and said nothing. The little boy slipped by me and entered our home. The mother, frustrated with both of her children, said, "They want to know if you'll buy a magazine subscription to help their school."

I thought to myself how many times my husband had told me we didn't need any more magazines around. I said nothing, but my husband invited them in. The little boy was looking around at our home. "You have a beautiful house," he said. Guilt filled my heart as I thought back to the earlier conversation with my husband about our frustration with this house.

Soon our toddler came into the room and again the little boy spoke, "You have a pretty baby." This little visitor was like an angel, there to remind us to look around and notice how much we had been blessed.

Much to my surprise, my husband chose a magazine, and I wrote the check to the children's school. The mother went on to tell us that she had four more children at home and that she was already a Grandma. She looked so tired; I wanted to do more for her than buy a magazine subscription. As I was thinking these thoughts, she gathered her children, said "Thank you," and they were gone.

I was quiet and reflective. I thought about the home to which they would return, perhaps to a husband and father who was not helpful or tender. And I wondered how justice would come to this family. And then I remembered the young boy's words about our home and our baby. I recalled the sweetness in his voice. He probably didn't have many treasures on earth, but he knew how to be kind and to recognize the beauty of a child. He knew how to teach us that our real treasure is in heaven, not in a big spacious home.

Faithful God, help us to listen to the tender young voices of your children who teach us about the treasures you give, and lift our eyes to the real treasures to come eternally in heaven. Amen.

Patricia Stuart Jacobs

Suffering With

Two are better than one...For if they fall,
one will lift up the other; but woe to one who is alone
and falls and does not have another to help.
—Ecclesiastes 4:9-10

The novel *Cold Mountain* by Charles Frazier tells the story of a soldier's dangerous and painful journey during the Civil War. At one poignant point in the narrative, the soldier encounters a young widow, her husband lost to the war. She gives him food and shelter, inviting him to her bed rather than the corn crib. She needed a presence, someone to be with her. As they lay side-by-side, nothing more, she wept. She began to talk about her husband. What she needed of this soldier, this stranger, was that he "bear witness to her tale." We all need someone to listen, hear with the heart, bear witness to our suffering.

We do the work of Christ when we are listeners, when we bear witness. We are called to be a loving, compassionate, and caring presence for one another, even when we cannot heal or change the circumstances. Compassion (to suffer with) is not to stand on the outside looking in. It is not pity or sympathy. It is a willingness to take upon oneself the suffering of others, to enter into their pain, to cradle them in their dying.

Michelangelo's Pieta shows Mary cradling the body of Jesus. The embrace is a dramatic declaration about relationship. The sorrowful Mary knew she could not heal her beloved son's wounds or prevent his physical death. But she could be present, to comfort and cradle him in his dying.

In times of grief and loss, in our woundedness, we want and need to be held. We need to be in relationship with another; we need to be in relationship with God.

We are called to be present to others, especially in their time of greatest need. Whether it is a stranger with a story to tell or a beloved one who is near death, we are called to listen to others in their sorrow and in their joy, to cradle their heads when they die, that they might see in us the face of Jesus.

Gracious God, who calls us into relationship with you and all people, help me bear witness to the stories that need telling, that none must bear suffering alone. Amen.

Emilie J. Aubert

Gifts

*He looked up and saw rich people putting their gifts into
the treasury; he also saw a poor widow put in two small
copper coins. He said, "Truly I tell you, this poor widow
has put in more than all of them; for all of them have
contributed out of their abundance, but she out of
her poverty has put in all she had to live on."*
—Luke 21:1-4

We found a department store in Honduras where we wanted to
buy Venancia de la Cruz and her family a housewarming gift.
But what do you get for a family who lives in a remote mountain
village without electricity and running water? We quickly discovered that Honduran department stores don't cater to poor mountain people.

Our group had traveled to Honduras in November 1999 to build
a house for Venancia and her family because her home of sixteen
years—constructed by her husband—had washed away in Hurri-
cane Mitch's rains in late 1998. The family escaped harm but lived
in the remains of the house until local authorities ordered them out.
In a community where wages amount to $3.50 per day, Venancia's
family income barely covered the necessities.

When Venancia arrived at our work site one morning carrying a
large, blue bowl filled with homemade sweet bread and an even
bigger, steaming metal pot of coffee, we stopped, set down our
tools, and stared in disbelief. Her daughter followed with a hodge-
podge of faded plates and cracked cups under one arm and a toddler
under the other. We were hungry and readily accepted their gifts on
that day and every other day we spent at the work site.

At the department store, we were stumped. Nothing seemed
right. Several times we passed over a set of plain green dishes that
could have replaced Venancia's faded, cracked dishes. We were
searching instead for something brighter, something more attrac-
tive. Finally someone said, "The only reason we're not buying those
green dishes is because they're not stylish enough." Silence. "Yes,"
someone else finally replied.

We returned to the village, presented Venancia and her family with their house and a new set of green dishes, hoping we were capable of offering our gifts in the spirit in which she gave her gifts.

Thank you, God of all that is good, for reminding us where true gifts come from. Amen.

Angela Herrmann

Fear of the Unknown

*I hereby command you: Be strong and courageous;
do not be frightened or dismayed, for the LORD
your God is with you wherever you go.*
—*Joshua 1:9*

Several years ago, and a short time after the student protests, I visited Beijing, China, as a member of a People to People tour for public health nurses. In addition to our professional visits to hospitals, clinics, and homes, we enjoyed sightseeing. One stop was on Tiananmen Square. Our local guide shared information on several points of interest and then encouraged us (forty nurses) to explore the square on our own in small groups for about thirty minutes. Prior to leaving us on our own, our guide gave us directions to find our bus by using our last site as a point of reference.

After a few minutes of walking around the area, there was increased security activity on the square. Several busloads of soldiers arrived in front of one building. The soldiers stood shoulder-to-shoulder and began to march across the square, clearing it of all visitors. Everyone had to move in a direction away from where we were to meet the bus and our guide. Our small group looked for familiar faces of other tour members in the crowd. We finally spotted a few friendly faces. Our hearts and pulses were pounding, since no one could tell us what had happened to initiate this clearing of the square. Eventually, all of the tour members found their way to our bus. Our local guide learned that the square was cleared merely to prepare the area for the arrival of a visiting dignitary.

This experience with the unknown is probably the most frightening experience I have ever had in a foreign country. It was very disconcerting to be denied freedom of movement without knowing what was happening or why.

Christian women in many countries experience this kind of fear and oppression daily. Their movement is restricted, as are their outward expressions of faith. My own experience of fear, even in what was a relatively safe setting, has increased my awareness of the uncertainty that many women live with throughout their lives.

Dear Lord, thank you for the freedom that I enjoy in America. I pray in Jesus' name for Christian women throughout the world who do not have this privilege. Amen.

Marilyn D. Harris

Journey toward Hope

But many of the priests and Levites and heads of families, old people who had seen the first house on its foundations, wept with a loud voice when they saw this house, though many shouted aloud for joy, so that the people could not distinguish the sound of the joyful shout from the sound of the people's weeping, for the people shouted so loudly that the sound was heard far away.
—Ezra 3:12-13

Ms. Taylor sits inside the cool of the FEMA camper trailer. Nine months earlier, floodwaters had ravaged her house and left it in ruins. We first met several weeks earlier when I had arranged a meeting with her and her daughter. Being a widow, well into her seventies with an income of $600 a month, she had surrendered to her daughter all the legal matters and red tape of flood relief. I had come to bring hope. We were discussing the building of a new house with volunteer hands. If all went well, Ms. Taylor's new home would be built in a one-week blitz in mid-July, which was six weeks away.

Today, however, while Ms. Taylor hibernates indoors, a group of energetic and enthusiastic youth volunteers labor outdoors. With joy, vigor, and shouts of camaraderie, the home place is dismantled, piece-by-piece. This sacred dwelling that housed family and friends—where holidays had been celebrated, pictures taken, and birthday candles extinguished—had been reduced to a heap of busted wood and broken glass. The old upright piano that once filled the house with music was pushed onto the pile of debris. Every broken board holds a shattered memory.

The teen effort is genuine. Their hearts are good, their work valuable, and their services necessary. The contrast is striking. Sorrow and joy stand only a few feet apart. Youth and wisdom rehearse an awkward dance. Hope and despair intermingle as blood and water.

Following Babylonian captivity the Israelites returned home to rebuild their beloved temple. Ezra proclaims the elders wept as the younger generation rejoiced. More deeply than before, now I understand. Hope is a bittersweet journey.

Intermingling God, we are thankful for helpful hands and caring hearts. Remind us of the great losses so many have encountered. Make our hearts compassionate, our hands gentle, our eyes wide open. Guide us, as we seek to be companions on the journey toward hope. Amen.

Annell George–McLawhorn

My Sister's Keeper

The LORD works vindication and justice for all who are oppressed. He made known his ways to Moses, his acts to the people of Israel.
—Psalm 103:6-7

Yolanda, a young woman of nineteen, had many dreams. Dreams to be fulfilled with her husband and daughter, Elizema, eighteen months old. Her dreams were so strong that she ventured to cross the border of Mexico into the United States where her husband was working hard and had called her to be with him. So she went. Like the people of Israel coming out of Egypt, dreaming of a better future, she walked a long way from San Pedro Chayuco, Oaxaca, to Sonora.

She was not alone. With her, five men walked and shared her dream. However, unlike the people of Israel, they had no leader to guide them. The *pollero*, or the person they had paid to guide them, abandoned them, telling them that their walk through the desert would take just four hours. Instead, they walked for four days.

Yolanda felt weak with the extra weight of carrying her daughter, who got heavier with the passing hours, the scorching sun, and the hot, dry soil. The group had to be concerned also with the fear of snakes, the border patrol, and ranchers who might shoot without asking questions. Yolanda decided to rest. "I will catch up with you in awhile," she told the men. And they went on their way.

When that "while" became five hours, the men—in a spirit of community—worried and went back. They found her lifeless body lying on the ground, with Elizema in her arms.

Many people cross borders in our days and enter into physical or emotional deserts. And they too are left alone. God calls us to become our sister's keeper and feel the passion to serve, guide, and console those who are "harassed and helpless, like sheep without a shepherd." Beyond the many borders that separate us, we must look at people with the eyes of Jesus. Then we will understand the roots of suffering that move people to venture into the desert with nothing but a dream in their hearts and hope in their souls.

Dear God, help us to realize how to give hope to those in the desert and to help them find new ways in the wilderness. Give us strong hearts to believe in your dreams and to make all people our own people. Amen.

Doris J. Garcia-Mayol

Caregivers: Humble Advocacy

From there he set out and went away to the region of
Tyre. He entered a house and did not want anyone to
know he was there. Yet he could not escape notice, but a
woman whose little daughter had an unclean spirit
immediately heard about him, and she came and bowed
down at his feet. Now the woman was a Gentile,
of Syrophoenician origin. She begged him
to cast the demon out of her daughter.
—Mark 7:24-26

She simply wouldn't take no for an answer. What a model this Greek woman is for those of us caring for aging, ill, or disabled family members!

It's easy for patients to fall between the cracks of today's confusing health care systems. Every patient needs an advocate: someone who will double-check diagnoses, monitor care, deal with paperwork, seek more information, question, probe, insist, and persist.

It's a daunting job. We're grieving for our loved one's pain; we're dealing with problems we don't understand; and our presence is not always welcome. "Go sit in the waiting room," we're sometimes told.

Like an overburdened doctor who has gone too long without sleep, Jesus needed some time off. How difficult it must have been for the distraught mother to breach social custom and invade Jesus' seclusion. Not only that, she demanded unorthodox treatment. Why, the child wasn't even his patient!

Why did Jesus initially put her off? "I was sent only to the lost sheep of Israel," he tells her in Matthew's account. Did he want her to teach us something?

From her we learn to persist with grace and humility. I'll take the crumbs, she told the great physician. That will be good enough.

I read a news account recently about a man suffering from a rare affliction. His life was saved in part because his daughter was a persistent advocate as he lay near death in the hospital. "When my sons are her age, if they look after my interests the way she did, I'll be in good shape," said one of the man's doctors.

There's a boundary between earnest advocacy and in-your-face obstructionism. Both the Greek woman and the modern daughter recognized that boundary. As a result, their loved ones received the best possible care.

I pray that that through Jesus, our greatest advocate, I find the grace to persist for my loved ones in faith and humility. Amen.

Mary Koch

Running Scared

"Truly I tell you, just as you did not do it to one of the least of these, you did not do it to me."
—Matthew 25:45

Working late at the parish, I ignore the furious rain pounding on the window above my shoulder. Suddenly, above the storm's clatter, comes a loud hammering on the front door. I look at my watch: 11:15. All programs ended hours ago. My office light and my lone Saturn in the parking lot gave me away. Dear God!

In a flurry, I exit my computer, douse the lights, and slip into the dark corridor. I stare down the hall toward the windowless front door where the banging continues. Parishioners know there is no priest on the premises.

As the banging stops, I inch my way toward the reception area. Standing well back from the windows, I search the rainy lot. No one. No vehicle. Suddenly the insistent hammering resumes at the far end of the L-shaped building. I run to my office, grab briefcase and keys and head for the mid-building door. Before I get there, the pounding stops. I freeze.

It starts up again, louder, at this very door. As I turn back, it stops again. A familiar figure races past the window. Dear God, it's only John! He is a young, learning-disabled parishioner who comes to every event, then needs a ride home.

My fear quickly slides into anger, anger into blame. His meeting ended hours ago. Where are his parents anyway? How can they just presume he'll get home? Do I dare become another backup driver? And reinforce such irresponsibility? It is past eleven thirty, and icy rain is pelting the roof. As John bangs on the front door, I slip out and drive off.

Six blocks later, in shame and regret, I turn back. Too late. I cannot find him anywhere.

Though John still greets me today with a warm hug, I deliberately hold another image: Cold, soaking wet and desperate to get my attention, he rounds the building to see me drive away.

Compassionate Jesus, forgive me for the times I wall another person out of my heart, refusing to get involved. What I fail to do for the least, I fail to do for you. Help me to face my sins of omission with honest repentance. Change my attitudes that I may respond spontaneously, as you would, to anyone in need. Amen.

Josephe Marie Flynn

Translators of God's Word

When the day of Pentecost had come, they were all together in one place...All of them were filled with the Holy Spirit and began to speak in other languages, as the Spirit gave them ability... each one heard them speaking in the native language of each...Amazed and astonished, they asked,... "And how is it that we hear, each of us, in our own native language?...in our own languages we hear them speaking about God's deeds of power."
—Acts 2:1-11

It seems we spend much time these days
    pondering how to reach the young with the Good News.
Through different music? Worship? Cyberspace?
    —a matter of translation?

Wise men of long ago
    were vilified and killed
For changing dying words
    into the living language of the streets.

Why did some fear to hear about God's deeds
    in their own native tongue?
—a matter of translation?

Today we praise the names of learned folks
    who often spend their lives
        bringing Good News to obscure jungle tribes
        in their own languages.
World travelers, too, attest to their delight
    in worship that contains familiar words
    their minds can hear as caring.
— a matter of translation?

Now there are churches where
God's love is not just mottoed on the wall,
It's spoken in a language that includes
    not only men and man, mankind, and Father God,
    but women with their gifts,
        humanity and God beyond all male.
It isn't just what's fair.
It's knowing those who speak
    have cared enough to put the great Good News
    in words that feel like home,
    that open Scripture to your inner self.
— a matter of translation?

*Creator God, we thank you for creating women and men in your
image, and for helping us to hear the Good News in our own language. Help us to be translators of your words to all we meet. Amen.*
                                    Carolyn Hall Felger

Remembrance of Things Present

Remember those who are in prison,
as though you were in prison with them...
—Hebrews 13:3

Ragged children scavenging through garbage cans. Scarred survivors of genocide. Wives beaten by their husbands. Men living on the street. Christians tortured for their faith. Schizophrenics. Nursing home patients abandoned by family. Drug addicts. Sexually abused boys and girls.

There are many kinds of prisons. Too many, it often seems. Headlines clamor for attention. The six o'clock news can be overwhelming. So much calamity. What can one woman possibly do?

We can start with Hebrews 13:3—we can remember. Remembering the suffering of others isn't always the easiest thing to do. It can make us uncomfortable. It is often easier to turn the channel, turn the page, turn the other way.

But as we remember, we learn to empathize. We begin to see ways to reach out and help others. Maybe we can write a letter. Visit a shelter. Donate time or money. Be a friend.

And we can pray. If that were the only thing we ever did, it would be a great thing. "Prayer changes things" is not just a cute bumper sticker slogan. It is a wonderful and amazing fact.

The world is full of individuals who—one woman, one man, one child at a time—changed the world. We can be among those individuals. It all begins with remembering.

Dear Lord, please bless our minds and our memories, that we would remember those in every sort of prison and bring light to their days. Amen.

Sherry Elmer

Lost and Found

"But when he came to himself..."
—Luke 15:17a

It was two o'clock in the morning, and I had just sat down to take a breather. Within minutes my pager went off for the tenth time that shift. The extension flashing on the screen was that of the Trauma Center. I had only a few seconds to pray as the staff rushed a young man with a gunshot wound into surgery.

Hours later, I was at his bedside in Intensive Care. As the nurse tried to obtain some pertinent information, I learned he lived in a homeless shelter. He gave no next of kin, and there was no one he wanted to be notified of his condition. When we came to the question of religious affiliation, he shared that he had not gone to church since he left home as a teenager.

The doctor joined me at his bedside and shared some troubling news. The young man's leg might have to be amputated. They had done everything possible to save it, but now only time would tell. Already in poor physical health and weakened by the surgery, he lay there with a far away look in his eyes, not blinking, no tears. He just starred into space. Then came the words: "My past has caught up with me." We talked for a while, and he shared his story. I remained at the homeless man's bedside until daybreak as he drifted in and out of sleep. I was able to ascertain that he did have a family who cared for him. I telephoned them and they rushed to his bedside.

How often in the chaplaincy we encounter persons who are estranged from their families. On this occasion, I thought about the parable commonly referred to as "the Lost Son" (Luke 15:11-24). A few days later, I shared the story with the young man. In the gospel account, the young man's "lostness" was something he chose. He chose to leave home. He knew exactly what he was doing.

How was the lost young man found? The Scripture suggests it was not the result of some great spiritual revelation. Being found does not require getting your act cleaned up first or changing your lifestyle. God cleans the fish after God catches them. The turning point comes when this willfully lost young man "came to himself"

(Luke 15:17a). This simply suggests that he made a wise choice. He said, "This is stupid. I don't need to live like this. I have a home and a family." There was no mystical experience.

There are two truths in the story that are very reassuring. The first is that somehow you and I have a home in God. When we're lost, it's because we have strayed from the place we were meant to be. We were made for life at home with God. We can never feel at home in a far country, even though sometimes the only way to God is through the far country. The far country is the place where we become disillusioned with who we are. We are in the far country when we are disappointed with the world and say, "Is this all there is?" And our parent says, "Of course not. Come home."

The young man's leg was not amputated. Before he left the hospital, he shared this Scripture with me: "The LORD is good, a stronghold in a day of trouble; he protects those who take refuge in him" (Nahum 1:7). Then he said, "Thanks, Pastor."

Thank you, God for each opportunity to do ministry. Amen.
Evaleen Litman Sargent

What Child Is This?

When the angels had left them and gone into heaven,
the shepherds said to one another, "Let us go now to
Bethlehem and see this thing that has taken place,
which the Lord has made known to us."
So they went with haste and found Mary and Joseph,
and the child lying in a manger. When they saw this,
they made known what had been told them about this
child; and all who heard it were amazed at what the
shepherds told them. But Mary treasured all these
words and pondered them in her heart.
—Luke 2:15-19

"What child is this, who laid to rest, on Mary's lap is sleeping?" This, this is Christ the King.

This is Kugu Sengane, an eleven-year-old from South Africa

who nursed her AIDS-affected parents through their dying days as she also took care of her toddler brother. Most AIDS deaths in the world are in sub-Saharan Africa; children suffer both as orphans and victims of the disease.

"Why lies he in such mean estate where ox and ass are feeding?"
This, this is Christ the King.
This is eighteen-month-old Marishwara, robbed of her childhood because of protein-energy malnutrition and iron deficiency, at danger because she receives no immunizations against disease. Her family wanted a boy; she is fed less and fed last because she was born a girl.

"So bring him incense, gold, and myrrh, come rich and poor to own him."
This, this is Christ the King.
This is five-year-old Allison, the only child who still smiles in a group at Booger Branch Hollow in Appalachian Kentucky. Hope still shines in her eyes; the other children appear to be beyond their years.

"Haste, haste to bring him laud, the Babe, the son of Mary."
As we nurture the girl child (and all children) we bring laud to Christ the King.
What child is this? It is every child whose birth we celebrate.

On December 25, 1967, my older daughter, Sharon Elaine, was born. Thirty-three years ago I celebrated with joy and awe as I asked, "What child is this?" I continue to ask and continue to learn that each child from God is given as celebration and challenge. May the season that celebrates the birth of a child bring you joy, awe, and challenge.

What child is this, Holy One? We thank you for the child Jesus. We pray for the child Kuzu, and for Marishwara, and for Allison. We pray for all little girls and little boys who grow old before they can be children. Guide us, move us, use us. Amen.

Carol Q. Cosby

Sharing the Good News

For I am not ashamed of the gospel; it is the power
of God for salvation to everyone who has faith,
to the Jew first and also to the Greek.
—Romans 1:16

As the young Thai woman at the beach was beading my hair, I asked about her life. Surprisingly, she opened up and shared with me her years of pain from being married to an abusive and dangerous alcoholic. After discussing her options for finding safety and freedom, I asked her if she had ever heard of Jesus. She never had. There was a Gideon Bible in the hotel room, and together we looked up John 3:16. I told her that the God who had created her loved her. Unlike her husband, God would not harm her. I told her she was precious to God and that God never intended for her to be abused. She listened intently as I told her how she could know this healing love. She gratefully took the Bible home with her.

Samon had been braiding the hair of foreigners on that beach for five years, but she had never heard the story of Christ's love. It made me wonder how many times I have interacted with other aching hearts, unaware of their need to hear the Good News.

None of us alone is capable of reaching the whole world for Christ. I wonder, though, what impact we could have if all who know the love of Christ openly shared with those they encounter whether at work, at the supermarket, or on vacation. My heart cries for Samon, and I wonder where her life will lead her. Maybe the Good News of Christ will give her hope. Maybe in her lonely and painful days she will call out to God and find God's presence healing and reassuring. It's the least I can give her; it's the best I can offer her.

Lord, we know that there are women and children all over the world in great pain. Many of them have never heard of your love and your touch, which brings healing and wholeness. We ask and pray, Lord, that you would open our eyes to see the need, open our ears to hear the pain, and give us willing hearts to share from the abundance of love you have shared with us. Amen.

Annie Dieselberg

Becoming Less

John answered, "No one can receive anything except
what has been given from heaven.... The friend of the
bridegroom, who stands and hears him, rejoices greatly
at the bridegroom's voice. For this reason my joy has
been fulfilled. He must increase, but I must decrease."
—John 3:27;29-30

Last summer, my daughter and I volunteered to help pass out backpacks full of school supplies for needy children. Unfortunately, there were so many volunteers that there wasn't much for us to do. So when the director of the project came up to me at the end of the day and asked if I'd do public relations for the project next year, I was delighted. I'd been looking so long for a place where I was needed.

But while doing public relations was something I thought sounded fun, I soon learned it was not something I could do well. This was made clear to me when I was casting about for ways to alert the parents of needy children that they had to fill out and return applications for the supplies. Many of the parents didn't read the local paper, and it seemed the only way to reach them would be a story on the local TV news.

During a meeting with the school district to talk over the problem, the public relations person for the district volunteered to work with the local TV station to get a story on the air. Even though I really wanted to do the work, I realized that the school district people, with their vastly superior connections and experience, would do the better job and truly help the children of our community. I needed to join John the Baptist in playing a lesser role so that the work of the Lord could become more.

Dear God, let me remember, in the midst of my pride, that for you to become more, I must become less. And that by doing so, I come closer to your son Jesus. Amen.

Melinda McDonald

One in the Spirit

"...that they may be one, as we are one..."
—John 17:22

A couple of years ago I took a group of church people on a mission trip to the Czech Republic, where we worked on the grounds of the International Baptist Theological Seminary in Prague.

One night as we were taking a bus back to the seminary from the Old Town of Prague, a member of our group happened to sit next to a seminarian's wife. I noticed that the woman talked seriously to the member of our party, and I wondered what she could have to say to a stranger.

When we arrived at the seminary and parted from the woman, I asked my friend about the conversation. She replied that it was something about her baby being in the hospital for six months and not knowing whether or not the child would live. The woman was from Africa and had an accent, so my friend wasn't sure of the details or why the woman had decided to pour out her heart to a stranger.

A couple of days later, an announcement was made that one of the seminarians had just lost a child who had been in the hospital hovering between life and death since birth six months ago. I knew immediately to whom the announcement referred. I explained the story to the rest of our American group. They were very moved by the tragedy and felt that it was part of God's plan that the woman should unburden herself to one of us. They immediately gave me their spending money to deliver to the woman and her husband.

After presenting the grateful couple with the American dollars, I spoke with one of the administrators. I learned that this couple had very little money and that even insurance probably wouldn't cover all of the medical bills. I also found out that most of the students were on full scholarship and did not have money for any other expenses.

Upon our return home, we began fundraising to help the seminary provide for student emergencies. We had gone abroad to help, but we also learned. We now know what it means to be "one in the Spirit."

O God, help us continually to reach out to others so that we might truly be "one in the Spirit." Amen.

Martha Sobaje

A New York Lesson

"You received without payment; give without payment."
—Matthew 10:8b

Some twenty years ago, my daughter, Mary, and I left Philadelphia before daybreak on a train for New York City and a day of sight-seeing. One of my lifelong ambitions was to visit the Statue of Liberty. We had also scheduled a time to go to the top of the Empire State Building and to other places of interest. Then we would eat at Mama Leone's before heading for home. I knew that I would be spending more money than I had ever previously spent in a single day.

We arrived in New York Central Station with much anticipation and had just gone through the gate when I experienced something that was not in our plan. There on the station floor were a number of persons fast asleep. Most were huddled next to the walls, but one woman had found her place in the middle of the floor. Her paper bag of possessions had become her pillow; she wore a thin sweater but had nothing to cover her bare legs. I knew she was homeless. I knew she had few belongings. I knew the cold marble floor could not offer her a good night's rest. Her image remains with me to this day: this woman who had almost nothing while I was looking forward to a whole day of pleasure.

Mary and I did have a good time. We did all the things we planned and took some leftovers home from Mama Leone's that made a complete meal the next night. But ever since that day, when I saw up-close the plight of the homeless woman, I have recognized in a new way the riches that are mine: home and family, a comfortable bed, three full meals each day, a closet filled with clothes, money for pleasures, and much more. The image of that woman I passed on the cold marble floor continues to remind me that I want to be generous, that I want to help make life better for those who are poor and homeless.

God, continue to increase my sensitivity to the needs of all people, especially those who lack the basic human necessities, that I might share abundantly with them out of my affluence. Amen.

Marilyn R. Taylor

Loving Jesus

"Truly I tell you, just as you did it to one of the least of these who are members of my family, you did it to me."
—Matthew 25:40

On the wall above a concrete bathing slab hung a sign reading, "The Body of Christ." Three sisters laid the tiny body of an elderly woman down and began to pour water over her. When her anxious eyes fell on her caretakers' kind faces, she sank down into their arms and relaxed. One sister worked on her long braid, gently unraveling its crusty knots.

I stood against the wall watching and wondering who the woman was, where she came from, why her body was so diseased. The sisters worked slowly, their white saree blouse sleeves rolled up. They lathered every inch of skin and hair with a block of soap, re-lathering where the filth of weeks, months, or years had penetrated. It was clear that they, too, did not know who this woman was or where she came from, or why she had been left to die alone on the streets of Calcutta. But to them, it seemed, hers was in truth the body of their God, and they worked as if they were leaning over the broken body of Jesus, anointing it for burial.

During this first visit with Mother Teresa's Missionaries of Charity, I felt a certainty that I shared their calling. But it has been only recently that I have understood the essence of that call.

At times I have been tempted to believe that what makes the work of the Missionaries of Charity holy is their occupation: service to the poor. But I am reminded again and again that it is their *vocation*, their service to Jesus, that makes what they do Kingdom work.

In the ten years that have passed since that day in Kalighat, I have lived and worked among the poor in Africa and Bangladesh, taught wealthy children in private school, partnered with a husband, and mothered two boys. I have learned that *every* act of service, no matter how seemingly insignificant, finds sacred purpose when it is done unto Jesus. My work, too, whatever it may be at whatever stage of life, is holy when I love "the least of these" in my corner of the world as if I were loving Jesus.

Lord Jesus, help me see you in the faces of the people I encounter today that I may truly love you through loving them. Amen.

Christie A. Eastman

Pray for Us!

*At the same time pray for us as well that God will open
to us a door for the word, that we may declare the
mystery of Christ, for which I am in prison.*
—Colossians 4:3

Anna and Louisa rushed up to me with smiles I had come to look
for and to love during my thirteen days in their country. "We want
you to have these," they beamed as they placed their gifts in my
hands. "We made them for you. When you wear them, remember
us and pray for us."

I opened their package to find two beaded bracelets, two pairs
of earrings, and two necklaces. My heart was deeply touched.
Immediately I placed the bracelets on my wrist, promising to stay
in contact and to pray.

In countries where AIDS/HIV is rampant, economy low, education poor and often denied because of finances, affirmation of
women silent, and the quality of life hard, there still is hope. Where
does it come from? Knowing that as we pray for each other, we
open ourselves to how God can use us. Prayer unites us so that what
we can't do individually, we can do collectively.

St. Paul calls us to be living examples of the power of prayer.
We read in his letter to the Colossians: "Devote yourselves to
prayer, keeping alert in it with thanksgiving...Let your speech
always be gracious...so that you may know how you ought to
answer everyone" (Colossians 4:2,6).

When we say we'll pray for another, let's get serious. There is a
world out there that needs us to be united by God's love in order to
make a difference.

*Lord, as you unite us in prayer, open our eyes, our hearts, and
our hands that we might see how we can make a difference in the
lives of others. Amen.*

Cynthia E. Cowen

A Difficult Search

Vengeance is mine.
—Deuteronomy 32:35a

"Father, forgive them;
for they do not know what they are doing."
—Luke 23:34

As an advocate for adults who are mentally retarded or developmentally disabled and have been abused, I am frequently in contact with abusers. A call from a prosecutor, neighbor, or teacher—or a tearful plea from a victim—can send me immediately out into the unknown on a home visit. I have often been physically threatened.

Over the years I have struggled with myself and with God over the command to forgive. Evening after evening, as I took my prayer walks, I shared my anger, hurt, and grief at the abuse of these innocents. The same answer always came back: I was first to protect the victim and second to forgive the abuser, leaving vengeance to God.

Eventually, I became satisfied that God would take care of vengeance. Then God called me to further growth, saying, "Humanity is created in my image. Look for me in the abuser. I am there. Find me." Now that's a very tall order! I didn't even want to try. I had no compassion for the abuser. But the command was consistent: "These, too, are made in my image. Find me." Eventually I gave in and began the difficult search. I began each day with prayer requesting help in finding God in each and every person I encountered that day.

Amazingly, with God's help, I am now always able to find at least a tiny reflection of God in each and every person. Sometimes it takes a long time. I have developed the understanding that the abuser is indeed loved by God and that God longs for communion with him or her. I have learned to ask for abusers' stories. Some have limited intelligence and do not know how to discipline or to cope. Others have brain diseases. Many have experienced terrible abuse themselves. Always they are hurting deeply.

Yes, the victims must be protected, and that always remains the first priority. But the perpetrator is also a human being made in God's image and whom God calls back. What God really wants to give is forgiveness. God longs for each soul to come home, begging forgiveness, no matter the trespass he or she has committed.

O God of unconditional love, help me always to find you in all those whose lives intersect with mine. We are all sinners. They, like me, need your love and guidance. Help me to remember to pray always for them and to lead them toward you. Amen.

Dorinda K. W. Kauzlarich-Rupe

A Welcome in Our Hearts

Be hospitable to one another without complaining.
—1 Peter 4:9

I love having people in my house. I love meeting them at the door, saying, "Come on in! Make yourself at home!" I love it if they kick their shoes off and settle into the couch while I offer them a drink. I love sitting at the kitchen table chatting, laughing, crying, praying. I love the sound of ice cubes clinking, the teapot whistling, spoons stirring in mugs.

However, none of the books I've read on hospitality talk much about the sports equipment piled by the door, blocking the entrance to a messy living room. Few mention the spots on the tablecloth, the spatters on the stove you notice when you're fixing tea, or the dirty dishes in the sink. I have sat at my own kitchen table and noticed cobwebs hanging from the light fixture and dust on the sideboard.

You know what? In my house, there's life happening. A family lives here, whose members are sometimes going in four different directions. And it's into this life (sometimes chaotic, sometimes peaceful) that I invite people to enter, visit, and stay awhile.

Does hospitality happen when the house is prepared, the meal cooked, and the table set? Absolutely. Does it happen when you're spot-cleaning the sofa, the dishwasher stops working, and you don't have your makeup on? Of course. Does it happen when you're about to walk out the door to an appointment and your friend shows up with a tear-streaked face, needing your prayers and your listening ear? Yes, you'd better believe it does.

Hospitality is first and foremost a welcome in our hearts. We let people in. We say, "Sure, come inside, sit for awhile and let me serve you. You are important to me." You don't need a how-to book to show you how to be authentic and to let people into that realness. Just be. Just say, "Yes, come in." That's where real hospitality begins.

God, you let me see into your heart when you sent Jesus. Help me to see that hospitality begins when I let people interrupt me, see me as I really am, or enter a world that's not perfect. Even if perfection never comes, let me build relationships. Let my heart, and my door, always be open. Amen.

Martha Palmer Chambers

Empowering Women to Believe in Themselves

"If you are able to do anything, have pity on us and help us." Jesus said, "If you are able!
—All things can be done for the one who believes."
—Mark 9:22-23

While working in India, I visited a women's self-help project in one of the worst slums of Madras. Earlier I had seen projects organized by "do-gooders," politicians, and relief agencies that had the effect of diminishing people's dignity and belief in themselves. But one project manager, Shoka, had a different attitude: "People who live in slums are citizens too. They may not know that, and society certainly doesn't treat them that way. But they have the right to resources."

When I interviewed a young woman holding a baby, her eyes sparkled as she talked: "We always had many things inside us. But we were afraid to speak up for what we knew was right. When Shoka first met us, we didn't know if we could trust her. Many people have said they'd give us something. But Shoka didn't promise us anything.

She said we had rights and that she would help us learn how to get help for what we needed. We really needed a water tap here, but we didn't know where to go. Shoka helped us learn how to talk to government people and how to ask where their offices were located. Finally we were not afraid, and we were able to go by ourselves to the offices and ask for help."

An older woman concluded, "We're worried our community will soon be moved to another slum. But we're organizing ourselves to try to stay here. If we don't know where the housing office is, we'll go to the water commissioner's office and ask them where the housing office is. Then we'll take the bus and turn it around to the place we need to go. We believe we can ask and someone will help us."

Today the women of the slum can identify their own needs, discover what is available, and deal with problems realistically. Like Jesus, Shoka has respectfully helped the women believe in themselves and in their power to do things.

Compassionate God, help us to learn to be more like Jesus. Show us how to help empower those who have little belief in their own abilities so that they may feel a sense of their self-worth and dignity. Amen.

Joy Haupt Carol

Being Rescued

He reached down from on high and took hold of me;
he drew me out of deep waters. He rescued me
from my powerful enemy... the LORD was my support...
He rescued me because he delighted in me.
—Psalm 18:16-19, NIV

The girls looked so young, and yet there was no innocence left in their eyes. In their scanty costumes they moved their bodies to the rhythm of the music. Our missionary friends had taken us to the bars of Patpong, Thailand, the number one sex capitol in the world. Many of these girls had been sold into prostitution by their families. It was the only way the families could survive because of their extreme poverty. The girls would send money home from their work in the bars.

Waan was seventeen. She had been working in the bar for four years. My missionary friend had given her some things to read and had talked with her about Rahab, a Christian organization that could rescue her from this life. Waan visited the Rahab office and told them she wanted out. She said she would be back.

They didn't see her for weeks. When they finally met up with her, the women said she looked awful. Part of her show involved dipping a large stick in alcohol and lighting it into flames. Then she swallows it until the flame goes out. The alcohol had accidentally dripped down her chin and onto her chest burning her badly and causing a scar on her chest. The alcohol had also damaged her stomach and esophagus so she couldn't eat. Why couldn't she just walk away?

Waan had no citizenship papers, and she owed the bar 5,000 baht for a loan they had given her brother. She was expected to pay it off. If she left, the bar owner would come after her. She had no place to go, no money, no hope. She could be arrested if she went wandering around with no papers.

But God in his mercy sent my missionary friend Annie and others to rescue her.

They were able to come up with the money to pay off her loan and to help her to escape with another missionary to a safe place where she would be counseled, schooled, and provided the legal documents to live unthreatened in Thailand. There are thousands of these girls who need to be rescued. They feel that they are garbage. To be told by Christians that God loves them and delights in them is healing music to their ears.

Lord, help us to be sensitive to the lost women in our world. Give us the strength and ability to be your hands and feet and to offer hope. Use us as your rescue team and provide the way out for so many who are trapped. Amen.

Donna Buckles

The Girl at the Well

*"Let the little children come to me...for it is to such as
these that the kingdom of God belongs."*
—Mark 10:14

The hot wind blowing from the Judean wilderness ruffled the young
girl's thick brown hair. Impatiently she brushed it from her eyes.
She was hard at the task her family expected her to fulfill. The other
children were idly standing around the well as she worked to pull
the bucket of water from deep beneath the desert floor.

Is this a scene from two thousand years ago? No! It is a drama
embedded in my memory bank from May, 2000. As changeless as
the sketch seems, the clues that it is from a more recent time include
tourists standing around the well watching the girl; and the other
children holding out their grubby little hands expecting to get some
"goodies" from these foreign visitors who have come to their
Bedouin tent community. And in the background is a four-wheel
drive vehicle waiting to carry the onlookers back to their cool, clean
hotel in Jerusalem when they grew weary.

In anticipation of what we were to experience, our thoughtful
guide had alerted us to bring small gifts other than money or candy
for the children. I looked at my small cache of plastic, token gifts.
What could I give the girl? She was the one designated to be the
water drawer for the benefit of the guests, and she took her job very
seriously. I had nothing appropriate to give in return. I chose a small
mirror and gave it to her with a prayer that she would see in it the
reflection of God's beautiful creation.

Her gift to me, however, was enormous. Hearing about her life
brought new insight and new compassion for the world's marginalized children, those who have little physical and emotional support
to develop their human potential. It has been said that compassion
is sympathy turned into action rather than just pity. I am challenged
to find new ways to be God's presence in the lives of children.

*Loving God, grant that we may see with your eyes the needs of
the children in our lives. Give us hearts of compassion and courage
to minister to those across the street and across the globe. Amen.*
Gloria Marshall

The Mask

The LORD hears the needy...
—Psalm 69:33a

Wearing ill-fitting clothes and lugging dirty canvas sacks of food and bottles, she had moved quickly through the crowd of women. Seated, she organized the bags around her feet. When she looked up, I saw the mask—a soiled white cloth covering her nose and mouth. Unruly brown hair. No makeup. Mid-thirties, I guessed. Her blue eyes returned my welcome. "My name is Helen," she said, then returned to her bags.

When all groups were formed, the facilitator read Luke's account of Jesus healing the hemorrhaging woman, then directed, "Remember a time when you felt life draining out of you ... Perhaps you are still there, reaching to touch Jesus, or maybe you have felt his healing power, heard his reassuring words ... In your group, share whatever you feel comfortable sharing."

Helen was the last to speak. Hunched over, eyes on fidgeting hands, she began apologizing. For the mask: "I'm allergic to my environment." For the bags of food—also allergies. When asked to speak louder, she glanced up briefly, punching her words more forcefully into the mask. We shuffled our chairs closer. She leaned in, bunching her sweater to her throat: "Sorry, things are dirty. No wash machine." Understanding nods. Small, empathetic sounds.

Helen's story of abuse came out haltingly. When she choked up, we too cried, but no one violated her moment by touch or words of comfort. We simply listened. In response, she sat taller, lifted her face, spoke louder. Near the end, she pulled the grubby mask out of her way. Her voice became animated, eyes brightened, hands gestured freely. Each of us took time to thank her, to hug her. No one offered advice.

The late afternoon prayer service ended with a free-form dance. As music filled the room, a few leaders swirled into the group to draw in more dancers who, in turn, invited others until every woman was on the floor. Across the sea of dancing women, I saw Helen twirling freely, her arms raised in praise, the dingy mask bobbing like a necklace under her radiant face.

Listener-God, by listening with such deep love, you bring us to freedom and salvation. Fill me with gentle reverence for those you put in my path today. Help me let go of my own agenda to be fully attentive to them. May my listening convey your love. Amen.

Josephe Marie Flynn

How Can We Smile?

> *By the rivers of Babylon—there we sat down and there*
> *we wept when we remembered Zion.*
> *On the willows there we hung up our harps.*
> *For there our captors asked us for songs,*
> *and our tormentors asked for mirth, saying,*
> *"Sing us one of the songs of Zion!"*
> *How could we sing the LORD's song in a foreign land?*
> *—Psalm 137:1-4*

"Now smile! Say cheese."
> We made the request again and again as we aimed our
> cameras, ready to
> capture faces to go with our stories of the journey.

> Often they obliged, these people who were our hosts
> in the mountains and hollers of Eastern Kentucky.
> But did we know what we were asking of them?

> Smiles were produced—-smiles practiced with
> closed mouths.
> > Who wants to show gums with missing teeth?
> > mouths with gaping holes?
> > gum disease with no hope of treatment, no dentist availabl
> —smiles produced to cover the quiver of a split lip,
> > a broken jaw, a black eye.
> > Who wants to show the wounds left over from the
> > terror of the night?
> —smiles of the mouth only,

eyes and body proclaiming that life is hard, affirming
the everyday "not enough" that keeps people from
the health care,
the healthy diet, the comfortable surroundings we
all assume as birthright.

"Now smile! Say cheese."
But some produced no smiles.
Some seemed to be without smile muscles.
Hardest for us were the children.
No one had yet taught them to be "polite"—
to smile even though—
even though they were sad,
even though they were hurting,
even though they needed to *eat* cheese,
not *say* "cheese."

Yet many people did smile at us, genuine smiles—
people who knew and loved their land,
people who loved and were loved by their family,
people who were getting by,
working hard and able to make it,
people who could laugh at those of us
who think we are rich
when all we have is money and "stuff."

And many children smiled at us, genuine smiles—
children whose lives are being nourished
not only by enough food,
but also by lots of love
and by alternative schools, co-op day care,
places and people teaching them more than numbers
and ABCs,
places and people teaching them that they are
special, unique, cherished, loved.

Creator God,
Before we ask for a smile,
before we try to preserve the memory of a face,
before we beg, "Say cheese,"

Help us to look into our own faces, hearts, and lives
and to know what we are doing.
Help us to do those things that make it easier
for our sisters and brothers to produce genuine smiles.
Amen.

Carol Q. Cosby

Christmas Shopping Made Easy

"I was hungry and you gave me food, I was thirsty
and you gave me something to drink..."
—Matthew 25:35a

Each year, we all go through the process of deciding what to get for those who are on our Christmas list. A good book or subscription to a fine magazine is always a possibility. It's a sensible gift, something a person can enjoy year round.

Then I hear about a tornado in Bangladesh that leaves 1,000 people dead, 10,000 injured, and destroys all the houses, trees, crops, and power lines in a six-mile radius.

What about tickets for dinner or an evening out to see a show? Something just for the fun of it. A thoughtful gift, I'd say.

Then I remember that each year 15 million children die from starvation. Half of those who survive are permanently damaged from severe malnutrition.

Perhaps some nice cologne, or shampoo, or lotion, or soap, something a bit more personal.

Eighty percent of all sickness and disease in the world is caused by inadequate water or poor sanitation. Half the people in the world lack easy access to an adequate supply of pure, fresh water.

So many really good ideas, but so far no purchases. Can it be that my choices are wrong? That I don't have the Christmas spirit? That I bear responsibility for sharing the Good News of the arrival of the Prince of Peace?

The answer begins to come through. I have to do something, and what better time than Christmas. Dear friend, who also cares about the needs of the suffering, your Christmas gift this year went to Church World Service. Joy to the world, and peace on earth.

O God, giver of all that we have and are, thank you for giving us Jesus to show us how to live our lives. Forgive us when we refuse to follow his example. Help us to see the real meaning of Christmas. Amen.

Ellen A. Frost

The Hope That Is Ours

The Faithfulness of God

The LORD is my shepherd, I shall not want.
—Psalm 23:1

Two decades ago, she was director of the Older Youth department in the Sunday school of my home church. She was manager of the cafeteria at the elementary school I attended. Weekdays during lunch she negotiated the behavioral antics and feeding of groups of fifty to seventy-five children. On Sundays, she accepted the challenge of offering Christian education and spiritual nurture to thirty-five to forty teenagers.

But on this particular morning, she was a patient in the Critical Care Unit when I made my rounds as hospital chaplain. She was unconscious and unresponsive—still, quiet, and frail. There was just a hint of a human frame under the stark, white sheets. Plastic tubes formed a link to the latest in medical technology and equipment.

Standing at her bedside that morning, I prayed for grace for her journey and comfort for her family. I gently took her hand and quoted the Twenty-third Psalm. "Yea, though I walk through the valley of shadows, I will not be afraid . . . For my God is with me." As those words left my lips and sounded a counterpoint to the hum of life-supporting machines, I became aware of the powerful cycle of life and faith and the passing of missions and faith from generation to generation.

My words at her bedside that morning were the very words she had spoken to me many years before. Someday, when I am facing the end of my own journey, I trust that someone will pause at my bedside to hold my hand and voice those words of faith for me. "My God will comfort me and make a place for me in his presence."

The old hymn makes this promise: "Great is Thy faithfulness, Lord, unto me." And so it is. God is there as our lives are touched by women and men who serve as models of faith, as advocates who are sent into the fray to give comfort and support during the worst moments of our lives. God is there as we who are gifted and equipped minister to others. Christian Scripture becomes a well-spring of faith, hope, and joy for life: "Surely the goodness and mercy of God will follow me and I will abide in Him forever."

Eternal God, we celebrate your faithfulness to our world today, both to our youth who are searching for a path that is true and everlasting and to those who have lived faithfully and are now at the end of the path walking toward their dying. May your faithfulness to our world be made visible and concrete in the way we care for one another. Amen.

Linda G. Frost

Note: A version of this devotion first appeared in *Sacred Stories,* a publication of Catholic Health Initiatives.

Un-cloistered City

"Come to me, all you that are weary and are carrying heavy burdens, and I will give you rest. Take my yoke upon you, and learn from me; for I am gentle and humble in heart, and you will find rest for your souls. For my yoke is easy, and my burden is light."
—Matthew 11:28-30

One day, late in Advent, a friend and I spent time at the Cloisters—a section of the Metropolitan Museum just a few blocks from our Manhattan apartment. Music surrounded us as we enjoyed richly textured nuggets of medieval Christmas art celebrating the birth of the Christ Child, set among the white cyclamen and baby red roses, the narcissus and lilies of the valley. It was a hopeful, fragrant, joy-filled moment in an often too-hurried life.

In one room we found an enormous and magnificent hanging wreath made of wheat. The peasants, we learned from the silent printed tutor nearby, made wheat wreaths to symbolize not only the bread of the Eucharist, but the daily bread of life that continued to sustain them. The wreath was garlanded with red ribbon to symbolize the power of God in their lives, and with boxwood, an evergreen, to note with hope the joy of eternal life. Such simple beauty and profound meaning, such connectedness with the daily elements of our lives. Grain wrapped in goodness, bread wrapped in a baby's love, lived out in generous giving. So the story, the artful, homely story of Christmas, comes in old-new packages all the time, surprising us with joy!

Surely these are necessary connections—these links between hope and hopelessness, between sustenance and survival, bread and bounty. In spite of the lovely Cloisters, we live in an un-cloistered city—violence and cruelty cause much despair. Not too many years ago a loving, caring man, the principal of a school in the Red Hook section of Brooklyn, was tragically shot in the crossfire of a drug-related fracas as he was seeking a child who had left school. Gunfire still cuts short the lives of too many in our city. And the twin towers that once housed many workers in lower Manhattan are now dust, leaving anguish among families and friends—all of us— touched by the tragedy. Now we are a city in tears, a world deeply grieving. Yet somehow in the middle of all the anguish there are moments of hope and healing. At Christmas, those of us who are Christians celebrate the good news that God does make a difference through the gift of Jesus, child of Grace and Peace. In Christ's name, living and loving in God's gracious ways, we can make a difference, too. The connectedness, the compassion, the power of God in our daily lives, are gifts to share in community!

O God of rest and refreshment, stir our hearts to live compassionately in the daily places of our lives, and in the world you so love. Thanks be to you, O God of justice and mercy, for the gift of your beloved one. As we celebrate Christ's birth, may we be reborn with power and energy for building hospitable communities. Amen.

Kathleen Hurty

Practice Resurrection

"Consider the lilies of the field, how they grow;
they neither toil nor spin..."
—Matthew 6:28

Every year I purchase most of my perennial plants by mail order. Last year one of the shipments came quite early. I eagerly unpacked the little plastic containers, each with its somewhat travel-worn occupant, out of their shredded-newsprint nest. Imagine my disappointment when the last pot contained nothing but dirt! Its marker informed me that it was supposed to be a fern that I had especially wanted. Well!

Now of course I knew intellectually that this should indicate no more than a deep dormancy. The plant really *is* down there; it's just died down to the roots during the winter and the days have yet to lengthen sufficiently to awaken it. It's also (I told myself) from one of the oldest and most reputable of firms, one that surely would not send me just a pot of dirt. All the same, it was hard not to look at it and think, "This is just dirt! I've been had! Is anything *really* going to come up in this pot?" Despite these misgivings, I dutifully watered the dirt whenever it dried out and put it under the skylight in a tray close to the houseplants. A couple of weeks passed, and my skepticism increased.

But by Easter Day, my plant had been up for at least a week. It began with an almost imperceptible, shy showing of miniature fronds curling up from the surface, and then became recognizable as an especially lovely small fern.

Perhaps our Creator, knowing our doubting nature, has arranged for a world where the skeptic can be surprised by the yearly resurrection of spring, which for us in the Northern Hemisphere so happily coincides with the seasons of Lent and Easter. "Behold the lilies of the field"—not only are they clothed in beauty, but they die and arise from the dead year after year after year. God has given us these gentle messengers of life to encourage us each spring. Perhaps we are also to emulate their gracious radiance and grace-filled acceptance of rain and sun and drought and frost. Let us give thanks for these fellow creatures and attempt to follow their ways. As Wendell Berry wrote, "Practice resurrection."

Dear God, help us through our times of skepticism, our times of doubting what we cannot see and yet know is surely there. Amen.

Nancy Adams

It's on the Way

For a work is being done in your days that you would not believe if you were told.
—Habakkuk 1:5b

God is on the verge of working miracles in your current situation. It doesn't matter who you are, where you are, what your concerns are; God is on the verge of doing something unexpected that will turn everything around! How awesome, amazing, exciting, maybe even frightening it is to consider that God is so concerned about you that God is willing to intervene in your situation.

Like the prophet Habakkuk, we sometimes think that God has forgotten us. We are holding on to a vision that seems to have been lost. Habakkuk cried out, "How long, O Lord, how long?" (Habakkuk 1:2a). We also cry out "how long?" as we stand in the midst of ministries that are not bearing fruit, as we try to solve problems that seem to have no solutions, and as we hold on to promises that never materialize. Our cry seems to be heard only by the wind that echoes it back to us, "How long, O Lord, how long?"

But even when God is silent, God can still be on the case. Even when we see no effects, God is often working. We must live with confidence that the answer is on the way. We are called to live with confidence that God is growing us into the vision, preparing us for something we do not yet see. The delay is not really delay but active work on God's part to shape and mold us for the work ahead.

So wait with joy, even if God seems slow in answering. Wait on God even if others say that you have waited long enough and you should take another path. Wait on God because God is going to do something awesome in your life. You have a burning bush experience ahead of you. There are "children" to birth even if you think you are well past childbearing years. There is a sea that God will roll up for you so that you can cross on dry land. There are prisons from which you will be released. There are walls that will come tumbling down.

Wait on God because God is going to do something amazing for you. Be blessed as God sends joyous surprises your way and as your ministry unfolds beyond all you could ever have imagined.

God, help us to live believing that the miracle is on the way and that wonderful surprises are coming to us. We know that you give gifts to us not because we are good, but because you love to give us joyous surprises. Amen.

Marsha Brown Woodard

Remembering My Best Friend

"Do not let your heart be troubled. Believe in God,
believe also in me. In my Father's house there are
many dwelling places. If it were not so, would I have
told you that I go to prepare a place for you?"
—John 14:1-2

I lost my best friend to death. Her name was Barbara. We were very different. She never married; I did and have children and grandchildren. She was a Roman Catholic and I am American Baptist. She smoked for fifty years; I never have. She was very thin and I am overweight. Somehow the differences never mattered. If anything, they made our friendship stronger.

We shared our faiths with each other: I learned much about Catholics, and she learned about Baptists. When her illness did not allow her to drive herself to church for her beloved services, I took her and shared in her joy observing the sacraments. On many occasions she came to our church for special programs, and I think she learned from me the value of individual Bible study.

We shared our families. She lived with an older sister; I grieved with her when that sister died. She took part in the lives of my children and grandchildren; until the very end she never tired of having me tell her about their antics and experiences. She attended their special occasions: birthdays, weddings, and baptisms. I attended the same for her nephews.

We shared our professional lives. Both nurses, we had memories of experiences that no one else could appreciate. She specialized in obstetrics, and she worked with an organization benefiting disabled children.

We had a similar sense of humor. Sometimes that got us in trouble, for others did not always see the humor we saw. We loved retelling humorous stories of people and situations, knowing that we had a unique companionship.

How does one get through the grieving process when one loses such a special best friend? Every day little things remind me of her, and I have the urge to call her to tell about some family happening. Or I read a book and think how much she would enjoy it. Or I go to a restaurant and am brought to tears by a basket of onion rings, one of her favorite treats.

So I pray, relying on her faith and mine, knowing that she has only gone on to await a wonderful reunion some day. Friendships are a special gift from God, and they are not destroyed by death.

Gracious God, thank you for the precious gift of friendships that multiply our joys and divide our sorrows. Amen.

Kathleen A. Moore

God Is With Us

"And remember, I am with you always, to the end of the age."
—Matthew 28:20

Since September 11, 2001, I have heard over and over, "Everything has changed, everything has changed forever." Yes, our world, our lives, our environment, and the way we live has changed. Yet one fact is constant: God is with us. It may not *feel* like God is with you, but according to a major theme throughout the entire Bible, God is present with us at all times. God does not abandon us, but is present with unconditional love in the midst of every aspect of our living and our dying.

The terrorist acts of September 11 caused many to reevaluate and to re-think some of their theological beliefs. As I spent time with people in the weeks following the tragedy, leading church group retreats and seeing individuals in the ministry of spiritual direction, I heard many questions and comments such as: "If God is all powerful, why did God let this happen?" "My loved one died because it was his or her time to die." "God certainly was with my friend as she made it out alive." These comments stir up a variety of thoughts, emotions, and actions in the persons who say them and those who hear them.

Throughout my years of theological and spiritual contemplation, reflection, and prayer, I have come to believe that God is the one constant who is with us always. God weeps with us over the pain and tragedy of that fateful day and every day in our lives when we experience pain and suffering. I believe that God was present on September 11 with every person who died and with those who lived. And God is here today.

God is with each of us now as we are called upon to change some of the ways in which we live our lives. It is up to us to choose to acknowledge God's presence.

Gracious and loving God, help each of us to be aware of your presence with us always, which comforts, guides, and nourishes us. May we claim that you are with us as all of the changes take place in our world and that you weep with us in our sorrow as well as laugh with us in our joy. Amen.

Sara J. Davis-Shappell

The Secret Is Out

Jesus said to her, "I am the resurrection and the life.
Those who believe in me, even though they die,
will live, and everyone who lives and
believes in me will never die."
—John 11:25-26

What are we most afraid of? What are we preoccupied with more than anything else? I believe that there is a universal fear of abandonment, separation, and death—a fear of bodily destruction and abandonment at the hands of the community (being put in a nursing home and forgotten; being a prisoner of war, etc.).

Because of these fears, the physician has become "God." With the advent of so much medical technology and expertise, we have come to see suffering and death as absolute evils instead of as a part of life. And we see the doctor as the only one who can save us, or at least prolong the inevitable.

As Christians, we need to remember that we know the rest of the story! We know that Christ has come and will come again. We know that what was once the universal enemy was conquered when Jesus came out of that tomb. In Romans 6:9, Paul wrote these words: "For we know that since Christ was raised from the dead, He cannot die again; death no longer has mastery over him."

Jesus makes an incredible claim in the above passage from John 11. He also declared in John 10:10, "I have come that they might have life abundantly, now." I have struggled with the meaning of "abundant life." It is not the absence of pain or suffering. Jesus did not promise to "grease the skids" so we could slip through life effortlessly. To me, abundant life means that I have been given the freedom and the responsibility to live my life experiencing a wide range of emotions and events. However, I have the option of experiencing them differently from people who do not know Christ.

With Jesus as our ever-present friend, we have the strength and courage to face life head on. When Jesus the Christ is the center of our lives, we live with a different kind of awareness. We know a secret: what we once saw as evil is not the ultimate reality. God is our ultimate reality. In God we live and move and have our being, confident that whatever we face we can handle bravely. Facing and overcoming a tough challenge is in fact a "natural high."

We live with the assurance that God, who created the earth for us, also created the conditions for our continued manifestation after we leave our earthly bodies. The resurrection of Jesus is the pledge that love will be eternally victorious! Paul wrote in Romans 8 that nothing can ever separate us from God's love. Death can't and life can't. The angels won't, and all the powers of Hell cannot keep God's love away. Not even our fears can come between God and us. Even when we don't allow ourselves to experience the love of God, even when we are fearful and anxious, God loves us. Jesus came to conquer fear; he came so that you and I might not be afraid of life or death! Jesus came so we would learn to worship the one true God and not idols, as with our current "worship" of physicians and medical technology.

Amazing and eternal God, you have given us the secret to abundant life, now and abundant life forever. The evil that surrounds us cannot overcome us because your love is much stronger. Thank you! Amen.

Dorothy Lairmore Michel

Hoping for the Hopeless

He gives power to the faint, and strengthens the powerless. Even youths will faint and be weary, and the young will fall exhausted; but those who wait for the LORD shall renew their strength, they shall mount up with wings like eagles, they shall run and not be weary, they shall walk and not faint.
—Isaiah 40:29-31

In all honesty, the "hopeless" used to terrify me. They appear trapped in misery, consumed by the emptiness of their souls. How could I help those who seemingly do not want help? I have struggled in my work with others who appear stuck and unable or unwilling to grow.

Sometimes feeling hopeless is a temporary condition, perhaps following an unexpected loss of a job promotion, or not getting your way in an argument. Other times, the feeling of hopelessness lasts longer and is more difficult to shake. This might occur following the death of a loved one or when facing the realty of a permanent change in health. Regardless of the particular circumstances, it can become comfortable to adopt an attitude of hopelessness. Despair may subtly take control of your soul, and before you know it ensnare you into depression.

I have fallen into this pit when, out of my need to help the deeply wounded, I have relied on my own strength to motivate and inspire others toward a life where hope would be possible despite their circumstances. Over time, my well-meaning and apparent noble efforts proved unsettling to my conscience. I found myself living in two worlds: encouraging others to have hope and not give up on life while at the same time secretly maintaining a belief that perhaps *I* had been forgotten. Did I really believe there was hope in all situations, and could this be true for me personally? Where was the hope in my life? At that moment I felt artificial and alone.

Slowly over time, Christ revealed the truth to me gently through his Word and reinforced it through his people. Eventually I came to believe what the written truth had to say about hope for myself. Only much later was I able authentically to pass that reality on to others. I had become aware of something profound: I simply could not genuinely give to others what I had not first experienced for myself. Hope requires constant faith and patience. It too must be bathed in compassion—for both self and others. If we rely only upon our own abilities and energy, we will surely grow weary. Our hope cannot be in our circumstances or in our relationships with others. We must come to realize the Lord is our hope, and only he can sustain and strengthen us. As we keep our eyes upon him, our hope will naturally increase.

Lord Jesus, hear our prayer. We are feeling we have no hope, that there are no answers to our many problems and fears. Sometimes we even doubt you and your concern for us. Yet we know from your Word that you know each of us by name. Our own strength is often not enough, but your great power can move mountains. Lord, forgive our desire to be in control and not fully trust you. Overwhelm

us with your love and grace. Lift our weary hearts and bodies.
Teach us how to rely upon you for strength and hope for whatever
may come our way. Amen.

Amy Turner

Rejoice Anyhow!

> *Though the fig tree does not blossom, and no fruit is on*
> *the vines; though the produce of the olive fails, and the*
> *fields yield no food; though the flock is cut off from the*
> *fold, and there is no herd in the stalls, yet I will rejoice*
> *in the LORD; I will exult in the God of my salvation.*
> *—Habakkuk 3:17-18*

While listening to my sisters at transitional home share their stories during a group counseling session, I began to reflect on my own life. As members of the group shared some helpful tips for resolving their individual situations, I marveled audibly. I closed the session with some of the ideas contained in the following words of comfort.

Many of us have reached a point in our lives where everything around us seems to be falling apart. We have dropped a stone in the brook and the ripples fan out as if a boulder has been disengaged and dumped into the water from the side of the bank. When we try to do the right thing, our endeavors may fail. Friends that we trust in and confide in may disappoint us. For those of us who at one time had budding careers, our jobs may have been eliminated. Or as an entrepreneur, the business we worked so very hard to build may have crumbled.

In times like these, we need to halt in our steps and examine what is truly important. Yes, we must do everything right the next time around: strategic planning, budgeting, saving, and supporting each other. But in navigating these waters we cannot place our trust in our abilities alone.

Habakkuk witnessed the collapse of most of what gave meaning to his life and to his community. Through a period of questioning the Lord and reflecting upon the loss, failure, and disappointment, he was able to determine what had real meaning for him. Habakkuk could not make fig trees bud or produce figs. It was not within his power to control the viability of the animals that provided meat for his table. Nor could he manage the productivity of the soil that yielded crops in their season. He could not dictate how the people responded to him or to each other. This man's praise might not have come easily, as he watched his hopes and dreams fail. Even though the Lord did not live up to Habakkuk's total expectations, he came to the realization that even if everything around him failed, he would rejoice.

If things seem to be failing around you, and you feel as if you are being consumed by the strange noises and overgrowth that lurk in the swamps of life, you can still praise God. At some point in your life, your tap may have run dry and you had no running water with which to cook your food and to clean your body. But tonight, our stomachs are full and we can shower before bed, if we so choose. In despair, you may have cried yourself to sleep in an open alley way or a bus station bathroom. But by God's grace, tomorrow did come, and it will come again. And you can praise God and rejoice even in the midst of troubles, for with each new day life does begin anew.

Rejoicing in the Lord should not be based on the success of your endeavors, but on God's love and faithfulness to you. Ask the Lord to help you look past all the chaos and crises in this world so that you may understand the reasons you have to praise God. Then in this new light of God's presence and in your new frame of mind, you are more able to discern and to act on what you really need to do to accomplish your goals and God's divine will for your life.

Dear God, help us to handle the day-to-day rigors of life. And to learn the lesson of faith, which is to trust in your providence regardless of the circumstances. Amen.

Evaleen Litman Sargent

Help Our Unbelief

But Thomas…was not with them when Jesus came.
So the other disciples told him, "We have seen the
Lord." But he said to them, "Unless I see the mark of
the nails in his hands, and put my finger in the mark
of the nails and my hand in his side, I will not believe."
A week later his disciples were again in the house, and
Thomas was with them. Although the doors were shut,
Jesus came and stood among them and said, "Peace be
with you." Then he said to Thomas, "Put your finger
here and see my hands. Reach out your hand and put it
in my side. Do not doubt but believe." Thomas answered
him, "My Lord and my God!" Jesus said to him, "Have
you believed because you have seen me? Blessed are
those who have not seen and yet have come to believe."
—John 20:24-29

Thomas had doubts. Thomas had seen Jesus die. Thomas would believe Jesus was alive only if he could actually put his hands in the wounds caused by the nails and the soldier's spear. Thomas would not be called a fool. The others believed. Maybe they saw Jesus. Maybe they heard about Jesus. But they believed. Not Thomas, not until he touched Jesus.

We are like Thomas. Our souls hunger to believe. Our hearts want to believe. But our minds are wary, not sure, not wanting to be ridiculed, not wanting to hold false hope.

Jesus said those who can believe without seeing, without touching, without hearing his voice or looking into his eyes are the ones who are truly blessed. We have heard God's promises to be with us in the darkest of valleys. Can we believe? Do we have just enough faith to give us the courage to get out of bed tomorrow? That's all God is asking us to do: take one step, believing that God will turn our doubts and fears into something wonderful and powerful.

God of the strong of heart, God of the doubter, we bring both the strength and the weakness of our faith to you. We believe; help our unbelief. We pray in the name of our brother, Jesus, who lived and died and lives again that we might know the depth of your love for us. Amen.

Dianne L. Mansfield

Promised Paradise

"Truly I tell you, today you will be with me in Paradise."
—*Luke 23:43*

The justice of Jesus, revealed in this promise to the repentant thief, is as much mystery as it is mercy. As I struggle to understand the Scriptures, it is in life events that I come to realize their meaning. This verse came alive when I looked into the eyes of a dear friend who confided, "I'm afraid to die. What if God doesn't think I've been good enough. Do you think I will go to heaven?"

At forty-two, my friend was indeed a good person, fighting a fast-growing brain cancer. When it appeared that she would not survive, she asked these questions. I tried to reassure her: "When you die, you'll rest in the arms of God."

A number of our conversations centered around what she would have done differently had she known her life would be shortened. Perhaps the repentant thief might have lived differently had he been given the chance. Who knows what led him to Golgotha?

I walked with my friend through the shocking experience of her diagnosis. I also witnessed the unkind effects of two brain surgeries, radiation, and chemotherapy on her body, mind, and spirit. What impressed me most was her determination to get well despite a dismal prognosis. She outlived what doctors predicted by at least eight months.

A fierce desire to be there for her three children sustained her hope. Her faith grew, as did a tremendous ability to persevere through every kind of affliction and challenge.

When her husband informed me that her death was imminent, I went to her bedside and sobbed: "You've been robbed! Cancer cheated you out of life."

With her every labored breath, I wondered how much longer she would have to suffer. Suddenly, the words of Jesus broke through my distress: "This day, you will be with Me in paradise." My heart became still. Through teary eyes, I noticed that my friend, lying peacefully in her white gown, resembled an angel. I began to envision her in God's eternal embrace.

When a loved ones dies, we get a glimpse of the crucified Christ. Faith assures us that God's justice and mercy prevail in the end.

Lord, when we accompany our sisters and brothers to Golgotha, may our prayers and tears help guide them to the paradise you promise. Amen.

Mary Beth Krainz

Golden Years

The steadfast love of the LORD never ceases, his mercies never come to an end; they are new every morning; great is your faithfulness. "The LORD is my portion," says my soul, "therefore I will hope in him." The LORD is good to those who wait for him, to the soul that seeks him. It is good that one should wait quietly for the salvation of the LORD.
—Lamentations 3:22-26

It was a beautiful autumn day. The air was warm and the sky clear blue. My three-year-old son, Samuel, and I were visiting my mother at the nursing home where she was living. We had taken her outside to enjoy the afternoon. Mom seemed content sitting quietly watching Samuel play in the leaves. It was a day when few words were necessary. We were enjoying each other's company and taking in nature's beauty.

A gold-colored leaf floated slowly from a tree and came to rest on Mom's lap. It prompted me to consider that these were supposed to be Mom's "golden years," but she was trapped in her body by an illness that shows no mercy: Parkinson's Disease. Interrupting my thoughts, little Samuel came rushing to the side of Mom's wheelchair and asked, "Grammy, do you want to die?"

Mom looked to me for some clarification as to where this question was coming from, and I explained. Samuel had recently begun asking questions about death and had learned that as Christians we look forward to seeing Jesus when we die. He then asked Mom and me, "Don't you want to see Jesus?" Mom's face lit up and she laughed. It was clear that she was thrilled to know her grandson was looking forward to meeting Jesus. It was also obvious to me that she knew these were not really her "golden years." Those would be the years of eternity she looked forward to spending with Jesus, her Savior. Her faith was strong enough to realize that her God would never leave her or forsake her. She never gave up hope in her earthly struggles, and she was confident as she waited on her God to deliver her.

O God, give us strength and courage to never lose faith in your love for us. Help us never to lose sight of the "golden years" that lie ahead when we will spend eternity with you. Amen.

Jane E. Shumway

The Miracle of Holy Saturday

When it was evening, there came a rich man from Arimathea, named Joseph, who was also a disciple of Jesus. He went to Pilate and asked for the body of Jesus; then Pilate ordered it to be given to him. So Joseph took the body and wrapped it in a clean linen cloth and laid it in his own new tomb, which he had hewn in the rock. He then rolled a great stone to the door of the tomb and went away.
—Matthew 27:57-60

I was standing at my desk in my office when the call came. My youngest sister, at age thirty-five, had just been diagnosed with leukemia. I knew that my family's life was about to change forever. Fear gripped my heart. I heard the tomb door slam shut. Winter descended.

The Friday of Christ's death is called "Good Friday." The Sunday of the Resurrection is called "Easter." But what of Saturday? Saturday—when the tomb is cold and dark—shutting out all life and holding only death? The church is made barren and dark. The altar is stripped. There is no celebration of the Eucharist.

And the tomb was sealed. It was surely a devastating time for Jesus' followers. It had to have been a time of excruciating loss, confusion, terror, utter helplessness, shock, horror, and disbelief. How many of us have experienced those same feelings resulting from a loss? It is a time when our grief doesn't do any good. A time when everything we have has ended and nothing is left.

Many people of faith refer to the Saturday before Easter as "Holy Saturday," holy meaning "belonging to or coming from God," "sacred," "spiritually perfect or pure." "Holy: to be made whole."

My beautiful sister had become unrecognizable: not a strand of hair left anywhere on her body, bloated from chemotherapy, suffering from radiation burns, and hallucinating from the morphine. She fought for life. It was medicine and it was torture. A few days before she died she said to me, "I want you to know how important this has been. I have been healed. I'm so proud of how I've fought. I look like a monster. I am horrified at what I see; it isn't me. My beauty is gone, and still so many people are praying for me. Friends and people I don't even know. I know that I am loved."

The tomb of my sister's death sentence amid the horror of utter agony became the womb for her rebirth. In it she was born even as she died. There are no words adequate enough to describe the pain of such a devastation. One simply endures. We are in God's hands.

Just as my sister died, I saw her spirit. It was a few hours later. She was well. She lived! Out of the wounds of our devastation comes the healing, and we are made whole again. And we are made holy.

On this day, when Jesus was laid in the tomb and it was sealed, something happened. Holy Saturday was unique. Winter came and left by sunrise.

God, help us to sustain strength and faith when the tomb door is sealed. Help us to wait expectantly for the time when we know it will be opened again—this time forever. Amen.

Gwynne M. Guibord

Living Water

"I know that Messiah is coming"...
"I am he, the one who is speaking to you."
—John 4:25-26

The Samaritan woman's encounter with Jesus shatters expectations and conventions from beginning to end. That this funny Jewish man should ask her, a Samaritan woman, for a drink of water was strange enough. Most Jews looked down upon the Samaritans as heretics, polluted with foreign blood and bad theology, because they were descended from Israelites of the Northern Kingdom and their foreign conquerors. Unlike the Southern Israelites of Judea, who worshiped at the temple in Jerusalem, the holy site of the Samaritans was Mt. Gerizim in the north. Most Jews would never consider even talking to a Samaritan, let alone drinking from the same vessel!

Then this weird Jewish stranger begins babbling about the "water of life." The Greek words that are literally translated as "living water" were also used idiomatically to mean flowing water or running water, as opposed to water from a well or cistern.* Like most of us, the Samaritan woman is inclined to take him literally. God is my help; therefore, he should improve my material lot in life. Ah now *that* sounds good! Answered prayers that lead to prosperity and success. No more dragging around with this stupid bucket, journeying far from home. Water delivered right to your doorstep, that's what we want. We are seldom interested in the water of life that springs from within; we'd prefer ease and comfort. The Greek word that describes this water, *hallomenoi*, can mean not only the action of the water as it wells up from a spring but also "to leap up or jump." So we can think of God's Spirit working in us as not only coming from a deep source, but also as rather boisterous in action.

Jesus' next words discombobulate the Samaritan woman even further. He knows all about her life, present and past. This knowledge opens the woman's eyes, for to her mind there is only one way that he, a stranger in this place, can have such knowledge. "I perceive, sir, that you are a prophet" (v. 19). The Greek word translated here as "perceive" and in some other versions as "see" is not the everyday verb for see (*horao* or *blepo*), but the verb *theaomai*, from which we get the word "theater" and which means "to gaze upon, behold, discern with the eyes." Not merely to see, but to look at with intention and discernment. It's as if Jesus' words have lifted the curtains of her mind's eye and revealed to her his status as a prophet. She then makes a great intuitive leap of faith, asking him indirectly if he is the Christ: "I know that the Messiah is coming, the one who is called the Christ. Whenever he comes, he will report all things to us." His answer must have blown her mind: "I who am speaking to you am he."

The idea that God knows every thought, every experience, is one that I find enormously comforting, yet all too often difficult to believe. So I hope against hope and pray that God will help my unbelief. That God should know all our weaknesses, foibles, hatreds, and prejudices, yet still offer to us the water of life, sounds too good to be true. Let us pray in the words of Psalms 139 and 42 (paraphrased):

> Lord, you have searched me out and known me;
> you know my sitting down and my rising up;
> you discern my thoughts from afar.
> You trace my journeys and my resting places
> and are acquainted with all my ways.
>
> As the deer longs for the water brooks,
> so longs my soul for Thee, O God.
> My soul is athirst for God, athirst for the living God.
>
> *Search me out, O God, and know my heart;*
> *try me and know my restless thoughts.*
> *Look well whether there be any wickedness in me*
> *and lead me in the way that is everlasting. Amen.*

Nancy Adams

*This information comes from Dr. Glenn Koch, retired professor of Greek and New Testament at Eastern Baptist Theological Seminary.

Assurance of God's Love

All we like sheep have gone astray;
we have all turned to our own way,
and the LORD has laid on him the iniquity of us all.
—Isaiah 53:6

I heard a crash and screams. I looked outside to see my neighbor sitting on her step, cradling her head in her hands, rocking soundlessly. From inside, her son was whimpering.

I went over to her house. "I heard a crash," I offered. She looked up, tears running, and replied, "It's Jimmy. He's been playing with matches again, and I told him if he got into them just once more, there would be dire consequences."

"What happened?" I asked.

"I put the matches on top of the china cabinet. As soon as my back was turned, he climbed up, lost his balance, and pulled the cabinet over. He broke every single piece of my wedding china and crystal, and he bruised himself all over. I was so angry I knew I couldn't touch him, so I sent him to his room. He screamed and screamed, and when I told him to stop, that he wasn't hurt that bad, he cowered down beside a chair and wailed, 'I'm not crying because I hurt. I'm crying because you don't love me anymore.'

"Can I ever make him understand that I'm angry with him for disobeying, but that, of course, I still love him? After all, he's my little boy! I just want to hold him in my arms and reassure him that I love him."

Is this what God is trying to tell us? There are consequences for our stubbornness, but Jesus, God's own Son, has paid the costs. Our heavenly Father, like that earthly mother, longs to hold us in his arms and reassure us of his love and grace. Like the disobedient children we are, we, too, long for that forgiving embrace.

Loving God, we keep "turning to our own way," doing what we shouldn't do and "forgetting" to do what you have commanded. We deeply regret our willfulness and seek your peace and forgiveness as your children. In the name of the One who bears our punishment, Christ our Lord. Amen.

Fair C. Meeks

A Path to Wholeness

For surely I know the plans I have for you,
says the LORD, plans for your welfare and not for harm,
to give you a future with hope. Then when you call
upon me and come and pray to me, I will hear you.
—Jeremiah 29:11-12

The pathway to wholeness comes in many forms. When I was a mother with young children, I was just learning about God's power to bring healing and wholeness to our lives. Through participation in a community Bible study group, I became close friends with another mother of young children.

One day in the group, my friend told us that her doctor had found a cancerous lump in her breast. Naturally, she was consumed with anxiety. We were led to lay hands on her and pray for healing. We were confident she would be healed. In October of that year she was back in the hospital after surgery because of the pain. Cancer was still present, and she was still very anxious. But one night she had a dramatic experience of the presence of Christ at her bedside. All fear and anxiety disappeared. She came from the hospital filled with the assurance of God's presence.

In the months following, she touched the lives of many people, including my own, as she gave witness to her experience of God's love. She was radiant—almost other-worldly. Less than four months after her experience of Christ's presence, she died and entered into the Church Triumphant. Actually, it seemed as if she had crossed over into heaven before she left this earth.

No, my friend had not been healed of the cancer in her physical being as we had so hoped. But she had been made whole. She had met Christ face-to-face and had entered into the heavenly realm. She changed forever my concept of healing, wholeness, and heaven. When I was diagnosed with breast cancer twenty-five years later, there was no anxiety, only a deep sense of God's presence.

God does know the plans God has for us, to give us a future and a hope—no matter the circumstances. Let us learn to trust God's Spirit to lead us into the future that has been prepared for us that we may experience the fullness of life that God has prepared for us.

All powerful and loving God, we thank you that you know our future. Even when the way seems dark, may we be open to experiencing your loving presence, filling us with light and hope that we may grow toward the wholeness you have planned for us. Amen.
Norma S. Mengel

Forgetting to Hope

For you, O LORD, are good and forgiving, abounding in steadfast love to all who call on you.
—Psalm 86:5

Recently I faced a difficult choice: continue in a job I loved or end a commuter marriage. A move to the city where my husband worked, and where many family members and longtime friends also lived, would probably mean changing not only my job but also changing a satisfying career path.

For over a year, I had commuted two hundred fifty miles across Missouri every weekend from Kansas City to St. Louis. Although my husband was tolerant of this weekdays-apart arrangement, I felt something important had been lost: a sense of family and of belonging to a place. Increasingly, I felt that a return to St. Louis represented not only wholeness, but peace. Yet the field I had worked in for some twenty years had brought me considerable satisfaction and success, even a measure of prestige. How to resolve these conflicting feelings?

Often when I face difficult decisions like this one, I feel stuck, as if I were living in a shrinking box. Even my prayers are marked by a feeling of futility. I lose sight of the depth of God's love for each of us—the depth of God's love for me.

Despite my lack of hope, breakthrough inevitably comes. This time, during an activity-packed weekend with my husband, when I barely had time to glance at the newspaper, an employment ad caught my eye. The job, though in a new field, felt right to me.

Apparently it felt right to my new employers too. I am now applying old skills to new projects and tasks, finding the work satisfying. In fact, there are even times when I feel joyful about the change.

I find myself smiling at myself, wondering how many such situations will cause me to lose hope before I remember to think *first* of God's love for me rather than to recognize it only in retrospect.

Source of all being and Eternal Word, the One who is called Emmanuel—God with us—help me to remember that you, though far greater than myself, are part of me, closer to me than my own heart. Help me to remember in difficult times that you are aware of my needs and hopes before I speak them to you. Give me faith to believe that when I don't feel you at my side, it is because you have gone ahead of me to open new doors. Amen.

Pamela Schaeffer

Pointed toward Life

For to this end Christ died and lived again,
so that he might be LORD of both the dead and the living.
—Romans 14:9

Our son's varsity basketball team's successful season and post-season play had paved the way for a trip to the state tournament. The shadow of my father's brief illness was all that kept our excitement in check. When we learned that Grandpa had to endure yet another surgery, we ached, knowing the pain he bore so courageously.

I was torn. Go to be with my parents and sister some 400 miles away? Go to watch my son's team compete? I knew my dad had rallied many times previously. With no indication that this surgery might lead to his death, and at his urging, I went to the tournament. "There is nothing you can do here. Tell Dustin to win." Those were the last words he would say to me. No phones in ICU.

I take some notion of comfort that he was never out of my mind as I prayed quiet little prayers amid the din of the crowd. I thought about the contrast of my father and those young men, struggling for every breath, but for very different reasons.

We lost the championship in the final game. My father survived the surgery. And he seemed to rally afterwards. But within a few days I received word to hurry and come. I arrived at his bedside, too late for him to speak but in time to be with him as he took his final breath.

Later I learned that as they wheeled him off to surgery, he said, "I hope Dustin wins." He had lived a long and full life; he wanted his grandson to do the same: to always seize the day, because the day may never come again.

My father's legacy lives on in this wide-eyed son of ours. He never hesitates to seize the moment and knows, from his grandfather, that God points us toward life, wants us to seize each moment as if it were our last. It is God's gift to us; it was my father's gift to me and to my son.

Keeper of all life, who creates and sustains, thank you for the exuberance of youth and for the wisdom of age. Point us toward life. Amen.

Emilie J. Aubert

A Teenage Daughter and God's Abiding Love

"Abide in me...If you abide in me, and
my words abide in you, ask for whatever you wish,
and it will be done for you."
—John 15:4a,7

I was a teenage girl, once. I remember doubting that a boy would ever ask me out on a date, feeling insecure about my looks, and being impatient with parents who denied me what I thought were long overdue privileges. I remember what it was like to be a teenager. But even that remembering did not prepare me for the turmoil I encountered when my own little girl—my sweet princess—crossed the line and entered those turbulent teen years herself.

"This is more than I can take," I wailed to my husband late one Saturday night after a difficult day with my daughter.

"The Lord never gives us more than we can bear," he assured me, obviously believing such a gentle reminder would comfort me. It did not.

"Then the Lord thinks too much of me," I replied as I sank my head onto the pillow and cried.

But the next morning, the Scripture lesson in Sunday school confirmed the comfort in my husband's words: "Abide in me...If you abide in me, and my words abide in you, ask whatever you wish, and it will be done for you."

Suddenly the message seemed obvious. When we abide in the Savior's loving care, then we will never feel overwhelmed by what we encounter in life. Nothing will be more than we can bear when we abide in his all-powerful, all-knowing, and ever-present love. We can release our burdens and give everything over to God, knowing that he will respond to our needs and see us through to victory.

Here is the comfort: Those teen years will, eventually, end. God's abiding love never does.

Lord, the truth in your promises is real. Help us to release our burdens onto you as we abide in you and know the goodness of your comfort and love. Amen.

Jean Alicia Elster

Courage for Living

I believe that I shall see the goodness of the LORD in the land of the living. Wait for the LORD; be strong, and let your heart take courage; wait for the LORD!
—*Psalm 27:13-14*

In my Bible at home, I have the words "Yes I do!" written beside this Scripture verse. I believe. And yet some days, the waiting is hard, the courage is faint. My heart grows weary. Let me share a prayer from my journal, written on one of "those days," so you'll know what I mean:

> My soul is longing for the glory of You! My heart aches for the tenderness of your touch. Babies are near death today—babies with names: Hannah, Tonya, Monique, Kellie. Babies are struggling for life. Children by the hundreds and thousands suffer floods, wars, hunger, pain, abandonment. In Mozambique, land mines float along the currents of flooded rivers; mosquitoes carry malaria and death. In Nigeria, Muslims and Christians kill each other in your Name. My soul longs for your Spirit's comfort. Wayne lies in intensive care. Drake waits for his doctor to enter the hospital room and give him news. Dottie, in her wheelchair, paints cabinets. Life continues its steady, relentless cycles of pain and relief, struggles, beginnings, and endings. And pastors have no magic words. I have no extraordinary wisdom or amazing grace, only a will and desire to serve and obey you. My soul longs for you to transform, to re-create, to inundate your people with hope and expectancy and joy—with faith that outlasts, out-shines, out-endures every desperate, disappointed, discouraged moment.

Maybe you've had days like that one, days when it's hard work just living in the world. If so, let your heart take courage. You are not alone. You and I and every other person who gets worn down and weary have been given a great gift. We are a part of the Body of Christ, part of a community. We have a God who sighs with us, waits with us, enters into our deepest longings and prayers. We have sisters and brothers who cry when we cry, tremble when we fear, and long with us for God's righteousness to reign for eternity.

Thank you, God of grace and glory and great expectation, that when life gets heavy you are there. Fill us with your hope as we wait patiently for what your Spirit will do among us. Amen.

Karen Ann Selig

You Are Mine

*"Do not fear, for I have redeemed you;
I have called you by name, you are mine."
—Isaiah 43:1*

My work, as chief ecumenical officer for my denomination, requires that I travel a great deal both domestically and internationally. It is not uncommon for me to fly several times a month as I traverse the heavens helping to create ecumenical bridges toward the goal of building up the beloved community of the church.

With recent air tragedies, the growing volume of aircraft in the skies, and the ever-present threat of terrorism, my fear of flying has increased significantly. Carrying fear on any level is depleting and cancerous to one's soul. I've managed to combat my fear with a pre-boarding, boarding, and in-flight liturgy of prayer, meditation, and favorite hymns (softly hummed). For the most part it has worked, except that in the deepest part of my spiritual integrity, I have felt confessionally that my fear of flying is somehow an affront to my trust in God.

On a recent flight, as I sat buckled in my seat, fear gripping my heart, hands sweaty and cold, intoning an intercessory prayer to steady myself, a wave of calm settled over me as a voice in my head said, "God knew you before you were born; you have been marked by God as God's own." My heart resonated and my soul sang with the safety that comes from knowing that God has called me "by name," that each of us enjoys an intimate relationship with God that transcends fear even unto death. As the plane ascended, I felt a deep sense of peace, knowing that I (as is all creation) am God's own from the beginning, now, and forevermore.

Loving God, let us remember that each of us has been named and claimed by you as your own, that we are forever yours. As yours, we are safe even unto death. Amen.

Gwynne M. Guibord

Keep Your Eyes on the Lighthouse

I will instruct you and teach you the way you should go;
I will counsel you with my eye upon you.
—Psalm 32:8

As women, we constantly find ourselves in situations that require our immediate attention. We are challenged to have an answer for every question posed to us. We are expected to meet seemingly impossible deadlines. Yet because of our gender, our decisions are often questioned.

Often, we put our own personal wants, needs, and desires on the back burner—sometimes we put God back there as well. For example, when was the last time you had a physical, had your blood pressure checked, had a mammogram? When was the last time you set aside quiet time to spend with God?

We do need to care for others, but God also wants us to take care of ourselves. Our attention is focused on many other responsibilities, on spouses requiring a bit of attention, on children demanding undivided attention, and on bills screaming for all of our attention. God didn't promise the road would be easy. But our Creator did promise never to leave us.

As long as we can hold onto our anchor of faith and know that we are planted on a firm foundation, we can ride out waves that rise up in our lives. When you think you have reached your limit, keep your eyes on the lighthouse. When you have lost both of your oars and you cannot depend on anyone or anything else, keep your eyes on the lighthouse. God, who is so loving and who knows your limitations, will extend hands of mercy and kindness. The unconditional love that God has for you will protect you and guide you back toward the shore of that firm and solid foundation, Jesus the Christ.

God, thank you for illuminating our hearts with your lighthouse of love. May we always look toward this light and follow its leading. Amen.

Inga D. Green

Morning Tears

Weeping may linger for the night,
but joy comes in the morning.
—Psalm 30:5

Why, wrote the psalmist,
Weeping's for the night,
"but joy comes in the morning"?

It's often in the morning
    that I weep,
sometimes for deep-held sorrow,
    astonishment at
      God's great steadfast love.

Tears come like early dew
    or rain-washed grass
    of summer dawns,
gentle and quickly gone.

How can it be
God's waiting for our "Yes,"
ready to comfort fears,
and calling,
    calling us into true being,
that scariest of states.

Creator God, open us to hear you whenever you call. Guide and prepare our hearts and minds to be ready to receive you, whatever the morning brings. Guide us in being there for each other. Amen.
Carolyn Hall Felger

Faithful Christian Living

Who's in Charge?

Then [God] led out his people like sheep,
and guided them in the wilderness like a flock.
[God] led them in safety, so that they were not afraid...
and [God] brought them to [God's] holy hill...
—Psalm 78:52-54

I was sitting in the aisle seat. A grandmother was in the window seat, and between us was her three-year-old granddaughter. The child was wearing a new dress. Her feet, in black patent Mary Janes and lace-edged white socks, stuck straight out from the seat. It was obviously her first plane trip, and she was both excited and intensely curious. She fastened and unfastened the seat belt, turned on lights and air vents, examined magazines, and asked constantly, "What is this for?"

Suddenly the plane began backing away from the gate. She sat straight up, whirled toward her grandmother, and asked, "Grandma, are you driving?" Grandma said, "No." The girl turned to me and asked, "Are *you* driving?" When I, too, said I was not, she raised her voice and called out loudly, for all the plane to hear, "Who's driving this thing?"

Some days I want to yell at the universe, "Who's driving this thing?" It all seems so out of control, so confused, so wrong. In my younger adult days, I imagined that I might myself be able to exert some control, to shape the course of events through sheer will or intense effort. Several years ago, during an opening exercise at a meeting, we were instructed to tell the person sitting next to us the most important lesson we have learned in life. I heard myself say, "That I'm not in charge."

That day in the airplane, after we reached cruising altitude, the flight attendant came back and said to my little seatmate, "Come with me, honey. I want you to meet the person who's driving." A few minutes later, a happy child climbed back into her seat, clutching a wings pin and babbling about the cockpit and the pilot. What I need in my life are friends and colleagues who cut though my stress, frustration, and deep discouragement to remind me of—even reintroduce me to—the One who is driving, who is in charge, who "guides us through the wilderness in safety."

O God our guide, we do know who's driving this thing. In our moments of inflated self-confidence, as well as our times of fear and despair, send companions who remind us of your love and constancy. Amen.

Peggy Halsey

Culture Shock

I will not set before my eyes anything that is base.
—Psalm 101:3

I returned from an extended trip to a nation in another hemisphere, another time zone, and what seemed like another world. But arriving back in America was when I felt the culture shock. The wealth, the abundance, the choices! There were far fewer options for the people I'd left on the other side of the globe.

In an attempt to overcome my jet lag and adjust to my Pennsylvania time zone, I turned on the TV to try to stay awake for at least a while. I was astounded by what I saw on the screen. Oh yes, they had TV where I'd just come from, but only state-owned channels, which meant that no commercials accompanied the programs, which included, believe it or not, 1960s American shows like "Leave it to Beaver," with subtitles. Three months in another place was enough time to begin to acculturate, and what I saw on TV that first night back home shocked me. What shocked me was not so much the programs, but the commercials. I was being told I needed to own this, buy that, or get a better one of these, so that, seemingly, I could then be a fulfilled person.

These commercials used to seem normal to me, but I suddenly realized it is not normal to be continually bombarded with that kind of life-shaping manipulation. I'd never before seen how preoccupied we Americans are with ownership, with more, better, bigger.

When our thoughts are on God, when we continually adjust our lives to what God says is of value, when our desire is to do God's will, we call it worship. Consumerism was unmasked to me in that moment as a religion by which too many Americans "live and move and have their beings." Appalled by the subtlety of the idolatry I had just witnessed, I lunged toward the TV, pressed the control button, and banished that spirit from my home. I've never missed it since.

Lord, forgive us for entertaining ourselves with what is an abomination to you. Please purify us and restore us to the simplicity of devotion to you. Rescue our society from manipulation motivated by pride and greed, and restore us to enjoyment in each other and in you. Amen.

Lonnie Lane

The Power of Prayer

*I thank my God every time I remember you,
constantly praying with joy in every one of
my prayers for...you, because of your sharing
in the gospel from the first day until now.
—Philippians 1:3-5*

Several years ago I received a note in the mail from my friend Louise telling me that for some time I had been on her personal prayer list and that she prayed for me daily. How blessed I felt!

Those of us who are clergy are "in the business of prayer." We get asked to pray for others a lot: to open meetings with prayer, to do the grace before a meal, to do an invocation at a public event, or to pray with someone over the phone. We pray in homes, at bedsides, in hospitals, at gravesides. Often others think clergy prayers are somehow more beneficial than theirs.

There is great power in prayer, especially intercessory prayer. Sometimes a word to God, offered by a woman of God, changes things. Attitudes, decisions, priorities, and even disease can be altered. I have seen and felt the effect of prayers offered by the people of God on behalf of others with amazing, and sometimes miraculous, results. At those times in my own life when I was too anxious to pray for myself, I depended on others to uphold, carry, and pray for me.

Ever since Louise told me she prays for me daily, I have felt different—blessed. The knowledge of her prayers is a secret strength I tap into as I go about the tasks of parish ministry. To me, Louise is a "woman at the well" who, having received the living water from Jesus, passes it on to others. I cherish her and her prayers. Who prays for you?

For whom do you pray?

Dear God, thank you for Louise and for others like her who uphold us in their prayers and support us in so many ways. Like the woman at the well, having encountered your Son, Jesus, they believed and went to tell others of him. May we be like them. Amen.

Janet K. Hess

Shoes of Readiness

Therefore, since we are surrounded by so great a cloud of witnesses, let us also lay aside every weight and the sin that clings so closely, and let us run with perseverance the race that is set before us.
—Hebrews 12:1

God calls each one of us to follow in the way of Jesus Christ in a race toward the goal of a world made whole and holy. We are called to stand firm and to step out in faith, recognizing that we have a role to play in bringing about a world where justice and peace kiss. For women, especially, what we wear on our feet often determines how far we can go.

The stories of the great cloud of witnesses told in Hebrews 11 sets the pattern that Jesus exhibits and that we must expect in our own lives: triumph achieved through trauma, joy gained through suffering. New life from the tomb, miracles of transformation, closed hearts wrenched open, brokenness bound up into wholeness, injustice become justice, animosity turned into peace. All require unthinkable sacrifice, yet God's grace is sufficient and the joy beyond reckoning.

The letter to the Ephesian church exhorts us to wear as shoes the readiness to announce the Good News of peace. In other words, what we wear on our feet determines whether we are able to follow Jesus toward the goal he sets before us. Sometimes when faced with injustice, I feel like wearing stomping boots to obliterate opposition. Sometimes when confronted by squabbling and polarized Christians, I want to put on mommy shoes to set them straight. Sometimes when dealing with closed hearts, I want to put on running shoes to run right over skepticism.

But the witness to the church at Ephesus reminds those who would walk in the way of Jesus that we are to wear the shoes of readiness to announce the Good News of peace. Now we know that when Jesus wore those shoes, they took him to the cross. Our journey will take us there as well, because it is the only way to the other side. That way will demand more than we ever knew we could give; yet all that we need will be given unto us.

Holy One, we would stand fast but not still; we have places to go where you are summoning us. Ground us in the assurance that we are held in love that will never let us go, no matter where in the name of that love we are sent, in the name and the way of Jesus Christ. Amen.

Kate Harvey

God's Gift of Others

How very good and pleasant it is
when kindred live together in unity!
—Psalm 133:1

I can't imagine living alone, without companionship. From the beginning God created us as relational beings. We are reminded in Jesus' prayer (see John 17) of the divine desire for all of God's creation to live together in unity. There was once a time in my life when I didn't want anyone close to me. Those were hard and very wounded times. Yet, as I tried to push people away, God just held on to me tighter. In my struggles I have learned many things. One of the great lessons is the importance of others in our lives.

My lesson began with the recognition of personal need. As I

sought healing from child sexual abuse and later in learning to live with cancer, I found that I needed other people in order for me to heal. I needed people to listen to and understand me. I needed people to help guide me, to physically heal me, to do for me. I needed people to just be with me. In time I found that I could trust other people, allow others to come closer and get to know me. I discovered joy and peace in companionship, and I learned how not just to need others but to enjoy the presence of others. Today I still value my times alone, but I cannot live without the presence of others. Indeed, how good and pleasant it is when we can live together in unity!

We have been given a great gift and blessing in others and in the need to nurture relationships. It is time to stop letting our differences separate us, time to acknowledge our differences as gifts and blessings. God created every single person who lives, has lived, and will live. We are all God's children and it is God's will that we live in unity, as Christ and God are one. It begins with each of us reaching out a hand, in God's love, to a person who is ill, or to someone we have shunned or not accepted or not loved; reaching out in friendship and unity as God reaches out to each of us.

Loving Lord, thank you for loving and accepting me. Help me to not turn away from others but rather to learn to love all people and accept them as you do me. Amen.

Debbie H. Deane

The Race

Therefore, since we are surrounded by so great a cloud
of witnesses, let us also lay aside every weight and
the sin that clings so closely, and let us run with
perseverance the race that is set before us, looking to
Jesus the pioneer and perfecter of our faith...
—Hebrews 12:1-2

There are many aspects of our life of faith that are similar to a race. Each of us has a journey to complete.

People have various goals when they enter a marathon. Some want to dress up in special outfits. Others want to prove their bodies are still young. Many are concerned with their speed and finishing time. Minimally, however, it is everyone's goal to finish.

When you are running a long-distance race, you can't see the finish line for most of the way. However, in my experience running marathons, there is never a long stretch of time when I don't think about finishing. When I am in a race, I am constantly assessing my pace, the way my body is feeling, how much liquid and energy bars I need to consume to finish well.

There are times, especially at the beginning of the race, when racers feel so invincible that they can be oblivious to what the future holds. It is especially important at these times to keep up the food and water intake and to monitor energy output.

It is easy in our Christian journeys, especially when we're still fresh and strong, to feel so invincible that we forget about the end we can't see. We take our eyes off Jesus, who is at the finish line waiting to welcome us home. We don't put much of a priority on building a life of faith or investing in God's kingdom. Some of us even stop and get out of the race altogether. Paul encourages us not to make this mistake. God desires that we finish strong and make the right provisions to do so.

God, help us to fix our eyes on Jesus and to run with determination and perseverance the race marked out for us. Amen.

Carolyn Iga

Learning to Forgive

"For if you forgive men when they sin against you,
your heavenly Father will also forgive you.
But if you do not forgive men their sins,
your Father will not forgive your sins."
—Matthew 6:14-15, NIV

Many times I have heard people say, "I'll just never forgive." When I hear this statement, I feel pain in my heart. To know that holding back forgiveness from someone who has wronged me will keep the Lord from forgiving me, is more than I can stand. For I want to be as sure as possible that when I sin, I can ask for forgiveness from the person I have wronged and receive forgiveness also from my Lord.

When I was about eight years old, I learned very well what God's forgiveness for a "sin committed" really meant. I don't remember what I was being corrected for, but I do remember being angry and talking back to my mother. In our household that was a "no-no." My mother told me to go to my room and not come out until I could tell her I was sorry for the way I had talked to her.

I went to my room still upset. But after thinking about it for a while, I began to realize I was wrong. The hardest part was going back to my mother and saying I was sorry, even though I knew full well I could not leave that room until I did just that.

I prayed, asking God to help me go downstairs and tell my mother I was sorry for talking back. I knew I could not do it alone. I prayed for a long time. (To a child of eight, it seemed like it was all day.) I remember vividly walking down the steps, praying all the way for help to say the words.

When I was in front of my mother, I asked her to forgive me. I told her I knew I was wrong for what I had said. She took me into her arms so that I knew immediately that I was forgiven. And love shined all around us that day.

It was this feeling of forgiveness that to this day has helped me to forgive others and to seek forgiveness from God and others. The feeling of God's love for me no matter what, the joy of his forgiveness, and the knowledge of his grace keep me always mindful that I am a child of God.

Almighty God, whose loving hand has given us hearts and minds to know right from wrong, guide me to seek you in all that I say, do, or think. Help me grow in your love so that I can fulfill your will for my life. Amen.

Lou A. Nutter

Level Ground

Then Peter began to speak to them:
"I truly understand that God shows no partiality,
but in every nation anyone who fears him and
does what is right is acceptable to him."
—Acts 10:34-35

One Sunday morning years ago, two men went forward when the invitation was given at Calvary Baptist Church in Washington, D.C. Both had decided to confess that they were sinners in need of God's grace.

One of the men was an immigrant, a Chinese laundryman. He worked hard all week cleaning the clothes that others soiled. The laundry was hot, and the humidity was high. The man who stood beside him at the front of the church, responding to the same invitation, was highly educated, well-to-do, and esteemed throughout the country. He was a justice of the United States Supreme Court.

They were two very different people, one at the top of the social ladder, and the other often ignored and frequently belittled. Neither could boast of his goodness before God; both were in need of grace. They knelt together in front of the sanctuary. The pastor stepped forward to greet both men. "At the foot of the cross," he said, "the ground is level."

It is easy for us as Christians, in all our humanity, to count ourselves superior to others. Most of us go along with politicians who claim that ours is "the greatest nation in the world." Many of us have been socialized to believe in the superiority of our own ethnic group or economic class. Some of us have internalized bias against our own group and struggle to consider ourselves and others in our group to be as worthy as others.

We ought not boast of our own accomplishments, superior goodness, creativity, ethnic background, occupation, or other characteristics, for all of us are alike in the eyes of God. God's grace is a gift offered equally to all persons, whoever they may be. God calls us to see the good in everyone we meet and to treat everyone with respect.

Loving God, thank you that you seek out and offer your grace to each person. Help us to respond to your love and acceptance by loving and accepting everyone we meet. Forgive and instruct us when we fail to be instruments of your grace. Amen.

Wilda K. W. (Wendy) Morris

Beyond Boundaries

But she answered him, "Sir, even the dogs
under the table eat the children's crumbs."
—Mark 7:28

Jesus was tired, oh so tired. He found a place to rest in the territory of Tyre. He wanted to be *incognito* for awhile—away from the crowds, those demanding crowds. Away from all the suffering, the deaf, the blind, the mute, all clamoring for healing.

Jesus was tired, oh so tired. He found a place to rest away from the crowds in the territory of Tyre. He wanted to be away from the Pharisees and the scribes, their probing questions, their transparent intentions. Away even from his disciples, who seemed so dull, unable to comprehend the simplest teaching.

Jesus was tired, oh so tired. He found a place to rest away from the crowds in the territory of Tyre. But no! There was no rest! For here was a woman asking him to go beyond the boundary of his own physical fatigue. Pushing him for more than he wanted to give. And for what purpose? A sick child, a demon-possessed child.

And this woman, this woman, a Gentile—a Syrophoenician, had no right to the grace meant for Israel. She was a foreigner. This woman was pushing Jesus beyond his own religious boundaries, beyond his own national boundaries. And for what purpose? A sick child, a demon-possessed child.

How dare she! How inappropriate, how unconventional! Where was her husband, father, elder brother? That's who should have come. The woman pushed Jesus beyond his own gender boundaries, beyond the boundaries of convention.

But Jesus said, "No! I won't be pushed! It is for Israel that I come—my energy and gifts are too precious for dogs!"

But the woman—the unconventional, pushy, frantic, bold, child-loving mother—contests our Lord! Is this not the same Jesus who says that religious customs should not stand in the way of doing good for those in need? Now this Jesus must be taught that social conventions, national boundaries, religious affiliations should not stand in the way of doing good for those in need.

And our Jesus, tired, weary in body and soul; our Jesus, shaped and formed by his own culture, his own gender, his own religious affiliations, his own nationality, listened to this unconventional, pushy, frantic, bold, child-loving gentile woman and learned how to move beyond his own boundaries. He listened. A child suffered. He listened. A mother willingly suffered indignity and abasement, begging for the child she so desperately loved. Jesus listened.

"Go to your daughter. The demon has left." Jesus listened, learned, suffered, and healed.

O God, help us to be like Jesus. Help us to listen, learn, suffer, and heal. Amen.

K. Joanne Lindstrom

"Why Me, O God?"

"Therefore I have uttered what I did not understand,
things too wonderful for me, which I did not know."
—Job 42:3b

"Why me?" was my cry when a rock hit the windshield of my car. A dump truck had just driven past me. "Why me?" I cried again when the window proceeded to crack. "Why Me, God?" I cried again as I reminisced about the miserable week I had just experienced. When I caught my breath, I heard, "Why *not* you?" I wanted to rebuke that voice in the name of Jesus, but I could not, because I recognized the voice. So, for the next month I pondered, "Why *not* me?"

The realization of what I was requiring God to perform transformed into a picture in my mind. I realized I wanted God to create a bubble to protect me from all the "Why mes?" As I pictured myself in this protected bubble, I recalled a story I heard on television about a boy who had to live in a protective plastic bubble so that other people's germs would not harm him. The thought of not having anyone who could be physically close to me was more than I could bear. I remembered thinking, "That poor boy will never experience life with all its bumps and turns." That would cancel all my freedoms and choices. Did not God create me with a free will?

Can you imagine! I wanted God to create this perfect environmental bubble that I would inhabit. I would be a prisoner isolated in my own environment. This is not what I prayed when I chose to follow God. I did not cry out "Why me?" this summer when I was fishing with the children, or having a wonderful time with my nieces, or receiving garden-grown vegetables and fruits. Overall, I had a wonderful summer. My health was not too great. I did what I could. I decided that my prayer would be to live through my miserable experiences by faith and discover the mysteries of God's love. Walking by faith means living life with all the whys: the good and the not-so-good times.

Why not *me, O God? Amen.*

Theodora A. Boolin

Justice and Grace

*He has told you, O mortal, what is good; and what does
the LORD require of you but to do justice, and to love
kindness, and to walk humbly with your God?*
—*Micah 6:8*

*So speak and so act as those who are to be judged
by the law of liberty. For judgment will be
without mercy to anyone who has shown no mercy;
mercy triumphs over judgment.*
—*James 2:12-13*

Justice and Grace. Complete opposites? Are they? In a society of "eye for an eye," how often do we feel that justice was done when an offender walks away pardoned? In an age of self-help, self-interest, and the promotion of rigid personal boundaries, how often do we deal justly in our relationships by being gracious, forgiving, and forbearing? And in our churches, where grace is foundational to our faith, how often are we just with one another especially during periods of reconciliation?

We speak of justice and grace as opposing concepts in our society, in our relationships, even at times in our churches. But God speaks of them in the same breath. We find in the Bible many stories of the deceitfulness and faithlessness of God's people, detailing how the poverty of their actions requires consequence and discipline. And yet through the prophet Jeremiah (50:20) God proclaims, "I will pardon those whom I preserve."

This is a new kind of discipline, the discipline of grace. God sees through our actions to what we need rather than what we deserve. And so God chooses to heal rather than to demand a restitution that we could not actualize. Within God's character, justice and grace complete each other.

So how then do we live? In such a way that we embody the unity between justice and grace: accountable to God and accountable to each other, but drenched in the love that overrides what justice would demand.

Lord, help me to be more like you. Help me to love beyond

definition and to see through what being right would demand to what love would require. Amen.

Rachel Matheson Ommen

Family Matters!

Speak to all the congregation of the people of Israel and say to them...you shall reprove your neighbor... but you shall love your neighbor as yourself.
—Leviticus 19:2,17-18

It was the hottest summer in the Middle East in forty years. I was in Israel for the birth of my first grandchild. My daughter Ellen and son-in-law, Tamir, named her Gili, which means "rejoice" in Hebrew. Needless to say, I rejoiced in her arrival.

A familiar traditional Israeli song is titled "Gili Maod." Anyone asking the inevitable question about a new baby, upon learning her name, immediately began to sing, "Gili maod, bat Zion": "Rejoice greatly, daughter of Zion." Each time this happened, I considered it a prophetic declaration that this child was very special, even to God.

When Gili was three weeks old, we took a drive to visit her other grandparents in Safed. On the way home I sat in the back of the little orange Volkswagen holding Gili, who cried. A lot. It was very, very hot. In that dry climate the breeze blowing in through the window of the VW as we drove along was like a hair dryer blowing in your face.

Coming down from Safed along the road to Tiberius we made a turn and suddenly before us—clear, blue and wet—was the Sea of Galilee. Tamir pulled the car over, reached for the baby, walked straight into the water and dipped her in. The shock made her gasp for a moment, squall for the next few seconds, and then grow quiet as she cooled off in her abba's arms.

Immediately several women who were sitting on the beach nearby began yelling at Tamir, in Hebrew of course, as if he had done something horrible to the baby. "What are you doing to that baby? You can't do that." They attacked him as if they were a gaggle of Gili's own grandmothers, protecting her like she belonged to them. He assured them the baby was fine and now much more comfortable. Still they continued to chatter at him as if they had some relationship with him that entitled them to such opinions about his baby—and for that matter, him. No American isolationist boundaries here, I thought.

The Old Testament draws a picture of a people who sense they belong to one giant family with one common, God-ordained destiny, accountable to and for one another. These women on the beach gave every indication that this idea still exists as they considered this a family matter about which they had every right to give their opinion.

We in the Church believe that we are, every one, God's own very special children. But perhaps we could do with some more of that good old-fashioned Old Testament sense of family and caring for one another as a people who belong to each other.

Lord, you've made your people into a family. Teach us to tone down our American individualism and let down our cultural boundaries in order to provide a safe place in the caring community of God's people, that we might "rejoice greatly" in one another. Amen.

Lonnie Lane

Magnifying God

Then Mary said, "Here I am, the servant of the Lord;
let it be with me according to your word."
—Luke 1:38

"My soul magnifies the Lord and my spirit rejoices
in God my savior, for [God] has looked with favor
on the lowliness of God's servant."
—Luke 1:46-48

There are so many times in my life and my work when I feel inadequate. How can God be asking me to meet with some of the great religious leaders of our time? I didn't even begin seminary until I was over fifty. But then I am reminded of a young girl who wasn't even fifteen when God spoke to her about bearing the child who would change the world. She didn't look at her inadequacy. Rather, she looked at God's majesty.

It is our ability to meet God on God's terms that allows Christ to be born. Wherever we find God and honor God, even in the harshest of times, Christ is born. God is bigger and more complex than we in our finite selves will ever be able to comprehend. God is always working in and through us. Our egos often keep us from even beginning to comprehend that reality. We often get so caught up in the "us" and the "me" of our lives that we miss the miraculous that is happening all around us. By the same token, there are times when we feel inadequate and undeserving of blessings that come to us.

Mary, as a young girl of perhaps thirteen, so loved God that she looked directly to the greatness of God even as God burst into her life, turning it upside down. Unlike so many of us, she never asked what it would cost her. She never stopped to consider what others would think of her. According to her time and place, she could have been stoned to death or cast out to fend for herself.

Mary responded with a song: The Magnificat. The song resonates from the depths of her soul. Mary, the poor, young, unwed girl became the mother of the Son of God. The ordinary became the extraordinary. Christ was born. Some thirty-three years later, the child she bore would forever change the consciousness of the world. And, she sang, "My soul magnified the Lord."

Beloved God, let me understand the meaning of the moment. When you call, let me respond, that the Christ may be born yet again within me. Amen.

Gwynne M. Guibord

Strength in Weakness

Therefore I am content with weaknesses, insults, hardships, persecutions, and calamities for the sake of Christ; for whenever I am weak, then I am strong.
—2 Corinthians 12:10

We all have weaknesses. This may be hard to admit, but it's true. Take a moment to examine yourself. Remember that argument, that defiant thought, the "attitude," the uncontrolled eating, the fear that keeps you from doing, or the pride that pushes you to do?

Weaknesses aren't bad, according to Paul. In this passage, he is rejoicing in weakness because he sees it as another opportunity to bring glory to God. Even though the thorn in his side (see v. 7) came from a "messenger of Satan," God is using it to keep Paul from being reduced to pride, arrogance, self-righteousness, and self-worship.

The Lord said to Paul, "My grace is sufficient for you, for power is made perfect in weakness" (v. 9). God uses our weakness to show us our need for him daily and to keep us humble in his presence. He gives us grace each day that is sufficient to keep us from falling to our weaknesses.

Satan wants us to use our weaknesses to destroy us, to batter us, and to keep us in bondage to sin. This is why we need to depend so completely on God for his strength when we would fall.

We don't have to let our weaknesses rule us. We don't have to give in to them. They are not our Lord, our God, or our Savior! We don't have to allow them to be our master by doing their bidding and then living in perpetual guilt and shame.

I am sometimes tempted to allow cigarettes to slither back into my life. I walk down the street, smell the smoke, and the desire tells me, "One won't hurt!" One such day I began to call on the Lord for strength to fight the desire. I had to stop chasing the smoke and call on God to help me. He did, and he will every time! God gives grace to face each weakness, no matter what it is, every day of our lives!

Dear God, your grace is sufficient for me every day of my life. I fully depend on your strength. Amen.

Nneka Best

The Secret of Having Plenty

*I know what it is to have little, and I know what it is to
have plenty. In any and all circumstances I have
learned the secret of being well-fed and of going hungry,
of having plenty and of being in need. I can do
all things through him who strengthens me.
—Philippians 4:12-13*

When I visited Gladys for the first time in more than a year, it
was as if no time had passed. Our conversation was warm and
easy. She explained how she had come to be at the assisted living
facility she now called home. Though small, her room felt familiar because she had brought along a few of her beautiful things:
a small chest she had painted, a red wooden horse, and one of
her easy chairs.

After her fall, she had spent several weeks in the care center in
her home town. "No one wants to go there," she said, and I knew
it was true. Few private rooms, not much space for personal items,
notoriously bland food, and a large number of bed-ridden residents
who would eventually die right there. I had sent her a note of
encouragement when I learned she was there, hoping that it would
lift her spirits. But I needn't have worried.

She smiled and in a soft voice told me, "People asked me how I
could stand it there. But it was really a nice place. I had plenty to
eat and plenty of room. And God needed me there. You see, so many
of those girls, the ones who worked there, they didn't know anything about Jesus, and I needed to tell them. I did tell them. I think
they were glad."

"And now you're here," I added, "and this is a beautiful place,
with more room for your own things, and more privacy."

"Yes," she agreed. "And I'm happy here, too. This is where God
needs me now, because some of the people here need to know about
Jesus, too."

Gladys is old, weakened by strokes, unstable on her feet, and
easily confused. She slurs her words now and doesn't keep her
hair "just so" like she used to. No longer does she live in a
spacious home, brimming with beautiful things. But she has

Jesus in her heart and longs to share him with others. She knows the secret of "having plenty."

Loving God, show me the deep contentment that comes from trusting you. Put me where you need me, and in that place let my life speak to others about the joy of your presence. Amen.

Jennifer M. Ginn

Following the Call

Orpah kissed her mother-in-law, but Ruth clung to her.
So [Naomi] said, "See, your sister-in-law has gone back
to her people and to her gods; return after your
sister-in-law." But Ruth said, "Do not press me to leave
you or to turn back from following you! Where you go,
I will go; where you lodge, I will lodge; your people
shall be my people, and your God my God."
—Ruth 1:14-16

Ruth's self-sacrifice makes her one of only two women honored to have an Old Testament book named for her.

For family caregivers today, she is an icon. She sets a standard that is almost impossible to match. Neither guilt nor societal pressure dictated her choice. In fact, she was out of step with her culture.

She had only one motivation: love.

But what of Orpah, the sister-in-law? She returned to her people, which was the expected thing to do, the cultural norm. Presumably it was the easier route. We don't know; we never hear of her again. All we know is that Ruth had a very clear call from God to stay with Naomi. Perhaps God had other plans for Orpah.

Initially she wept and insisted she too would stay with Naomi. But her mother-in-law dissuaded her. Still weeping, Orpah kissed Naomi goodbye. She must have walked away with a heavy heart. Did she needlessly add to her burden by comparing herself unfavorably with Ruth, blaming herself for not taking on the challenge Ruth was confronting?

Do we too needlessly compare ourselves with others who bear

a larger burden? Do we belittle our own efforts even when we're doing our best?

Caring for family members frequently involves making difficult choices. One of the hardest is deciding whether or when to move a loved one to a nursing home. Sometimes what may seem the "easy" choice to others is really quite painful. We can only listen and then take the route that God places before us.

I pray that I remember God gives me a calling that is mine alone, and that I follow the path that is true for me. Amen.

Mary Koch

Gifts from the Father

Now there are varieties of gifts, but the same Spirit;
and there are varieties of services, but the same Lord...
—1 Corinthians 12:4-5

One sunny fall day, a friend and I skipped lunch to take a walk in the park. We enjoyed the breeze that swirled around us, as well as the colorful falling leaves. I stopped and picked up a multi-colored leaf and, while showing it to my friend, mentioned how beautiful it was. She quickly commented that there were small holes in the leaf that detracted from its beauty. I didn't think the flaws made the colors less vibrant or changed its shape, so I responded, "It's like us, not perfect!"

God loved us into existence and chose this time in history for you and me to be exactly where we are in God's world. God has made each of us different in beautiful ways by giving us personal gifts that we can use throughout our lifetime to glorify God. Needless to say, these gifts won't make us perfect, so we must first accept our flaws, which resemble those holes in the leaf. And in spite of the flaws, we must go forward, using our gifts to share God's love with our sisters and others.

I can think of many women who have outgoing personalities and who are always cheerful, smiling, always ready to help anytime and anywhere help is needed. Being cordial and pleasant is a gift to share, one that is easy to use. With constant use, it can become a habit for a lifetime.

There are also women who have extended and enhanced their gifts through education and practice. Because of their dedication they have helped improve the lives of many people in their communities and their country while at the same time glorifying God. How fortunate we are that they ignored their flaws and instead built the future on their gifts. In doing so, they both achieved their own goals and helped others as well.

Lord, help me to see the best in the people and things around me, and use me to encourage others to do likewise. Bless me with a positive attitude to deal with whatever comes my way today. Amen.
Marie Compton

More Than I Can Handle?

Are they ministers of Christ? I am talking like a madman—I am a better one: with far greater labors, far more imprisonments, with countless floggings, and often near death. Five times I have received from the Jews the forty lashes minus one. Three times I was beaten with rods. Once I received a stoning. Three times I was shipwrecked; for a night and a day I was adrift at sea...
—2 Corinthians 11:23-25

Have you ever thought of just giving up? Just quitting? Has life ever dealt you such blows that you just didn't think you would recover? When you get a chance, read the entire list of "trials" that Paul experienced in 2 Corinthians 11:23-33. It is a wonder that Paul didn't cry out, "This is too much! I cannot deal with this! God has asked too much of me this time!" But there is no record that he ever cried out in this fashion.

Rather, Paul is known to have said, "I have learned to be content whatever the circumstances" (Philippians 4:11, NIV). That is not always an easy thing to hear, is it? This is especially the case if we have gained an extra thirty pounds or more, or if we have a skin disease that people are prone to stare at or if an operation has left an unsightly scar.

What Paul said in 1 Corinthians 10:13 probably has something to do with the fact that he did not complain: "No testing has overtaken you that is not common to everyone." Whatever you are dealing with in your life, it is not so unique that no one has ever dealt with the same problem. God is faithful and will not let you be tempted beyond your strength. In Isaiah 41:10 we read, "Don't be afraid, for I am with you. Don't tremble with fear, for I am your God. I will make you strong, as I protect you with my arm and give you victories" (paraphrased). God is saying that we can depend on him to help us in time of trouble and need.

Paul had learned that God is faithful time after time after time. Turn that idea around, and what it says is that if you are facing some struggle, you can handle it with God's help, because if you could not deal with it, God would not let you be faced with it.

So when a problem, trial, or struggle walks up and looks you square in the eye, remember what Paul learned: "God is faithful, and he will not let you be tested beyond your strength, but with the testing he will also provide the way out so that you may be able to endure it" (1 Corinthians 10:13).

Oh loving Lord, we ask for the patience to endure those events in our lives that lead us to despair. We seek your strength and your wisdom to remain faithful at all times. Amen.

Elizabeth Oikkers Killeen

Removing the Blindfold

"Woman, behold your son!"
—John 19:26, NKJV

Lenten tradition has called this verse the "word of affection." But as a mother myself, I wonder how Mary heard those words. She is in anguish as she watches Jesus struggle for each breath. Her beloved son is dying, and in these moments, Mary's entire being is centered on him.

"Behold your son"? "*You* are my son," her heart whispers in bewilderment. But Jesus is looking at the disciple beside her, offering that man in his own place. A substitute even while she watches her own son die in agony? How could Jesus of all people be so callous, so disrespectful of Mary's grief?

How many mothers have watched their children dying . . . in hospitals, in prisons, in wars, in broken relationships, in broken minds, in prodigal lives? And how many of those mothers would hear affection in words such as these? Where is the love in offering a substitute while one's own child still struggles for breath and life?

Yet the Jesus I know is the incarnation of love, compassion, and sensitivity. So what purpose did he have in speaking these dying words: "Woman, behold your son"? What healing is there in such a salty salve? I am convinced that, like Christ's other last words, this so-called word of affection was fundamentally a word of ministry.

Like any parent facing the devastating loss of a beloved child, Mary is in danger of being crushed by her grief. So summoning his last breaths, Jesus says tenderly, "Woman, behold your son." In so doing, Christ turned his mother's attention to another who was equally grief-stricken and in need of her ministry. When in her grief Mary could see only Jesus, Jesus himself called on her to minister to the one who was at her side, one whom Jesus also deeply loved.

Especially in the Lenten season, when our hearts are rightly focused on our dying Lord, Jesus himself reminds us with a word of tender affection to behold the other. And to minister to those others as sons, daughters, mothers, fathers, friends.

Precious Jesus, thank you for the reminder that the truest act of worship I can offer to you is an act of service to the ones you love. Amen.

Rebecca Irwin–Diehl

Whom Are You Reflecting?

*And all of us have had that veil removed so that we can
be mirrors that brightly reflect the glory of the Lord.
And as the Spirit of the Lord works within us, we become
more and more like him and reflect his glory even more.*
—2 Corinthians 3:18, New Living Translation

Have you looked in a mirror lately? If you're like most people, during the course of the day you have glanced there a few times. For some of us, it is a daunting task to view the effects of time, while others are content with what they see. If we look long enough, we are bound to notice the most minuscule things—a hair out of place, perhaps the first stage of an unwanted blemish, or certain body parts succumbing to the laws of gravity. Whatever the case, we are focused on improvement, and we do what we can to make sure we like what the mirror reflects.

There is nothing wrong with improving ourselves physically. But we should put at least as much effort into improving ourselves spiritually and to making the changes necessary to do so. God made it clear in the beginning that we are made in God's image (Genesis 1:27). We are patterned after God's likeness. Not only do we represent God, we also embody God's glory (1 Corinthians 11:7). It is God's glory that those around us need to see.

We are God's mirrors. A mirror is a surface that reflects light to form a true and accurate image of whatever is before it. Two things are necessary in order for a mirror to function: light and an object to project. As God's mirrors, we need to allow the light of the Holy Spirit to reflect upon us, thus projecting the image of Christ. To properly produce God's image we need to study the Word and imitate Jesus in every area of our lives.

Let's allow the fruit of the Spirit to reign in our hearts so that our words and actions reveal God's inner workings. Let's allow the Lord to have his way in us so that when others look, they will see him. If we do this—fashion our lives after Jesus—then our trips to the mirror will be more rewarding.

*Heavenly Father, in the matchless name of Jesus, help me to
walk in the full understanding of who you've created me to be. May*

*the words that flow from my mouth be words that heal hearts,
encourage souls, and speak the truth in love. May my thoughts line
up with your Word, so that the fruit of the Spirit will spring forth in
every action and deed I perform today. Amen.*

Lisa R. Jackson

Standing against the Crowd

*When he heard that it was Jesus of Nazareth,
he began to shout out and say, "Jesus, Son of David,
have mercy on me!" Many sternly ordered him
to be quiet, but he cried out even more loudly,
"Son of David, have mercy on me!"*
—Mark 10:47-48

Blind Bartimaeus hears that Jesus is coming and begins to call out.
The crowd surrounding him doesn't just tell him to be quiet; they
sternly order him to be quiet. Bartimaeus can do as the crowd
orders, or he can continue calling out. He chooses to call out louder
to Jesus. Bartimaeus wanted to be heard. Knowing that Jesus could
heal him, he was not going to let the crowd stop him. He used what
faculties he had—mainly his voice—to call out and be heard.

We too are given those moments of choice. Our communities
bear witness to the wounding effects of racism, prejudice, intolerance, evil, and injustice of all sorts. We are called to see with God's
eyes and be awakened to the reality of the world around us. We are
also called to be God's presence in this world, to be a part of the
answer to its problems. We are not to be silent but are called, in
some way, to take a stand. So often the world tries to silence us:
"Don't rock the boat; don't initiate change." Yet as Christians we
are called to stand up for truth and justice. We are called to bear
God's love to all of God's creation. When the world tries to silence
us, we are called like Bartimaeus to use whatever faculties and
talents we have to call out even louder until our voices are heard
and God's will is done.

Loving Lord, help me to see the world through your eyes. And

*help me to be a vehicle of your truth and love to a world broken
and yearning for you. Amen.*

Debbie H. Deane

Institutionalized Faith

*These people draw near with their mouths
and honor me with their lips, while their hearts
are far from me, and their worship of me
is a human commandment learned by rote.
—Isaiah 29:13*

In some countries, expressing religious faith is prohibitive and
dangerous. In America we have a different problem. Our faith is so
close to our culture that it can become empty and unexercised. Our
economy promotes in-kind and charitable contributions. Our consumerism is based on a forty-hour workweek and then a sabbath
rest, preferably spent shopping. Our creeds and litanies often make
it into our civil ceremonies, and our civil creeds very often make it
into our religious experiences.

But at an even more personal level, the majority of U.S. citizens
are familiar with church services, petitional prayer, and the Scriptures. Perhaps so familiar that we fail to personalize our faith, fail
to value it, fail to take the next step from being God's privileged to
choosing to be God's disciples.

In the Old Testament Scriptures God tells and retells of his
exhaustion with his "chosen" people. The progression of faithlessness went from the crucible of faith to an institutionalized faith to
acts of idolatry and the internalization of new belief systems. Why?
Because their faith had become little more than their culture.

It does an injustice to God, to ourselves, and to others when we
reduce our faith to the experience of culture. Culture is what we
make of life. It is our fingerprint in this human drama. But faith,
true faith, runs deeper. It supercedes what culture can contain. Faith
is our living litany with God. Faith is not something we do, nor is
it an association we belong to. Faith is what we know of God at the

most basic level. Eugene Peterson puts it best in his version of Romans 3:28 in *The Message*: "What we've learned is this: God does not respond to what *we* do; we respond to what *God* does. We've finally figured it out. Our lives get in step with God and all others by letting him set the pace, not by proudly or anxiously trying to run the parade."

Lord, be my all in all. Enter into my culture, my life, with your life. Break open these confining and rote ways in which I have been experiencing you. Amen.

Rachel Matheson Ommen

On Being Remembered

"Why do you trouble the woman? She has performed
a good service for me…Truly I tell you, wherever
this good news is proclaimed in the whole world,
what she has done will be told in remembrance of her."
—Matthew 26:10b,13

In Matthew's Gospel, this woman who anoints Jesus has no name. In another parallel passage (John 12), she is Mary of Bethany. The importance is not in who she is but in what she does. She prefigures Jesus. Broken and spilled out, the costly perfume in her alabaster jar suggests the very body of Jesus that will be broken, his blood spilled out for us. She knew what she was doing. By going to the dinner and entering men's forbidden space as they reclined and ate, she broke all the rules and violated her society's taboos. She transgressed for a greater good, that of marking Jesus as the anointed one of God.

By touching a man who was not related to her by birth or marriage, this woman put herself in jeopardy. By using the costly pound of pure nard on one person, she was being generous beyond what anyone else could comprehend. Surely she was not being the kind of steward of resources that others expected her to be. Her extravagance was a shadow of the sacrifice that Jesus would make.

By wiping Jesus' feet with her hair, she was touching Jesus in a

341

way that no woman of her time and place would ever do in public. It was a wanton gesture born of her profound belief in Jesus as Messiah. Her disregard for the opinions of others parallels Jesus' single-minded devotion to doing the will of God.

The woman who anointed Jesus points to and prefigures what happens to him. Her sacrifice and extravagant demonstration of her love sets the stage for Jesus on the cross and for his death so that we might have eternal life.

"What she has done will be told in remembrance of her," Jesus said. And so it has been. I wonder what will be told about me, about my words and deeds. What will be told about you? I'd like to be remembered in a similar way as the woman who anointed Jesus. May it be so.

Dear God, thank you for the wonderful women of the Gospels, those with and those without names. May their courage be ours; may their boldness be ours; may their heritage to us be preserved. Hear us for your Son's sake. Amen.

Janet K. Hess

Note: Dr. Louise Shoemaker retired recently after many years as Dean of the School of Social Work at the University of Pennsylvania in Philadelphia. She is a strong Lutheran lay person and a mentor to social workers worldwide.

Keeping Up with the Joneses

Teach me, O LORD, the way of your statutes,
and I will observe it to the end. Give me understanding,
that I may keep your law and observe it with my whole
heart. Lead me in the path of your commandments,
for I delight in it. Turn my heart to your decrees
and not to selfish gain. Turn my eyes from looking
at vanities; give me life in your ways.
—Psalm 119:33-37

How many times I have envied my siblings or friends for that new dress, that new couch, or new car, or home, or the vacations they could afford! How often I have longed for their luxuries in my life. Yet God in his wisdom and sovereign will had other plans for me, plans I didn't understand. So often, I have discovered only later that many of those same friends had pain in their lives of which I wasn't aware and from which I had been spared.

When Jesus encountered the disciples on the beach in John 21, Peter asked Jesus what his plans were for John: "Lord, what about him?" Jesus said to him, "If it is my will that he remain until I come, what is that to you?" (John 21:21-22). How convicting that statement is! God is infinitely wise and sovereign in his plan for each of us. God places us in different stations and arenas as testimony to him.

Focus on following after God and not envying what God has given others. Undoubtedly there are thorns in their paths, too. The less God gives you of the world, the more you have to depend upon God, and the sweeter your intimate knowledge will be of God's love. God's plan for you is unique. Trust God with every detail of your life.

Lord, forgive my desires for selfish gain. Turn my eyes away from the worthless luxuries of this world and help me to follow close after you. Forgive me for envying those who seemingly have more than I have. Help me to glorify you with what you have given me. May I honor you in all ways—with or without possessions—and be grateful for all you have given me. Amen.

Lavonne Hall

That All May Go
Well with You

Honor your father and your mother,
as the LORD your God commanded you, so that
your days may be long and that it may go well with you
in the land that the LORD your God is giving you.
—Deuteronomy 5:16

In 1995 I had the opportunity to travel to mainland China with an international bioethics delegation. One of the most enduring images I have from that trip is of a Chinese nurse, the director of nursing for a small hospital in a rural area. Lighting there was limited, the humidity was high, and the conditions were poor. Nevertheless, it was evident that this place was rich with love. The nurse took great pride in telling us how the staff cared for patients and how she educated the young doctors to respect their elders. She required doctors to be present with patients on their birthdays and to spend time with them in order to learn the value of wisdom that comes with age.

We miss so much of that in our Euro-American society. We separate those who are ill and those who are aging from their family members, as well as from the rest of society. We often treat doctors with respect beyond the wisdom of their years. We have made aging a disease to be avoided at all cost rather than considering it a natural part of life. We have taught our young to fear age rather than respect it. We spend outrageous amounts of money on products that will make us look younger and are willing to replace body parts to maintain the image of youth. Yet none of us will leave this life alive in body.

Until we are able to see all people of all ages—sick or well—as part of the whole body of humanity, we will experience only a fragment of God's wonderful creation. The Ten Commandments instruct us to honor our parents [elders] "that your [our] days may be long and it may go well with you [us]."

Lord God Almighty, help us to learn to understand and follow this commandment. Help us to regard aging and illness as natural parts of life.

Help us to see those who are aging as honored ones who have learned from their years and who can impart to us the wisdom of those years. Amen.

Jackie Sullivan

"'Tis a Puzzlement"

The wise woman builds her house,
but the foolish tears it down with her own hands.
—Proverbs 14:1

As women, especially mothers, God endows us with gifts for nurturing. When our children are infants, they depend on us for virtually every need. Little by little, as they mature, their dependency decreases. When our children reach adulthood, one would think it would be easier to stand back and allow them to place the pieces of their life in order. Unfortunately, for many of us, it is not.

As a teenager, I baby-sat for a family in the neighborhood. On one occasion, the father had set up a card table with the early stages of a very large puzzle. Normally, caring for these children was fun, but I became distracted with that pile of disconnected art. I found myself drawn to the puzzle in an effort to find one or two pieces to link with his connected pieces.

After hurrying the children to bed, I feverishly went to work. Excitement grew with each little jagged piece of cardboard placed in its proper position. I was amazed at my ability to spot and connect, and I was baffled by his inability to do the same. By the time the parents returned, the puzzle was nearly completed. As they walked into the living room, I looked up in pride and anticipation.

The mother was diplomatic. However, the husband was noticeably silent, his lips and jaw clamped so tightly shut I thought he might crush a molar. I don't recall them ever asking me to baby-sit again.

Our heavenly Abba has given each of us pieces to complete the puzzle of our lives and desires us to come to him to find and connect the pieces. There is no greater satisfaction than seeing the pieces of our lives transformed into a beautiful picture. God may use us to find a piece or two in someone else's puzzle. But we should never deprive any person of the joy and satisfaction of working on his or her own puzzle.

Thank you, Abba, for helping me with my puzzle. I trust you to find the pieces in my life. Help me to allow others, especially loved ones, to seek your help in putting together their own puzzles. Amen.

Terri Gillespie

Wholeness for a Samaritan Community

"I have come to call not the righteous
but sinners to repentance."
—Luke 5:32

Others avoided traveling through Samaria because of the prejudice against the Samaritans. But Jesus took no short cuts. Traveling the back roads, it took about two and a half days to get from Judea to Galilee: a distance of about seventy miles. Jesus walked through Samaria.

Weary, exhausted and thirsty, Jesus sat to rest at Jacob's well. A woman approached and began to draw water. Jesus asked if he might have a drink also. Recognizing his apparel—and astounded that he even spoke to her—she replied, "You aren't to have any dealings with me."

The Samaritan woman tried to avoid those who taunted her for the unwise choices she made about the men in her life. Jesus had a physical need: he was thirsty. But she had a spiritual need to drink from the life-giving stream of living water, which would quench her spiritual thirst forever. He looked beyond her faults and saw her need.

Jesus began to engage in conversation with the woman. He said, "If you only knew who I am. He imparted the message of salvation to her: "Go call your husband and come back," he told her.

"I have no husband," she said.

Jesus responded, "You have answered correctly. Even the man you are currently with is not your husband."

She quickly changed the subject by talking about the Messiah who was to come. Jesus reaffirmed her suspicion by saying, "I am he."

"Sir, give me this water; quench this thirst I have. Make me whole."

The woman received the Word of God, left her water jar, and ran into the city, shouting words about "a man who told me all the things I've ever done even in my private life and forgave me and made me whole."

Despite her reputation, other Samaritans heard her testimony and came to know Jesus.

Lord, teach us to face our fears, to tell our story and not be afraid to go through our Samaria. Sometimes our journey takes unwelcome paths, but you, Lord, always go before us and remain with us until the task is done. Help us as we commit to making our communities whole and to remember that wholeness begins with you. Amen.

Portia George

Forgiving Daily

"And in anger his lord handed him over to be tortured until he would pay his entire debt. So my heavenly Father will also do to every one of you, if you do not forgive your brother or sister from your heart."
—Matthew 18:34-35

Anne Lamott writes in her book *Traveling Mercies*: "Not forgiving is like drinking rat poison and then waiting for the rat to die." The biblical view of forgiveness appears in the story of a slave who owed the king an amount of money so great that it could never be repaid. The king demanded payment but then was gracious and discharged the debt when the slave begged for more time to obtain the money.

However, the slave immediately demanded payment of a small debt from a fellow slave. Even though his friend pleaded for more time, the lender refused, and the borrower was thrown into prison until payment could be made. When the king heard this, he was furious. He turned the evil servant over to be tortured until his debt was paid in full. Then Jesus said: "So my heavenly Father will also do to every one of you if you do not forgive your brother or sister from your heart." Wow! That's a tough sentence! What could Jesus possibly mean?

I believe that the torture comes from within ourselves from the damage our lack of forgiveness does to us. We have no peace. We have no joy. We may exhibit physical, spiritual, and emotional problems that are directly related to our unwillingness to forgive. We poison ourselves bit by bit.

The 2000 Easter issue of *Parade* magazine featured a lengthy article on forgiveness. The writer interviewed several people who were hurt so deeply by the actions of others that their lives changed permanently. The trespasses included rape, murder of a parent, murder of a child, and paralysis resulting from a gunshot wound. But instead of expressing their hostility, all those who had been wronged spoke of their need to forgive. Forgiveness for them wasn't a one-time event. Rather, it was something they needed to do daily.

We are called to forgive over and over—both for our own benefit and for the benefit of those who need our forgiveness. Let's take the antidote to a slow death by practicing forgiveness.

God, thank you for the forgiveness you continue to offer us. Help us to work through our woundedness so that we are free to forgive those who hurt us. Amen.

Jo Ellen Witt

Seeing Through God's Eyes

When Elizabeth heard Mary's greeting, the child leaped in her womb. And Elizabeth was filled with the Holy Spirit and exclaimed with a loud cry, "Blessed are you among women, and blessed is the fruit of your womb. And why has this happened to me, that the mother of my Lord comes to me?"
—Luke 1:41-43

If it isn't one thing, it's a half-dozen others. Problems never seem to come one at a time. Elizabeth, mother of John, had what we call a plateful. First her husband, Zechariah, loses his speech. This could be tough for a priest. How could he perform his duties? Did they have disability insurance?

Then Elizabeth discovers she's pregnant. Sure, she's thrilled, but it's a late-in-life pregnancy—risky for both mother and child. In such delicate condition, Elizabeth spends five months in seclusion. Then who should show up but her young, unmarried, and pregnant relative, Mary?

Elizabeth begins to feel activity in her womb—not a good sign from a modern medical point of view.

From our perspective, Elizabeth's situation looks desperate: An aging couple with a disabled wage earner, no Social Security or Medicare, stiff medical bills ahead, and another family member in even bigger trouble seeking aid and comfort.

But Elizabeth doesn't see it that way. She recognizes the activity in her womb as her baby leaping for joy. And she declares to Mary, "Blessed are you among women and blessed is the child you will bear."

Elizabeth is looking at the situation through God's eyes, from God's perspective.

How often are we faced with "desperate situations" only because we're looking at them from the wrong perspective? What happens when we step back to see things through God's eyes? At the very least, our half-empty glass becomes half-full.

The realities that faced Elizabeth and Mary were daunting. Yet they were thrilled. "The Lord has done this for me," declares

Elizabeth. "From now on all generations will call me blessed," exults Mary.

First, these women accepted God's assignments. Then they could do nothing but rejoice.

Dear God, I pray that when I am burdened by problems, I will be given eyes to look anew. May I accept God's calling and see my reality as a piece of divine wisdom. Amen.

Mary Koch

Repay with a Blessing

Do not repay evil for evil or abuse for abuse, but,
on the contrary, repay with a blessing. It is for this that
you were called—that you might inherit a blessing.
—1 Peter 3:9

Have you ever noticed the expressions on the faces of people caught in a traffic jam? How about people standing in line at the grocery store? What do their faces reveal? Why are we always in such a hurry? Now ask yourself: how patiently do I wait?

Think about Jesus. The Father gave him a most important task, a limited time to fulfill the mission, and insurmountable obstacles to overcome. Yet Jesus knew what he had to do, and he did not repay evil for evil or abuse for abuse. He repaid with a blessing. During his ministry he went about loving, healing, forgiving, and encouraging. We are to do likewise.

If Jesus were caught in a traffic jam, how do you think he might react? He would probably pray for the cause—perhaps an accident or a car that has broken down. I suspect he would ask God's safety and mercy for each person involved. While you are waiting, pray. Here you are with this free time, so why waste precious moments getting agitated?

Picture our Lord standing in line at a grocery store; the line is long and moving slowly. What might he do? I can see him striking up a conversation with the person next to him, sharing faith stories. Not long ago I was praying in a public place and was unaware I was praying out loud. A woman next to me asked if I was talking to her. I apologized and told her I was praying. She said, "Don't apologize for praying. Prayer is the answer." She was a real blessing. God is so good!

Someone has said that we live in "an age of rage," an age in which so many are in such a hurry and are so easily agitated. Let's remember that life is too fragile and short to rush through. Let us purpose in our hearts to ask what Jesus would do in one of today's stressful situations. How would he respond?

Dear God, help us to slow down, to learn patience, and to remember the value of prayer at all times. Help us also to be instruments of your peace. Jesus is our peace. Inspire us to be like Jesus, for we pray in his name. Amen.

Betty Susi

Of Discipleship and Discipline

*Then Jesus told his disciples, "If any want
to become my followers, let them deny themselves
and take up their cross and follow me."
—Matthew 16:24*

About fifteen years ago, I bought my piece of the American dream. It's a Victorian cottage built in 1902 on a tree-lined street near a park. I was an avid viewer of PBS, including the home shows where the experts take an architectural eyesore and in six thirty-minute segments turn it into a showplace. Well, I signed the deed and assumed that with a little sweat equity and creative design work, my old house would take its place on the home tour. In retrospect, I can only say I was idealistic, impressionable, and ignorant.

Some good things have happened in fifteen years: the floor furnaces and window air conditioning units have given way to central air and heat. The kitchen has been remodeled. Layers of wallpaper have been stripped and rehung. I have stripped and refinished hardwood floors and trim work, replaced dry-rotted carpet, patched cracked plaster, rewired light fixtures, and painted a score of ten-and-a-half-foot ceilings.

But some days it feels like every success is followed by two or three setbacks: shattered window panes, rotting gutters, hail damage, leaking roof, hissing toilet, broken water pipes. My old house is a fifteen-year investment of energy, creativity, and resources. In the course of this experience, I have learned something: Nobody can restore an old house in six thirty-minute segments. I am now certain that it will take more resources, time, and energy than my lifetime will ever afford.

The same long-term commitment and constant vigilance is required for discipleship. It doesn't happen with an hour here, a couple hours there, a few Bible study sessions, overnight retreats, or crusade rallies. Spiritual growth occurs as God's Spirit renews, restores, and refreshes the spirit of God's people and energizes us for community, and identity, and mission.

Eternal God, may your Spirit move in us to be patient, to create our own vibrant spirit that carries hope, that believes in peace, and that is filled with your goodness. Amen.

Linda G. Frost

Mary's "Yes"

Then Mary said, "Here am I, the servant of the Lord;
let it be with me according to your word."
—Luke 1:38
(Read Luke 1:26-38 for the full context.)

The story of Mary is familiar: how the angel appeared to her saying she had been chosen to bring the Messiah into the world and how she responded with a simple "Yes." As I meditate on this story, I often wonder how many Marys there were before this Mary of Nazareth. Is it possible that the angel appeared to others with the same message, but due to fear or lack of faith they were not able to listen or give their affirmation?

Just a few verses before we read how Zechariah did not believe the angel's message, and so he was struck mute and had to watch in silence as God's divine plan unfolded. Perhaps there were others

waiting, watching in silence, unable to participate actively. But
Mary was different. She listened, pondered, questioned, and listened some more. Then she gave herself. She didn't say, "Okay, *I*
will do it." She said, "Let it be with me according to your word."
She let go of control and allowed God to do with her as God desired.
With her willingness, God began the greatest miracle of all. God
took on human form so that we might know divine love.

God calls us with a similar message: to let go and let God take
control, to be transformed. Our response is not to be made
lightly. We, like Mary, need to stop, listen, and prayerfully
ponder. We have the choice to refuse, for whatever reason, or to
take that next step by saying, "Yes, I am willing to be used in
whatever way you desire." Often God calls us to step into the
unknown, promising to remain with us and to give us the necessary faith and courage. By letting go, by being willing to say yes
to God, we become God's healing hands stretched out to a world
in need. We become God's servants of love, bringing healing and
wholeness to all of God's creation. We need only be willing to allow
God control of our lives.

Loving Lord, help me to give myself to you. Use me to bring your
love and healing to this broken world that all may know you and
your love. Amen.

Debbie H. Deane

The Significance of a Name

"Blessed are the merciful, for they will receive mercy.
Blessed are the pure in heart,
for they will see God. Blessed are the peacemakers,
for they will be called children of God."
—Matthew 5:7-9

Naming and its significance are of great importance in biblical
stories. Remember Abram who becomes Abraham; Jacob who becomes Israel; and Saul who becomes Paul. If you know people from
Africa, you know the importance of naming in their cultures. I think,

for example, of a friend born in what was then Rhodesia. His name meant, "Before I die, we shall have prevailed." While I knew him, Rhodesia became Zimbabwe. My friend was an historian and activist who had assisted in that transition.

Another friend from South Africa was studying at a seminary in central Pennsylvania. With her was her adopted daughter whom she had found abandoned as a baby in the slums of Soweto. In typical African style, our friend had chosen her daughter's name with care, knowing that names have significance and can influence behavior.

The child was about twelve and was attending junior high school in the city where her mother was studying. There were few persons of color in that community, and the youngster found she was receiving some harassment. One boy in particular bullied her. She told her mother, who offered to talk to the boy's parents.

The next day the daughter said to her mother, "Please don't talk to his parents. I cannot make trouble for him. Remember, my name means 'Mother of goodness and kindness.' I cannot cause him any harm. I'm sure everything will be all right."

Our friend shared this story with us, in amazement at her daughter's sensitivity, maturity, and compassion.

Do you know the meaning of your name?

God—our mother of goodness and kindness, our father of compassion and wisdom, our sister of warmth and forgiveness, our brother of strength and support—help us all to remember that we are called as your children to be merciful, to be peacemakers, to be pure in heart. Help us to remember our true names. Amen.

Elizabeth V. McDowell

Holy Bothering

"In a certain city there was a judge who neither feared
God nor had respect for people. In that city there was a
widow who kept coming to him and saying, 'Grant me
justice against my opponent.' For a while he refused;
but later he said to himself, 'Though I have no fear of
God and no respect for anyone, yet because this widow
keeps bothering me, I will grant her justice, so that
she may not wear me out by continually coming.'"
—Luke 18:2-5

Our world is so often an unsafe place. It is unsafe especially for women overseas who have few rights and even fewer resources. As I write these words, four women—all service wives—were recent victims of domestic violence, brutally killed by their Army husbands at a nearby fort. And a woman from Nigeria, accused of adultery, awaits her fate: to be stoned to death as soon as she finishes the breastfeeding of her out-of-wedlock baby.

The violence is not limited to women, as snipers on the East Coast of the United States proved in the fall of 2002. Not all senseless acts of violence garner national publicity. But it seems that virtually every day we hear reports of someone who was young and caring and had so much to give whose life was cut short as a result of the epidemic of violence.

We ought to be so bothered that, like Luke's persistent widow, we take up the cause and press—again and again in whatever ways we can—for an end to violence. It is a holy cause, one in which we can make a difference.

Late in 2002 the World Health Organization gave us some help. It issued its landmark "World Report on Violence and Health," noting that violence around the world killed 1.6 million people in 2000. This first-of-its-kind report is not just a grim cataloging of human suffering. It helps people see violence as a global health issue. It posits that, as other "diseases" have been eradicated or mitigated, the same can be true of violence.

This report and its concrete objectives are designed to help governments and people view violence as a preventable health problem. Noting the common patterns that accompany various kinds of violence, the report observes that we as a world have what it takes to prevent violence. Possible initiatives range from anger management training in elementary schools to limiting the availability of weapons. In sum, violence is something we must never accept no matter how long it may take to eradicate it.

Oh, God, help us to be as persistent as Luke's widow. Open our eyes and ears and voices to our role in helping to combat violence. Help us to do the holy work of bothering the specter—and the reality—of violence until, with your help and power, we wear it down and out. Amen.

Nancy J. Stelling

Sticks and Stones...

...admonish the idlers, encourage the faint hearted,
help the weak, be patient with all of them.
See that none of you repays evil for evil,
but always seek to do good to one another and to all.
—1 Thessalonians 5:14-15

In Exodus 34:1, God told Moses he would replace the tablets "which you broke." Each time I read this passage, I imagine how that statement must have smarted to Moses. God himself inscribed his commandments for all humankind, and in a temper tantrum, Moses hurled them onto the rocks, smashing them to bits. I am so glad it wasn't me!

But when I think about it, how different am I? God calls us living epistles, human letters. Surely these living letters are more valuable to God than words written on stone. Yet I, in times of anger, frustration, pain, or disappointment, have shown myself capable of breaking God's living letters. No, I never smashed anyone against a mountain, but each time I throw negative, hurtful words at someone, I am splintering something God created.

Proverbs 18:21 says that death and life are in the power of the tongue. With my tongue I have the power to build up and the power to tear down. When I use words to wound others, I am no better than Moses was the sorrowful day he shattered the Ten Commandments.

Dear God, please help me to watch my tongue. Let the words of my mouth edify and encourage my family, friends, and everyone you place in my path today. Amen.

Sherry Elmer

At the Crossroads

They wept aloud again. Orpah kissed her mother-in-law, but Ruth clung to her.
—Ruth 1:14

Orpah and Ruth were Moabites by birth. They married foreigners in their country, sons of Naomi and Elimelech. Elimelech's death is followed by the deaths of both his sons. Naomi is left with the two young wives in her household. The famine she and her family had left their homeland to escape was long over, and Naomi longed to go home to her people.

Both daughters-in-law head out with her. But Naomi has second thoughts and tells them to return to the homes of their parents, to remain in their own homeland.

That was a big decision for two young women. Orpah decides to go home to that which is familiar. An understandable and honorable decision. Ruth, on the other hand, wants to continue on with Naomi. She boldly states, "Where you go, I will go; where you lodge, I will lodge, your people shall be my people." Her story is important enough that a separate book in the Old Testament is named after her.

Ruth and her sister-in-law had choices. They each made a different choice. One chose the familiar, the other the unknown. Having lived in various towns, I am often amazed at the number of people who live where they were born. I have chosen to heed callings that have taken me many places. Something within us either sends us forth or keeps us in the familiar. One choice is not "better" than the other.

There are times when we are at the crossroads as were Ruth and Orpah. In those times, may the God of all goodness give us the courage to make the decision God would have us make.

God of compassion, you created the world to change constantly, sometimes gradually, sometimes suddenly. As the transitions come into our lives, help us to make the necessary choices, keeping in mind your ever-present love. Amen.

Julia D. Shreve

Defining Success

This book of the law shall not depart out of your mouth; you shall meditate on it day and night, so that you may be careful to act in accordance with all that is written in it. For then you shall make your way prosperous, and then you shall be successful.
—Joshua 1:8

You volunteer to chair committees at your church or PTA because you want things done right. As a young woman you were taught that if you want something done right, you have to do it yourself. Therefore, you are the first to commit to make costumes for the children's holiday play or organize the car pool. Striving to be successful in the corporate world, you stay late and arrive early. In business, all your projects are completed "on schedule and under budget."

You go out of your way to make sure that every aspect of your life spells success. You attend the successful parenting seminars at the church to make sure your children reflect what a good mother you are. Maybe you don't have kids, but you make sure that you never miss your nieces' and nephews' birthdays, and you can be counted on to give the best Christmas presents. At church you are always ready to "bless someone" or to help out whenever you can to ensure that parties, fundraisers, and other social events are a success.

Successful mother, successful wife, successful businesswoman, successful Christian. Does your drive to succeed include your relationship with Jesus Christ? But who's defining your success? When you allow others to define your success, you have to follow their rules. In our desire to be successful, we run the risk of becoming people pleasers, and we set ourselves up for failure. We end up falling short of others' expectations as well as our own unrealistic standards of success.

However, God's Word provides us with a foolproof plan for success. God tells us not to let the Book of the Law depart out of our mouth. We are to speak God's word over our lives and life's circumstances. We must do what God says we should do, not what others think we should do. As women of God we are to look to God, not to those around us, to determine our success. We must abandon our need to carry everyone's burdens. We are truly liberated not when we take on additional cares and responsibilities, but when we cast the care for our families, church, and jobs on him (1 Peter 5:7).

God promises you that if you follow his plan, you will be successful. From this day forward, meditate on God's way of thinking and being. Begin to see yourself in Christ and know that in him, not in your own striving, you can do all things (Philippians 4:13).

Father, I commit right now to see myself as you see me. I won't look to others to determine my success. I will no longer define my worth based on society's standards or limited understanding. I will look to you and your boundless and steadfast love for my definition of success. Thank you for giving me the grace to do and be everything you say that I am. My ongoing and continuing success is sealed and secure in you. In Jesus' Name I pray. Amen.

Pamela R. Lucas

The Path of Life

You show me the path of life.
In your presence there is fullness of joy;
in your right hand are pleasures forevermore.
—Psalm 16:11

While I was on a prayer retreat this spring, I took a walk in the arboretum, following a well-worn path. The sun was shining, filtering through the trees, and making a lovely mosaic pattern on the ground. Birds were chirping a good-morning chorus. I spied a female cardinal with her dusty red coat, flitting from branch to branch. The ground was bursting with new growth. Poking up through last year's fallen leaves were trilliums and daffodils and jack-in-the-pulpits (though Jack hadn't quite arrived in the pulpits yet). I was captivated by the beauty of God's creation and the promise of new life inherent in the awakening of spring. I felt so alive, and I sighed with release.

After a while, the path I was on narrowed and then disappeared. I realized that I had lost my way. I felt a momentary panic seize me—you know, the knot in the pit of your stomach, the bile rising to the back of your throat. I immediately retraced my steps, and within a very few minutes found my way back to the main trail. As I continued down the path, I found myself anxiously looking for signs along the way. I wanted assurance that I was still on the right path.

I thought about that walk and how easily my peace had been disturbed. The clenched feeling was all too familiar. It made me realize that I had been leading a clenched life. Gently, the Spirit reminded me that I am never lost to God. There is nothing that can separate me from God's love. I am called to rest in that reality, even when things around me seem strange and I don't quite know my way.

The Bible is full of images of path-finding. It's the narrow path that leads to life, and only few who find it. The Psalmist describes God's word as a light to our path. The choice to follow God's path involves a decision to reject anxiety and even "productivity" as the rules of the day. Jesus said, "My yoke is easy and my burden is light." God calls us to enter into rest. This is a rest that involves discipline that may be "counter-cultural," and that brings life.

Creator God, you know my thoughts. You know how easily they stray from the center of your peace. Continue to call me home, and do not let me go. Remind me that your path is life and joy. Amen.

Patti Kenney Fraser

Send for the Women

Thus says the Lord of hosts: Consider, and call for the mourning women to come; send for the skilled women to come; let them quickly raise a dirge over us, so that our eyes may run down with tears, and our eyelids flow with water.
—Jeremiah 9:17-18

In the Hebrew Bible, tears were most likely a form of submission, petition, or prayer and had a spiritual and religious meaning. Tears were both a divine gift and an offering to God. It is through the ministry of tears that women of old were allowed the only profession granted to them outside of prostitution: mourning.

Many believed that because of their gender women found it easier to weep. Thus they were perceived as being weaker. As a result men encouraged the development of professional mourners, wherein women were invited to express their tears and moans.

Our culture says that learning not to cry is one way we can control what we reveal to others. It is a way of masking how we feel and what we believe ourselves to be. The tears the mourning women shed can teach us that crying is how we communicate our pain and sadness. Crying is not a sign of weakness; it is how we show the depth of our emotion. Crying invites us into the spiritual discipline of "letting go and letting God."

When we turn it all over to God, our tears flow more easily; we set aside our need to take charge, to manage. In doing so we perform an act of faith. Jeremiah, known as "the weeping prophet," understood a lot about crying. Jeremiah was obedient to God when he became exasperated with the sin before him and the frustration of pleading with God's people. He obeyed God when told to call upon the mourning women to take up where he had fallen short. These women were called to arise, awake, and act. And so are we today.

Dear God, we praise you for cleansing tears. We praise you for trusting in us and for the gifts you have bestowed upon us. We praise you for being chosen vessels for service, with both the right and the duty to shed tears. Amen.

Susan R. Street-Beavers

Appearances Versus Possibilities

*"...the LORD does not see as mortals see;
they look on the outward appearance,
but the LORD looks on the heart."
—1 Samuel 16:7b*

When King Saul floundered as Israel's leader, God sent the prophet Samuel to anoint a new king. Samuel knew only that God had chosen one of Jesse's eight sons. As the first son, Eliab, was brought before Samuel, Samuel was sure that this man was the Lord's choice. Eliab's appearance was impressive: tall and regal. Surely a man of stature and dignity like Eliab would impress us, too. But God "looks on the heart." The Lord told Samuel that Eliab was not the right man.

David was just a boy when Samuel anointed him. Yet God saw in David the possibilities. God saw boldness, courage, leadership, faithfulness, sin, repentance, joy, praise. We don't know whether Samuel could see these qualities in the young David. All that he is reported to have noticed is a "ruddy" young man with "beautiful eyes" who was "handsome."

When we choose leaders from among us, what qualities do we seek? Do we choose the ones central casting would pick on the basis of height, weight, and body build? Do we look for the obviously talented in preference to the quietly faithful? Do we seek to learn whom God would have us select?

Is there a person in your life with possibilities that aren't apparent at first glance? Could that person be a "David" in God's eyes?

O Lord, who looks tenderly upon the hearts of all your children, grant us clear eyes to see the worth of every person. Give us grace to see the possibilities! May we be encouragers and anointers of those whom you send to lead us. Amen.

Amanda Palmer

Bloom Where You're Planted

"Consider the lilies of the field, how they grow; they neither toil nor spin, yet I tell you, even Solomon in all his glory was not clothed like one of these."
—Matthew 6:28-29

Where I live, the late winter brings forth a vibrant beauty with seemingly no effort. Along the roadsides delicate heads of small flowers begin to appear. They come in a full variety of pinks and an occasional white. They don't discriminate about where they grow. They appear in the empty fields, roadside ditches, and interstate medians.

I was told that these were wildflowers, not subject to cultivation in flowerbeds. A year later, when our two small grandchildren were with us, I took them to a nearby area where we picked some of the flowers in bloom. We brought them back to our home and laid them along our back fence. This allowed the seeds to fall from the flowers naturally and thus to "plant" themselves.

It took two years before I noticed the winter phenomenon in my back yard. Today the flowers are profuse and provide a subtle beauty to our landscape. Before their blooming season is over and they have delivered their seeds for the next year, I collect some of the small flowers and put them in my flower press for making greeting cards.

The lesson I have learned from these tender blossoms is the need to "bloom where we are planted." In our retirement years my husband and I have made difficult changes. We moved to a different area of the country, far away from family, friends, and church. We have had to form new friendships, including some outside our religious tradition.

The reality of life is that death comes to us all, but even as the little flowers fade away in summer, they will come again. We, like the flowers, are assured eternal life when we place our trust and faith in Jesus Christ. The Holy Spirit sustains us in our most difficult hours.

Teach me, O Lord, to be content wherever I am. Let me bloom and grow with your love for those around me. May I add color to the lives of my neighbors, who see me as your representative here on earth. Make me worthy of their confidence. Let the beauty of Jesus be seen in me. Amen.

Mary Jo Ferreira

Living Water

"As the scripture has said, 'Out of the believer's heart shall flow rivers of living water.'"
—John 7:38

I had known the name "Mother Teresa" for as long as I could remember. And now, at the age of twenty-seven, I was standing in a sweaty crowd in Bangladesh waiting to receive her blessing.

When I reached the top of the stairs, I saw a small jam of people in the narrow hallway. My eyes scanned the floor for an indication of where Mother Teresa might be. After a few moments I noticed that between two sisters was one tiny woman I had initially overlooked. This diminutive figure was stooped under the garment she was wearing, and the people were filing by her slowly, each stopping and kneeling in front of her. This was Mother Teresa.

The crowd pressed forward, and suddenly I was in front of her, on my knees, gazing up into her face. She looked into my eyes. Though her face bore the signs of illness and exhaustion, her eyes were alive with love, kindness, and eagerness to impart a blessing on me. Though mine was one face in a crowd of a hundred and in a world of six billion, I had the sense that she saw me as God sees me: as an individual person of deep value, worthy of blessing. For a brief moment it was as if she and I were all alone in the presence of God.

As she laid her large, strong hand on my head, I felt an overwhelming rush of God's love flow through her hand to my body. It felt as if I had been touched by the hand of the Divine, though it was simply the hand of an old woman. She gave me a small pendant of the Virgin Mary, and I was up, moving away to make room for the next person to come and kneel before her.

I joined the line that was moving away and down the stairs. I inched my way into a corner, turned, and gazed on her for a few more moments as she blessed each person who knelt before her.

The spiritual glow that seemed to radiate around the old woman was flowing out in the stream of people moving away from her and down the stairs, like a river flowing out of a spring and over a waterfall. My spirit was awakened, and I felt refreshed, as if the cool waters of God's joy had washed over me on that hot day. And for the first time I realized that anyone could be a "Mother Teresa," a person through whom God pours out his abundant blessings on the world.

Dear Lord, help me to believe in you, and to gain a heart from which streams of living water flow into the lives of each person I meet. Amen.

Christie A. Eastman

An Invitation to Abundant Living

"The thief comes only to steal and kill and destroy. I
came that they may have life, and have it abundantly."
—John 10:10

What steals you away from experiencing abundant living? As I
have prayed with this Scripture over the years, my focus has been
primarily on Jesus' claim that he came so that we might live
abundant lives. Recently I felt led to focus on the entire verse.
Abundant living is the desire and the focus, but beware of the
thief that comes to steal, kill, and destroy Jesus' invitation to
abundant living.

There may be a variety of thieves in our lives that steal, kill and
destroy our living. For me the big current thief is clutter. Piles of
paper invade my prayer time as well as my daily living. And they
are keeping me from living the abundant life that Jesus is inviting
me to live. So, prayerfully, I have begun the process of reducing the
clutter. I am moving toward more freedom and less bondage.

Thieves come in many forms. They can include feelings such as
resentment, hatefulness, jealousy, and the desire for revenge.
Thieves can come in the form of unhealthy relationships, clutter,
food, or television. Our thieves may change throughout our lives,
or we may have one or two thieves that hang around constantly
trying to destroy our lives and our souls.

I invite you to pray with this Scripture, to become aware and to
name what thief may be robbing you, and to see how Jesus might
be inviting you to live more abundantly.

*Giver of life, guide me in discerning if there is any thief that is
destroying me from living the abundant life you desire for me. Then
give me the strength, wisdom, and grace to find clarity on how to
respond to your ongoing invitation to abundant living. Amen.*
                                        Sara J. Davis-Shappell

The Best Time Is Now

This is the day that the Lord has made;
let us rejoice and be glad in it.
—Psalm 118:24

The memory of a conversation that took place almost thirty years ago remains with me. A group of mothers in their thirties and forties were conversing. One said she had been happiest in high school and remembered those days with nostalgic longing. Nothing in life, not even motherhood, has surpassed her teenage years. I, on the other hand, remembered insecurity and unhappiness and a longing to grow up, as well as the fun moments of parties and proms and promising relationships.

Once, for a discussion group we belonged to, my husband wrote a paper titled, "The Best Time is Now." I agreed with him! We often think of the "good old days" when we witness some part of modern life that appalls us, but we are realistic enough to realize that those days were not always wonderful. Life is, and always has been, made up of the good and bad, happiness and sadness, contentment and discontent.

Perhaps one has to live many years to realize that each day is a gift from God, whether it brings beauty and peace or storm and sadness. With sixty-some years behind me, I am still restless and uneasy at times, happy and content at others. But one thing I am sure of: I would not return to any part of the sixty years and relive them. The focus is on today—the time I have been given—and I should work at making each day the best day of my life. A day full of activity fulfills a purpose. A day full of worship gives us contentment. A day of meditation renews us for the future. A day of travel gives us a sense of adventure. Each day has a special place in our lives. It's up to us to make the most of our days and to use them as best we can for God's special purposes.

O Giver of Days, we thank you for those we have been granted already and resolve that we will live each of those to come with new purpose and appreciation for your gifts. We repeat a morning prayer learned at camp years ago:

God has created a new day, silver and green and gold,

Live that the sunset may find us, worthy this gift to hold. Amen.
Theodora A. Boolin

Vision Correction

"A nobleman went to a distant country to get royal
power for himself and then return. He summoned ten
of his slaves, and gave them ten pounds, and said to
them, 'Do business with these until I come back.'"
—*Luke 19:12-13*

Working in retail at one time, I had a manager whom I adored. I would do anything she requested, including working late shifts, at the drop of a hat. Even when Lynne was not present, I did my best to excel in selling and in keeping the work area clean and orderly. I was eager to please her.

It occurred to me that our Lord also asked us to work for him, even though he would not be physically present. As he returned to his Father, he charged, "Go therefore and make disciples of all nations, baptizing them in the name of the Father and of the Son and of the Holy Spirit, and teaching them to obey everything that I have commanded you. And remember, I am with you always, to the end of the age" (Matthew 28:19-20).

I confess that too often my attitude has been more like, "When the cat's away, the mice will play." Too often have I forgotten the parting charge of the one I love dearly and have committed my life to serving.

When he returns, will he say, "Well done, thou good and faithful servant?" Have I focused daily on the ways I can please my heavenly master? Have I served him well? Would I live differently if he were physically at my side each day?

O Lord, forgive my negligence in observing your commands. Help me to focus on your values and objectives. Enable me to faithfully serve you well, as though you were physically present.

Lavonne Hall

Meeting God's Need

The Lord needs it.
—Luke 19:31

"My God shall supply all my needs." "Ask and you shall receive." "God will give you the desire of your heart." These are the comforts of our faith. And so we pray with confidence, asking God to meet our needs, to provide the things, both great and small, that this life makes necessary or desirable.

However, Gardner Taylor, that great dean of African American preachers, illumines a different aspect of the character of our sovereign and generous creator. God, Dr. Taylor asserts with passionate eloquence, has need of humanity.

If you look at the life of our Lord Jesus, it is perfectly clear. He needed another's stable in which to be born. He needed another's boat from which to speak his word. He needed another's fish and bread in order to feed the multitudes. He needed another's house in which to hold the Last Supper. He needed another's animal on which to ride into Jerusalem. He needed another's tomb in which to be buried.*

One can argue the semantics of the word *need,* but it was Christ's own. "What if the owner asks questions?" the disciples asked. "Just explain that the Lord needs it," Jesus answered casually—and profoundly.

If God Incarnate had need of human resources, then how much more does God need us now? We were created in the image of God, not for aesthetic purposes, but so that we might be incarnations of God's spirit in the world God loves.

Why does God not act more decisively to remedy the wrongs of this broken world, to eradicate the injustices of institutional and individual racism, sexism, classism, poverty? I think the answer may be found within myself. When I fail to act on behalf of "the least of these," I fail God in more ways than one. I fail to minister to God, and I fail to perpetuate the ministry given to us all at Pentecost: to become the body of Christ in the world.

Dear God, you who are faithful in providing for my every need, forgive me for failing to recognize your need of me: to provide

material resources, committed companionship, sensitive comfort, discerning counsel, wise stewardship, and overdue justice. Make me your instrument, not only of worship, but also of service. Amen.
Rebecca Irwin-Diehl

*Gardner C. Taylor, *The Words of Gardner Taylor, Volume 5: Special Occasion and Expository Sermons,* compiled by Edward L. Taylor (Valley Forge, Pa.: Judson Press, 2001).

Where Is Hope?

Then he led them out as far as Bethany, and, lifting up his hands, he blessed them. While he was blessing them, he withdrew from them and was carried up into heaven. And they worshiped him, and returned to Jerusalem with great joy; and they were continually in the temple blessing God.
—Luke 24:50-53

Jesus was really, truly gone. The disciples watched him rise into the heavens and simply disappear. It hurt to think about what tomorrow would be like without Jesus. It was far easier to hold tightly to the good memories: the teachings, the healings, the joy. The days felt better when the disciples could spend them in the Temple praising God.

But that is not where our lives are lived. We live in the valleys where there is illness, where jobs are lost, children go astray, and relationships are broken. Our problem comes when we forget that Jesus is found when two or three come together in his name— right in the middle of the muck and the mess—where the pain is the worst, the fear is the greatest. Maybe that's why God gave us each other, that we might be Christ to one another in the darkest moments of our lives.

Yes, someday we will see Jesus face-to-face—in God's time, in God's way. Yes, we cling to that promise. But today we live in the reality of this moment, where hope is tough to find and joy seems as elusive as last night's dreams. But this is also where Christ is made known to me through the words and hands and hearts of others.

God of grace and God of glory, we offer you our thanks and praise for memories that bring us joy and peace, that carry us home, that bring meaning to our days. Lord, open our eyes to this moment and the promise it holds. Grant us the courage and strength to see your face in the eyes of our neighbor and to feel the gentleness of your touch in our neighbor's hand. In Jesus' name we pray. Amen.

Dianne L. Mansfield

Sowing the Seeds

"Other seeds fell on good soil and brought forth grain..."
—Matthew 13:8a

As a youth leader, I was particularly challenged by a girl in my group who I will call Alicia. She was rebellious and did any number of things to destroy the spiritual quality of our group. She would sneak off with her boyfriend when the meetings were over and try to find a private room in the church to have sex. She would often come to youth group meetings high on marijuana or drunk. She would tell her father that she was going to youth group meetings when in fact she would skip them and go off somewhere with her boyfriend. In short, this girl was a youth leader's nightmare.

She eventually graduated from high school and left the group. I was so pleased, as we now had "good kids" who would follow the rules. Alicia eventually married her boyfriend and had a baby. I was invited to the baby shower. I had another commitment and couldn't attend. I purchased a gift and sent it along with someone who was going.

It was a few weeks later that I received a card in the mail thanking me for the gift. As I opened the card, a letter fell out. Much to my amazement, I began to read: "You can't possibly know what a difference the youth group and youth leaders made in my life. I look back, and those are my most special memories. I want to apologize for all of the bad things I did, and thank you for never giving up on me."

Today Alicia is a college graduate, a wonderful mother, and, most important, a wonderful Christian woman raising her son in the church. What a lesson for me! Often we cannot see the fruits of our labors until much later, if ever. Sometimes it is up to us to sow the seeds and to someone else to reap the harvest. Just think, if someone in our own lives had given up on us, we might never have reaped any harvests in our lives. We are all equally important parts of the process.

Dear God, help us not to give up on someone when our efforts at witnessing for you seem futile. Help us to remember that sometimes we sow the seeds for another to reap. Amen.

Martha Sobaje

Resolving Anger

Be angry but do not sin; do not let the sun go down on your anger, and do not make room for the devil.
—Ephesians 4:26

Nice girls don't get angry. Even though no one ever actually told me this, somehow I learned it. My younger sister was often in trouble for exploding, and I didn't want that. As a result, I pushed my anger so deep within that I didn't know it existed.

As I grew older, I continued this pattern. I seldom expressed my anger, and when I did, I would feel terribly guilty and would apologize profusely.

At the age of forty-nine, I entered seminary and was given the MMPI, a psychological examination to ascertain students' psychological fitness for ministry. At the evaluation, the psychologist said: "The test indicates that you are a very angry person." My reply was: "I am not! When I am angry, I do something about it and work for change." I then explained how I had worked for change in the Southern Baptist Convention, for education of church leadership to avoid sexual abuse, and for improvement of people's perception of women ministers. When I left, I was angry with him for even suggesting that I was angry!

Not long afterward, God gave me my one and only vision. (I'll warn you in advance that it was a bit on the strange side.) In my mind's eye I saw a pink piglet in my living room. (I never had a pig in my house!) The pig had diarrhea, and my light colored sofa, chairs, and carpet were covered with slimy manure. I had brought the pig into the house when it was tiny, and even though I knew it needed to be outside, I couldn't put it out. I felt as if God said: "When you name the pig, you can get rid of it."

I prayed a lot that day. By day's end, I knew the pig was "anger" and that I had to get rid of it before it destroyed me. Ridding myself of anger is a never-ending job. But as God shows me my hidden angers, I receive the courage and strength to work through them and clean up my life.

God, forgive me for the sin of nurtured anger. May I become aware of my anger when it occurs so I can seek your help in resolving it. Amen.

Jo Ellen Witt

Here with Me

This resurrection life you received from God is not a timid, grave-tending life. It's adventurously expectant, greeting God with a childlike "What's next, Papa?" God's Spirit touches our spirits and confirms who we really are. We know who he is, and we know who we are: Father and children. And we know we are going to get what's coming to us—an unbelievable inheritance!
—Romans 8:15-17, The Message

People talking about your coming
Like it's the day after next,
But I'm standing here watching
The tulips break through the ground,
My newborn baby smile,

And I feel you here with me now.
You don't leave me waiting;
Don't leave me wanting the rapture of the sky.
People are praying with longing
For the earth to cease its turning
And this mortal theatre to end.
They say that violence testifies,
Your coming is just around the bend.
But when I close my eyes and fold my hands,
There you are again.
You don't leave me waiting;
Don't leave me wanting the rapture of the sky.

I can get so lost
In this, the business of salvation,
I forget that you are saving me now,
Saving me in the here and now,
In order to save me for heaven.
You speak to me in context and texture,
You set me truly free,
You don't leave me waiting,
Don't leave me wanting the rapture of the sky.

People are making claims to visions,
Say they can see the Scriptures revealed
In our time, in our seasons.
But what do we long to see
But you here with me?
We really know only in part,
But you know us fully,
You will make yourself fully known.
You don't leave us waiting.

Lord, Our Emmanuel, all of our longings are summarized by our need for you and your presence here in this human plane. You place eternity in our hearts and reveal to us the beauty in being alive. Restore to us the dignity of life in your time. Amen.
Rachel Matheson Ommen

Mary's "Yes"

Then Mary said, "Here am I, the servant of the Lord;
let it be with me according to your word."
—Luke 1:38

It's hard to get past my own twentieth century response: What?!
Are you nuts?! You think having a child out of wedlock is a sign of
favor? Nor am I fond of how Mary is often portrayed as a kind of
simpering, groveling little milk-toast. Rather I like to think of Mary
as a strong, active woman—a woman who is not afraid to listen to
angels; a woman who says "Let it be so" because she trusts the
promises that the angel bore, promises that God would truly do what
God promised.

She didn't say, like Moses, "I can't speak." She didn't say, like
Jeremiah, "I am too young." She didn't say, like Isaiah before he
got his mouth washed out, "I am not worthy, a sinful man in the
midst of a sinful people." She did not grit her teeth and say, "Yes."
She was not coerced. Rather it was through her own agency, her
own consent, her own life that she said, "Yes, let it be so," which
implies the ability to say, "No, let it not be!"

After Mary gives her consent, Gabriel leaves and Mary, alone,
decides she needs to talk to someone. The pool of candidates for
a conversation of this type is fairly small. So she chooses her
older cousin, Elizabeth, who, by the way, had a bit of visitation
of her own.

Upon greeting, Elizabeth affirms Mary. Then out pours Mary's
Magnificat. Mary is no politician, no radical. But as she is empowered by the Holy Spirit, she becomes an articulate radical and an
astonished prophet, singing about God's mighty works as if they
had already happened. Mary sings about restructuring social orders:
politics, economics, even religion. She's talking about a major
housecleaning, not just a little spot-dusting and vacuuming in the
middle. She is talking about moving the furniture and getting out
all the cobwebs and dust bunnies: a thorough upheaval. She is
singing a faith in things not yet seen.

We are called to be like Mary: God-bearers, revealers of God's
love and grace. We are called to embody God in the world, to be

the continual coming of God in Christ. We, too, are called, invited. God invites, and we choose. And in our choosing, we, like Mary, may be stepping outside acceptable boundaries and cultural patterns. To follow in her example, we are called and invited to new creation, new justice, new ways of taking risks; new ways of committing to God, each other, and the world.

Holy God, help us take the time to ponder Mary's "Yes" and our own "Yes." Help us to be articulate radicals and astonished prophets; busy creating a world where all are free to love and serve God, however God calls. Amen.

K. Joanne Lindstrom

No Easy Way Out

The woman said to him, "Sir, give me this water,
so that I may never be thirsty or have
to keep coming here to draw water.
—John 4:15

The avoidance method goes all the way back to Adam and Eve. To avoid a confrontation with God, they hid in the Garden of Eden. We've all used this method at some time in our lives. As children, to avoid medicine, we hid under beds or pretended to be well. To avoid spankings, we lied and ran, perhaps made promises to God that we'd "never do it again!" As adults, to avoid a conversation, we pretend not to see another.

The Samaritan woman was a master of the art of avoidance. We know her story, how she was the "talk of the town" due to her lifestyle. At a Sunday service my pastor used the account of the woman at the well to illustrate the need for evangelizing. The woman's response to Jesus' words struck me. She said, "Give me this water so that I won't...have to keep coming here." Now that's avoidance! She wanted to avoid the loneliness of going to the well alone. (She couldn't go with the other women because of her reputation.) She wanted to avoid the possibility of running into anyone.

True to form, our Savior wouldn't allow her to get away from her troubles that easily. She needed to identify her problem and to be delivered from it. Her asking Jesus for the water that only Jesus could give was his opportunity to help this woman.

Jesus first identified her problem (vv. 16-18), letting her know that he knew all about her (v. 29). God knows you, too. He knows all about you, and he loves you no matter what! God wants us to get to the bottom of whatever causes you to explode or break down in tears of sadness. God wants to free us from whatever pain we bear.

Don't avoid your issues. Deal with them! God really does give beauty for ashes and joy for mourning! (see Isaiah 61:1-3).

Dear Lord, I know that the process of becoming whole is not easy. It can be painful, but with you I can overcome! Amen.

Nneka Best

Discernment amidst the Clamor

Jesus stood still and said, "Call him here."
And they called the blind man, saying to him,
"Take heart; get up, he is calling you."
—Mark 10:49

Can you picture it? Blind Bartimaeus is sitting along the roadside, calling out to Jesus as the crowd tries to silence him. Jesus notices him and sends his disciples over to get him. Bartimaeus, bursting with energy, springs up to be ushered to Jesus. Jesus looks into his face and asks, "What do you want me to do for you? What are you in need of?" Bartimaeus, without hesitation, asks to be able to see again. Jesus heals him, and then Bartimaeus follows Jesus.

In this story there are at least two groups of people. There is the crowd that surrounds Bartimaeus and tries to silence him. And there is the group of disciples who are sent to bring Bartimaeus to Jesus. Bartimaeus heard but did not follow the first group. When the second group spoke, he listened and went with them. As a result, he stood face-to-face with Jesus and received his sight.

God often uses other people to speak to us. It is not always easy to discern whom to listen to and follow. It seems it was an easy choice for Bartimaeus since he knew exactly what he needed. That is not always so for us. The worldly crowd can often be loud, persistent, and very convincing. It can even seem to smother out the voice of those God sends to us.

We need to listen very carefully as we discern what is of God and what is not. We may not know immediately. Discernment may need much time and prayer as we seek to know how God is leading. In our seeking, God waits to bring us healing and sight. Sight, of course, has meanings beyond the physical. It may mean seeing through God's eyes or knowing God in a different, deeper way. As God grants us sight, we, like Bartimaeus, are led to follow the will of God and not the will of the worldly crowd.

Prayer suggestion: Imagine yourself as Bartimaeus, calling out as the crowd tries to silence you. Imagine being brought to Christ. He asks what you need. Allow yourself to respond. And listen to Christ's response to you. Amen.

Debbie H. Deane

Biographies

Nancy Adams is the catalog librarian at Eastern Baptist Theological Seminary. She was born in Tulsa, Oklahoma, and received her Bachelor's of Music from the University of Tulsa. A member of the Episcopal Church, she is currently working on a historical novel set in ancient Rome. (5, 286, 301)

Emilie J. Aubert is an associate professor of physical therapy at Marquette University in Milwaukee, Wisconsin, and a physical therapist who specializes in treatment of children with disabilities. She is a lay leader at her church, Faith United Church of Christ in Milwaukee. Emilie is married with two sons now in college. (12, 248, 306)

Jéneen N. Barlow's life mission is to be God's agent of change. Jéneen is a visual artist, writer, and passionate minister and teacher of sacred dance and prayer. She and her husband, Prince Omar, are the founders of A More Excellent Way Presenters, Inc., an organization that teaches people how to discover and fulfill their life purpose. The couple resides in Philadelphia, Pennsylvania. (10)

Catherine Patterson Bartell delights in being a wife, mother, mother-in-law, and grandmother. She writes out of her love of God and the desire to witness to what God is doing in her life. Jim, her husband of 41 years, constantly supports and encourages all her writing endeavors. (51, 62)

Joy A. Bergfalk is an American Baptist Churches pastor serving York Baptist Church half-time. In the other half-time plus she works as a spiritual director, therapist, retreat and workshop leader, and labyrinth facilitator. Joy enjoys the ten grandchildren she and husband, Jimmy Reader, have. She and Jimmy also enjoy their border collie, Pepper, and cats Petunia and Samson. (16, 147, 174)

Nneka Best is married. She is pursuing a Bachelor's degree in music at Eastern University and attends the Covenant Church of Philadelphia, Pennsylvania. (331, 376)

Theodora A. Boolin is pastor at First Baptist in Pierre, South Dakota. She describes her life and call to ministry as "a kaleidoscope of journeys with many twists and turns."She has lived through seventy-six moves, the miscarriage of an only child, and the death of a mother and husband. She writes, "The kaleidoscope turned as the pieces collapsed, and the power of 'the story' became a faith statement in my life, which created a colorful mosaic." (325, 367)

Lyn G. Brakeman is an Episcopal priest, pastoral counselor, and spiritual director. She also serves as Sunday Associate at St. John's Church in Gloucester, Massachusetts, where her marriage partner, Richard Simeone, is the rector. Lyn is the author of *Spiritual Lemons: Biblical Women, Irreverent Laughter & Righteous Rage* (1997) and *The God Between Us: A Spirituality of Relationships* (2001), both Innisfree Press Publications. (189)

Kolya Braun-Greiner, who holds an M.Div. from Union Theological Seminary in New York City, is currently a full-time mother and part-time consultant/writer of religious curriculum and devotional resources. She leads workshops on social justice issues, non-violence training, and children's concerns. Prior to motherhood she worked as executive staff on advocacy for children, youth, and families for seven years with the Women's Division of the United Methodist Church and served as past president of the National Farm Worker Ministry. (41, 127)

Dallas Dee A. Brauninger, an ordained minister, is a recipient of a United Church of Christ Disabilities Ministries citation. Dee edits "That All May Worship and Serve," the United Church of Christ Disabilities Ministries news insert in *United Church News*. The Nebraska Conference UCCDM Task Force member also uses her talents as a writer to help churches increase awareness of welcoming ministry regardless of personal ability. (165, 192)

Judy L. Brown is an Associate Minister of the First Central Baptist Church, Staten Island, New York. She is employed as a housing specialist for Project Hospitality Inc., Hospitality House for Women and Children, Staten Island, and is the CEO of Pursuing Excellences (www.womeninministry.biz). In November 2002, Rev. Brown was certified by the American Baptist Churches, USA as a New Church Planter. (37)

Donna Buckles is an ordained American Baptist minister who has served as an associate pastor in Arizona and as the program director for Tonto Rim American Baptist Camp. She has led numerous teams on volunteer international mission trips. She currently serves as the director of volunteers for the Child Crisis Center in Mesa, Arizona. (242, 272)

Cathie Burdick is a Presbyterian elder who leads an adult study group each week. She has been a publisher and editor, an agency district executive, a census taker, and a church secretary. She is now executive director of the Ticonderoga (NY) Festival Guild. Her volunteer activities are too numerous to list. (160)

Marjorie A. Burke is the chair of the committee on Status of Women of the Episcopal Church, USA, and former national president of Episcopal Church Women. She is a strong advocate for women's full participation in the church. A pharmacist by profession, she is a wife, mother, grandmother, weaver, liturgical dancer, and poet. (27)

Valora Starr Butler serves as director for stewardship and evangelism for Women of the Evangelical Lutheran Church in America. Her life, relationships, and work have renewed meaning after a recent bout with cervical cancer. (123)

Liza Marie Canino, a native of Puerto Rico, is a research analyst for Walgreens. She is very active in her church congregation, Shepherd of the Prairie, a mission start in Huntley, Illinios. (68)

Joy Haupt Carol is a spiritual director, counselor, and author. She leads retreats and workshops on spirituality, wholeness, caregiving, loneliness, and healing for dying at many places including medical schools, seminaries, and retreat centers. She is the author of *Towers of Hope: Stories to Help Us Heal* (Forest of Peace Publishing, 2002; published in Europe by Veritas Publications as *Finding Courage*) and *Journeys of Courage* (Veritas Publications, 2003). (234, 271)

Cathy Carpenter is an ordained minister in the Presbyterian Church (U.S.A.). She lives and works in southwest Virginia with her two cats, Abigail and Mink. (214)

Nona Kelley Carver began writing while recovering from an injury. God also gave her the gift of poetry to help her through this hard time. Her work is available on compact disk from Carver Country Poetry, Box 115, Mesa, CO 81643. (33)

Martha Palmer Chambers is a pastor's wife who lives in the

North Hills of Pittsburgh with her husband, Dave, and children Caity (15) and Keven (12). She is preparing to pursue an M.A. in Religion at Trinity Episcopal School for Ministry in Ambridge, Pennsylvania, and is looking forward to speaking and writing about the things that mean a great deal to her: the Trinity, contemplative and liturgical worship, and cultivating the inner life. (131, 180, 233, 270)

Jenny Chandler has known the Lord for twenty-five years. She is a stay-at-home mother of two. She does graphic design for her church and enjoys gardening, reading, and yoga. (58, 77)

Marie Compton is an ordinary laywoman blessed with extraordinary life experiences that help mold her writings and interactions with other people. She is a former member of the General Board of American Baptist Churches USA and holds leadership offices in American Baptist Women's Ministries on several levels. She lives in Williamsport, Pennsylvania, with her husband, Bob, and attends Calvary Baptist Church there. (111, 334)

Cherise Valdá Copeland, a native of Bronx, New York, is a licensed and ordained Baptist minister. She is a 1999 M.Div. graduate (*cum laude*) from the School of Theology at Virginia Union University. Cherise takes pleasure from reading African American literature, traveling, and ministering to young adults. (108, 126)

Carol Q. Cosby is on staff with the Office of Disciples Women, Christian Church (Disciples of Christ), working with social justice, service projects, mother-to-mother ministry, and the Disciples Peace Fellowship. She has two daughters and two grandsons, and is learning once again to listen for God's latest wisdom. (238, 261, 276)

Cynthia E. Cowen is an associate in ministry with the ELCA and a licensed lay minister with the Northern Great Lakes Synod. She is a published resource and devotional writer and a past member of the Church-wide Organization Executive Board of the Women of the ELCA. (87, 230, 268)

Susan E. Crane is the pastor of Henderson Memorial Baptist Church in Farmington, Maine. She also serves the American Baptist Churches of Maine as the Advocate for Women in Ministry, providing support for women in preparation for or new to ministry. (75)

Stephanie Buckhanon Crowder is associate minister at New

Covenant Christian Church and professor of New Testament at American Baptist College in Nashville, Tennessee. (106, 121)

Delores R. Davis attended The Baptist Institute in Philadelphia and Eastern Baptist Seminary's music department. She served as Registrar at Haverford College. She is married to Robert Evan Davis. They have two children, R. Evan Davis and Marcia Jessen, and three grandchildren. (100)

Weptanomah B. C. Davis is a licensed therapist and the author of inspirational books for women. She lives in Bowie, Maryland, with her husband, Rev. Henry Davis, pastor of the First Baptist Church of Highland Park, and daughter, Lilybelle. (177)

Sara J. Davis-Shappell, a United Methodist clergywoman in the Eastern Pennsylvania Conference, is the founder and executive director of Spiritual Renewal Ministries Inc., a nonprofit organization that invites persons to deepen their relationship with God. She is a spiritual director and retreat leader. (32, 289, 366)

Debbie H. Deane is a seeker, a spiritual pilgrim whose journey has brought her through such challenges as child sexual abuse and metastatic breast cancer. Her present focus is in gaining greater appreciation of time with family and friends and the importance of laughter. She is an ordained American Baptist minister whose ministry is in spiritual direction. (176, 205, 319, 339, 352, 377)

Sarah Verne de Bourg was ordained into Christian ministry on November 12, 2000. She is the mother of one son and two daughters—Bill, Kristina, and Shelley—and the grandmother of Kadeem, Jalen, and Ayanna. She and her husband, Clyde, reside in Rochester, New York. (104)

Annie Dieselberg is an American Baptist missionary in Bangkok, Thailand, along with her husband, Jeff. They have four children. Annie works with prostitutes, the poor, and the international community, teaching and sharing about God's love and mercy. (221, 239, 263)

Christie A. Eastman and her husband, Trent, spent the '90s living and working in Kenya and Bangladesh with Food for the Hungry International. The experiences gained during those years are often at the heart of her writings. Christie and Trent live in West Virginia with their two young sons, Jacob and Joshua. (220, 267, 364)

Judith Northen Eastman grew up in Virginia as the daughter of a minister. Married with two grown daughters and two grandsons, she works as a licensed clinical social worker and marriage and family therapist. She lives in Chapel Hill, North Carolina, with her husband, William F. Eastman, who is also a therapist. (31, 173)

Eleanor James Edwards is an assistant director at the National Transit Institute of Rutgers, The State University of New Jersey. She is the former Minister of Christian Education for the American Baptist Churches of New Jersey. She and her husband, Charles, live in Piscataway, New Jersey, where they attend the First Baptist Church of New Market and where she serves as assistant pastor. (223)

Sherry Elmer, after pursuing a Ph.D. in political science, returned to her first love: writing. She is working on her first novel. She has published poetry, devotionals, and articles in various publications, including *The Upper Room, The Secret Place*, and *U.S. Catholic*. She lives in Wisconsin with her husband, Jeff. (259, 356)

Jean Alicia Elster, a resident of Detroit, Michigan, holds B.A. and J.D. degrees and is the award-winning author of the children's book series "Joe Joe in the City," published by Judson Press. The volumes in this series consist of *Just Call Me Joe Joe*; *I Have A Dream, Too!*; *I'll Fly My Own Plane;* and *I'll Do the Right Thing*. She also collaborated in the manuscript preparation for *Dear Mrs. Parks: A Dialog with Today's Youth* by Rosa Parks (Lee and Low). She was the editor of *Building Up Zion's Walls: Ministry for Empowering the African American Family* (Judson Press). (307)

Carolyn Hall Felger, who lives in Hamburg, New York, is a Presbyterian elder, cancer survivor, wife, mother, grandmother, and thankful eleventh-hour worker in God's vineyard. She is writing again after letting many years go by since winning the Florence Annette Wing Prize for Lyric Poetry at Wellesley. (146, 257, 312)

Mary Jo Ferreira is a wife, mother, grandmother, and great-grandmother with extensive travel experience. She has served the ABCUSA on a variety of local, regional, and national boards. She and her husband are retired after thirty-five years of ministry in churches of the American Baptist Churches USA Great Rivers Region. She now resides in Leesburg, Florida. (210, 363)

Josephe Marie Flynn, S.S.N.D., is a Catholic Sister currently serving as Director of Adult and Family Ministry at St. Mary Parish, Hales Corners, Wisconsin. She is an artist, writer, and speaker. (256, 275)

Juana L. Francis is bilingual (Spanish and English). She has a

Master of Divinity Degree from Pacific School of Religion and is now working on the Certificate of Advanced Professional Studies in pastoral counseling with a concentration on grief and loss. She is an associate minister at Third Baptist Church in San Francisco, California. (103)

Patti Kenney Fraser has served as the campus minister/director of the American Baptist Student Foundation at Michigan State University since 1993. She is an ordained American Baptist minister and serves as editor for *Minister*, the American Baptist Minister's Council professional journal. She is currently researching clergy well-being. (360)

Ellen A. Frost, an ordained minister in the Christian Church (Disciples of Christ), has recently retired after thirty-nine years of active ministry. She served four Disciples and one United Methodist congregation, fifteen and a half years in regional ministry, and eight years as Director of Women's Ministries for the Christian Church (Disciples of Christ). Ellen has participated in global learning experiences in the Soviet Union (1987), the Philippines and Thailand (1994), Hong Kong and China (1995), and India (2002). (141, 278)

Linda G. Frost is currently director of chaplain services at CARITAS Medical Center in Louisville, Kentucky. An ordained minister, Dr. Frost has served in missions work in South Texas and has held associate minister positions in congregations in Kentucky, as well as other chaplain positions in Kentucky and Indiana. (219, 283, 351)

Doris J. Garcia-Mayol is a married Puertorrican woman with three children. Her family serves as a missionary family of the American Baptist Churches with the Mexican people at the Baptist Seminary in Mexico. They work with leaders and church members to develop holistic ministries in both urban and rural contexts. (253)

Portia George is the wife of Dr. William Gary George. She formerly served as marketing sales representative for Judson Press and has been active in Christian education for more than twenty-five years. The founder of "Kingdom Kids," a program designed to help children of all ages to know Christ, Portia is the sole proprietor of PG Enterprises, the author of four African American Christian children's books, and the director of the American Baptist Speakers Program. (346)

Annell George-McLawhorn, an ordained minister of the

Christian Church (Disciples of Christ), is currently Disaster Relief Coordinator for the Christian Church in North Carolina. She is founder and volunteer teacher for the Suzuki violin program in her county's public schools. The program introduces violin to low wealth, minority, and rural children. (252)

Anissa Danielle Gibbs is an assistant professor of communications at Nassau Community College in Long Island, New York. In recent years, she has served as the study director of the Christian Womens Fellowship (Northeast Region) and director of Christian education at the Williamsburg Christian Church (Disciples of Christ) in Brooklyn, New York. She is currently writing a collection of essays regarding race, class, and gender. (118, 140, 172, 197)

Terri Gillespie has been married to her Baruch (blessed), Robert, for 29 years. They have one daughter, Rivka (Rebekah), who is a professional singer. Terri fundraises for the Messianic Jewish Alliance of America and is active in her congregation Beth Yeshua in Philadelphia. She is also a speaker at women's retreats. (4, 30, 345)

Jennifer M. Ginn is a Lutheran pastor who serves St. John's Evangelical Lutheran Church in Salisbury, North Carolina. (171, 332)

Bernadette Glover-Williams, executive pastor of Cathedral International Church of New Jersey, serves the General Board ABCUSA as Chaplain and New Brunswick Theological Seminary as assistant professor of preaching. She loves ministry and is married to Edward W. Williams. (13, 203)

Inga D. Green, a native of Washington, D.C., is the wife of Carl and the mother to one son, Corey. She is an active member of Sixth Baptist Church in Richmond, Virginia. She is an aspiring writer and soon-to-be seminarian. (29, 102, 311)

Amy E. Greene is a certified supervisor of Clinical Pastoral Education with the Care and Counseling Center of Georgia. She is a graduate of Union Theological Seminary in New York and lives in downtown Atlanta with her husband and sons. (3, 25, 50, 168)

Rosalyce Grubbs has been married to James A. Grubbs for thirty-nine years. They have two adopted children, Laura and David, and three beautiful granddaughters—Miranda, Megan, and Hannah. In addition to ABW Ministries involvement, she enjoys music, sewing, crafts, crocheting, and bowling. (101)

Gwynne M. Guibord serves on the Commission of Ecumenicity for the Episcopal Diocese of Los Angeles. She has served as the past president of the California Council of Churches. Currently, she is vice president of the InterFaith Alliance and vice president of Southern California Ecumenical Council. She is also a trustee of the Council for a Parliament for the World's Religions. (299, 310, 329)

Lavonne Hall is a graduate of Philadelphia Biblical University. She serves as administrative assistant in the Doctor of Ministry office of Denver Seminary. She is married to a pastor and has four married daughters. (343, 368)

Peggy Halsey is executive secretary for Ministries with Women, Children, and Families for the United Methodist Church's General Board of Global Ministries. She is a member of the Justice for Women Working Group of the National Council of Churches and of the Bi-National Advisory Committee for the Center for the Prevention of Sexual and Domestic Violence. (198, 315)

Cheryl Gale Harader is currently pastor at First Baptist Church, Winfield, Kansas. She has been active in planning congregational transformation events in the Central Region and is the president-elect of the ABCCR Ministers Council. (63, 167)

Carmen S. Harris has had a love of writing for over twenty years. But it was only in the last seven years that she sensed God calling her to the ministry of writing in order to encourage, uplift, and strengthen others. (117)

Marilyn D. Harris is a registered nurse. She is a hospice volunteer, the current chair of the Interfaith Health Ministries Consortium of Southeast Pennsylvania, and a parish nurse at Hatboro Baptist Church. (24, 251)

Kate Harvey has served as executive director of the ABCUSA Ministers Council since 1995. She received a $2 million grant from the Lilly Foundation to form covenant groups among ABC clergy from 2003–2007. Prior to her current position, she pastored in Rhode Island, most recently at the First Baptist Church in America. (318)

Naomi Hawkins has served as an associate pastor at Our Saviour's Lutheran Church in Arlington Heights, Illinois, and is currently serving at the ELCA headquarters as coordinator of interpretation and support for a project called Fund for Leaders in Mission—an endowed scholarship initiative to help seminarians pay their tuition at ELCA seminaries. (163)

Angela Herrmann, affiliated with the Christian Church (Disciples of Christ), is a freelance writer, photographer, and website publisher. When she's not traveling overseas, she hangs out near the banks of the White River in Rocky Ripple, Indiana. (250)

Janet K. Hess is senior pastor of First United Methodist Church, Media, Pennsylvania. A second-career clergywoman, she served on the Board of Directors for the ecumenical Metropolitan Christian Council of Philadelphia (for ten years) and was its first woman president (1997–2000). She is one of the founders of the area's ecumenical Women of Faith. She serves on the Board of Ordained Ministry for the UMC and is also on the board of directors for Spiritual Renewal Ministries and Pilgrim Gardens Retirement Community. (22, 98, 317, 341)

Theressa Hoover is the former staff head of the Women's Division of the United Methodist Church. She is retired and lives in Fayetteville, Arkansas. (208)

Blanche Clipper Hudson is an associate minister at Metropolitan Baptist Church in Washington, D.C. As a member of the Interim Ministries Program of the American Baptist Churches, she recently served as appointed interim pastor of First Baptist Church in Saratoga Springs, New York. She is currently pursuing the doctor of ministry degree at Howard University School of Divinity; her dissertation is "Women in Ministry: Reclaiming and Strengthening the Legacy of Lost Leadership." (36, 61, 97)

Kathleen Hurty is a consultant, grant writer, and researcher for nonprofit faith-based organizations interested in collaborative approaches to justice and peace. Her previous experience includes teaching, school administration, and ecumenical leadership. A member of the ELCA, Dr. Hurty serves on a number of boards and holds a Ph.D. in education from the University of California, Berkeley. (284)

Carolyn Iga serves as pastoral associate at First Presbyterian Church, Altadena, California, where she oversees worship, Christian formation, and education. She was formerly associate pastor at Evergreen Baptist Church, Los Angeles. (20, 159, 321)

Rebecca Irwin-Diehl is assistant publisher at *The Other Side* magazine, former managing editor of Judson Press, freelance writer and editor, and mother of two young sons. She holds an undergraduate degree in English-writing and a masters degree in contemporary theology. (122, 194, 212, 336, 369)

Lisa R. Jackson currently teaches fourth grade in Jersey City, New Jersey. She is a part of Mantle of Power, Paulette Polo Ministries, a ministry devoted to bringing people closer to the Spirit of God through worship, preaching, and flowing in the gifts by divine diection. (338)

Patricia Stuart Jacobs serves as the interim pastor of Warren Baptist Church in Warren, Maine. She has held pastorates in Waterloo, Iowa, and West Chester, Pennsylvania. Jacobs is a graduate of William Jewell College and Central Baptist Seminary. She is the wife of Bruce and mother of two-year-old Hannah Grace. (247)

Annette L. James is a practitioner of Kinlein. She is also a member of the ABCUSA 2010 prayer team and the District of Columbia Baptist Convention's Intercessory Prayer Ministry. She is married to Rev. Ronald James and has two children. (96)

Natalie Jones is a freelance writer/editor who has a love for poetry. Her writings are usually of an inspirational nature, stemming from life and all the good and bad that it can offer. She resides in Atlanta, Georgia. (161)

Dorinda K. W. Kauzlarich-Rupe is a mother, daughter, wife, and grandmother. She does individual and systemic advocacy for persons who are mentally retarded/developmentally disabled. People she works with have been abused, neglected, and exploited. Some are interfacing the criminal justice system. She is currently focusing her systemic advocacy on developing alternate sentencing for the mentally retarded and developmentally disabled and on securing services for those who fall through the cracks. (78, 269)

Christine Dean Keels is District President of the Wilmington District United Methodist Women. She supports her husband's ministry at Newark United Methodist Church. She is also an executive in the federal criminal justice system and a former Vice-President of Christian Social Responsibility for the Women's Division of the United Methodist Church. She is committed to issues of justice and peace. (18)

Mary Kemen is a Sister of St. Francis of Assisi from Milwaukee, Wisconsin. She taught in early childhood and elementary education for seventeen years and is presently working in the area of mission effectiveness. She enjoys writing poetry. (244)

Woodye Webber Kessler is a wife, mother, grandmother, and great-grandmother. An American Baptist, she has been engaged in a jail and prison ministry for twenty-seven years. The ministry, supported by her husband, Orville, includes weekly Bible studies; a Christian newsletter, *Woodye's Witness*; advocacy; annual Christmas parties; an extensive letter ministry to current and former inmates and their families; and the provision of hospitality, support, and advice upon release. (240)

Elizabeth Dikkers Killeen has served churches in New Jersey (as a church planter) and Illinois, where she is presently pastoring the First Baptist Church of Tuscola. (125, 335)

Martha Ann Kirk is a Catholic Sister and a professor at the University of the Incarnate Word in San Antonio, Texas, who works internationally sharing stories focusing on justice and peace. Her books include *Women of Bible Lands* and *Celebrations of Biblical Women's Stories.* (201)

Linda Kirkland-Harris, who finds seagulls immensely inspirational, is an ordained ABC minister, pastoral counselor, and teacher. She is the mentor for the United Theological Seminary D.Min. Reproductive Choice Fellows in the Sexuality and Spirituality in the African American Church program. She is also working toward certification as a spiritual director. (15)

Mary Koch is a full-time caregiver for her husband, who survived a stroke. She writes about caregiving in a weekly newspaper column, available on the Internet at www.marykoch.com. (158, 232, 255, 333, 349)

Mary Beth Krainz is a wife and mother of two young adults. She has worked in the healthcare field for numerous years. She enjoys reflective writing and is a member of the Wisconsin Fellowship of Poets. (297)

Lesley Walsh Krieger is a student at Duke Divinity School, Durham, North Carolina, in the Master of Theological Studies program. She is the wife of John M. Krieger. (150)

Marlys Kroon serves on the Dakota Chapter of the National Multiple Sclerosis Society. She enjoys leading a Bible study, being an inspirational speaker, and traveling. Her goals are to inspire and entertain, as well as to praise the Lord. She has multiple sclerosis. (59)

Lonnie Lane is a Jewish believer in Jesus who leads a house church with her brother, Michael Lane. She hosts a weekly TV show called "Messiah's Hope," which shares the Jewish roots of Christianity for Jews and Gentiles. She is a speaker, teacher, and writer on the same theme. (76, 107, 231, 316, 328)

Margie Ann Patterson Latham is an ordained minister in the ABCUSA. She has served as interim pastor of First Baptist Church, Ithaca, New York; University Baptist Church, Columbus, Ohio; and St. Peter United Church (UCC), Houston, Texas. She is a member of Covenant Church (ABCUSA) in Houston. (228)

Grace Thornton Lawrence is a commissioned woman interim pastor for ABCOPAD. She is presently serving First Baptist Church, Lewistown, Pennsylvania, after serving First Baptist Church, Lykens, Pennsylvania, for nearly eighteen years. (69)

Hannah Leafshoots belongs to a Messianic Jewish congregation. She writes and speaks on the relationship between Judaism and Christianity. (57, 154)

Mildred A. Leuenberger, OSF, is a Sister belonging to the congregation of the Sisters of St. Francis of Dubuque, Iowa. She currently serves as the pastoral administrator of two Catholic churches in eastern Iowa—Sts. Peter and Paul in Sherrill and St. Francis of Assisi in Balltown. (74)

K. Joanne Lindstrom serves as the director of experiential education & field studies at McCormick Theological Seminary in Chicago. She is also coordinator for the Nueva Vida Initiative for American Baptist Churches of Metro Chicago. Nueva Vida is a two-year project funded by the American Baptist Churches' National Ministries division aimed at strengthening and revitalizing congregations through partnership and education. (324, 375)

Betty H. Long has an M.Div. from the Samuel DeWitt Proctor School of Theology, Virginia Union University. She serves as Minister for Youth/College Student Ministries at First Baptist Church of Hampton, Virginia. (182)

Pamela R. Lucas is president of PR Lucas and Associates, Inc., a sports management agency dedicated to helping Christian athletes reach their professional, personal, and spiritual goals. She is a member of Faith Fellowship Ministries in Sayreville, New Jersey, where she serves as a deacon and teacher. Ms. Lucas is the founder of Esteem Ministries, which is committed to helping believers live victorious Christian lives. She is author of *"A" Is for the Anoiting: Keys to Walking in Victory. (358)*

Evangeline W. Lynch retired after thirty years in public school teaching. She is active with the Tennessee Commission of Indian Affairs in addressing Indian concerns and issues. She also serves as an officer in Tennessee State Church Women United. (35, 73)

Dianne L. Mansfield, after spending fifteen years at home raising children, went to seminary and graduated with a Master's degree in both Christian education and divinity. She has been an ordained Disciples of Christ pastor for ten years and is now an associate at First Christian in Greencastle, Indiana. She and her husband take great joy in living near and spending time with their children and grandchildren. (28, 80, 296, 370)

Gloria Marshall and her husband served in Congo as International Ministries (ABC) missionaries for two terms. They have also served as pastor and wife for the International Protestant Church in Kinshasa, Congo, and two stateside congregations. They are currently involved in a ministry acting as representative payees for challenged adults and for children who need financial protection. Gloria is also the mission study tour coordinator for American Baptist Women's Ministries. (274)

Jean Martensen is a peace educator who has been employed as a teacher, writer, civil rights specialist, and advocate for women's domestic safety. She has been an activist in local community organizations and the international feminist, anti-apartheid, and peace movements. (178)

Nancee Martin-Coffey is an Episcopal priest serving as associate rector in a large urban church. The mother of three daughters and a son, she is also a licensed professional counselor, a spiritual director, and an emerging retreat leader. She and her husband, who is an atmospheric physicist, make their home in Boulder, Colorado. (14, 148, 202)

Dawn Nichols Mays is an American Baptist minister serving as South Area Minister for the American Baptist Churches of New Jersey. She is married with two grown sons. She loves to garden and make quilts. (109)

Carol K. McCollough is retired after serving many years as a professor of English, Christian educator with the United Church of Christ, and college administrator. She enjoys life on a farm with her husband, Charles, near Princeton, New Jersey. They have three children and two grandchildren. (45)

Janet R. McCormack is an ordained American Baptist Churches USA minister who earned her M.Div. at Southeastern Baptist Theological Seminary and her D.Min. in Leadership through Denver Seminary. She is employed at Denver Seminary as the director of the Chaplaincy and Counseling Training Centers.

She also serves as Marketplace Samaritan Inc.'s Vice President of Chaplaincy. McCormack, who retired from the Air Force after twenty-two years, is an experienced military, hospital, prison, police, and industrial chaplain. She is also a NASCAR Team Chaplain for a Winston West racecar driver. (112, 145, 169)

Gay Holthaus McCormick, a United Church of Christ laywoman, serves the denomination in the area of evangelism, focusing on accessibility advocacy, issues, and resources for persons with disabilities. (166)

Melinda McDonald is a writer and member of Cherry Hills Baptist Church in Springfield, Illinois. She is employed as communications manager at a beverage equipment manufacturer. She is married, has two daughters, and is writing a book for teenagers about faith. (44, 92, 134, 193, 264)

Elizabeth V. McDowell combines her interest in the arts, education, and the church as a consultant, a museum docent, and a representative of the Theological Education Fund of the Presbyterian Church (U.S.A.). Now semi-retired, she was a college professor and an arts administrator. (90, 353)

Fair C. Meeks is married and has two children and two grandchildren. She has traveled widely and lived in Asia for nine years, including three years in China under a Fulbright grant. She taught English and humanities at Minnesota State University Moorhead until retirement. In May 2002 she was licensed after completing the Regional Lay Ministry Program of American Baptist Churches of the Dakotas and was installed as associate pastor. (303)

Norma S. Mengel is ordained in the United Church of Christ. She formerly served as an associate for Program for the UCC's Council for Health & Human Service Ministries; as CEO of the Visiting Nurse Association of York County, Pennsylvania; and as a health educator in Taegu, South Korea. (72, 190, 304)

Dorothy Lairmore Michel is an ordained United Church of Christ clergy whose passions include social justice and spirituality. She is married to Rev. Alan Michel. She spent the last seven years of her ministry as associate pastor at First United Methodist Church in Jefferson City, Missouri. Due to a double diagnosis of Parkinson's disease and acute fibromyleja, she retired early. (119, 291)

Joanne T. Mild, wife of William H. Mild IV, is the mother of two healthy young boys. She currently resides in Bound Brook, New Jersey, where she teaches piano from her home studio in addition to caring for her family full-time. She attended both Marywood University and Westminster Choir College of Rider University. (138)

Mary L. Mild is the director of the American Baptist Personnel Services. She is also editor of *Songs of Miriam, Worthy of the Gospel,* and the first edition of *Women at the Well.* (8, 64, 187)

Julia Miller was a pastor for five years on the Hopi reservation in Arizona. She also pastored a church in Connecticut. She is currently assistant chaplain and house parent at Ranch Hope for boys in New Jersey. She has one grown son, two dogs, and four cats. (133, 184)

Kelly S. Moor is an ordained American Baptist minister who is currently serving First Baptist Church of Idaho Falls, Idaho, as co-pastor with her husband, David. Along with pastoral ministry, Kelly has served as a hospice chaplain and conference/retreat facilitator for youth and women's ministries. Two teenagers and one very pampered cocker spaniel keep her balanced and learning. (21, 130, 227)

Kathleen A. Moore is a past state and national Love Gift Chair for American Baptist Women's Ministries and is a retired registered nurse. She is a non-retired wife, mother, grandmother, American Baptist woman, crafter, and quilter. (288)

Wilda K. W. (Wendy) Morris is editor of *The Pebble*, the American Baptist Educational Ministries' children's ministry newsletter, and coordinator of Shalom Education, an ecumenical organization providing workshops and curriculum on justice and peace. She is also the author of the Judson Press book *Stop the Violence! Educating Ourselves to Protect Our Youth.* (6, 188, 226, 323)

Lou A. Nutter is a number of All Saints' Episcopal Parish in Frederick, Maryland. She is married and has two daughters and six grandchildren. She is active in her parish and is a member of the National Order of the Daughters of the King. (322)

Elizabeth Okayama is associate general secretary for Episcopal Services and also director of human resources for the General Council on Finance and Administration, business office of The United Methodist Church. Her responsibilities have allowed her to visit bishops' offices in the Philippines, Angola, Mozambique, and European countries where United Methodist bishops serve. (206)

Rachel Matheson Ommen has a social work degree from Eastern University in St. Davids, Pennsylvania, and a master's in social work from the University of Illinois in Champaign-Urbana. Currently, she serves on the board of directors for The Springfield Project (TSP): a neighborhood revitalization organization. She is married and stays at home with her two young children. She attends Cherry Hills Baptist Church in Springfield, Illinois. (327, 340, 373)

Amanda Palmer is a writer, hospital chaplain, and Benedictine oblate in Canyon, Texas. (26, 49, 362)

Amy Pearson graduated with a M.Div. from American Baptist Seminary of the West in Berkeley, California. She is currently minister of spiritual development at First United Methodist Church in Pendleton, Oregon, where her husband is pastor. She is in the ordination process in the ABC of Oregon region. (95)

Linda M. Peavy is acting publisher for Judson Press. She has been previously published in *The Book of Daily Prayer* and *The Women of Color Devotional Bible*. A native of Cleveland, she holds an M.B.A. from the University of Akron. (53)

Ethel A. Ragland is a native of North Carolina and a 1971 graduate of the University of North Carolina at Greensboro. She and her husband, Larry, residents of Raleigh, have two adult children. Ethel currently serves as director of women's ministry for the Christian Church (Disciples of Christ) in North Carolina. She belongs to the Network of Biblical Storytellers, an ecumenical group that learns Scripture in order to "tell the story" using storytelling techniques. She has led retreats on spiritual gifts and workshops on biblical storytelling. (196)

Joyce Anderson Reed is a writer, storyteller, American Baptist missionary and minister, mother of two sons, and a married woman! She has ministered in New Jersey, Massachusetts, Alaska, and Mexico. She accepted Christ and wrote her first poem at age seven. Her faith and gift for writing continue to grow. (47, 66, 93)

Rhonda Rhône is a dual degree (M.Div./M.A. in Christian Education) student at Princeton Theological Seminary. (157)

Diana Rodríguez is executive secretary for leadership of the Women's Division of the United Methodist Church. (211)

J. Esther Rowe is executive assistant and director of the Bible Institute at the Progressive Church of God in Christ in Rochester, New York. She is an ordained Baptist minister and currently holds a license as an evangelist with the Church of God in Christ, Inc. The Reverend Evangelist Rowe is a 1987 graduate of the Colgate Rochester Crozer Divinity School in Rochester, New York. (65)

Evaleen Litman Sargent, an ordained Baptist preacher, is president and executive director of The Mission Institute and "Your Choice" Center, Inc. in Atlanta, Georgia. She also serves as dean of the New Era Missionary Baptist Convention of the Georgia Congress of Christian Education and as director of personal development, Women's Department, American Baptist Churches of the South, Area III. (260, 294)

Jill Schaeffer, Ph.D. (theology), is a Presbyterian minister who worked in Geneva for many years at the World Alliance of Reformed Churches on human rights and women's issues. Returning to the States in the Fall of 2000, Jill joined the Presbytery of New York City, where she has been preaching and moderating sessions of congregations. She served for a year as director of the New York Disaster Response Interfaith Council, an interfaith coalition born out of 9-11. Jill is single, lives with her cats, and loves music, needlepoint, and liturgy. (70, 224)

Pamela Schaeffer, a twenty-five year veteran of religion news, is director of communications for the St. Louis, Missouri-based Society of the Sacred Heart, U.S. Province. Her former posts include religion editor, *St. Louis Post-Dispatch*; news editor, Religion News Service; and managing editor, *National Catholic Reporter*. She holds a Ph.D. in historical theology from St. Louis University. (305)

Bonnie L. Scherer, a retired pediatric nurse, is a children's author who has written and published three children's books. (85, 143)

Linda (Schulze) Scherzinger is a lay pastoral minister with the United Church of Canada in Cape Breton, Nova Scotia. She was previously on the staff of the United Methodist Board of Global Ministries. (91, 236)

Sandy Schmidt received a Master of Theological Studies degree from St. Francis Seminary, Archdiocese of Milwaukee. She is a trained healthcare chaplain. She is strongly committed to social justice and peace and has had a long-time interest in women's spirituality. (135, 204)

Karen Ann Selig has co-pastored First Baptist Church, Manhattan, Kansas, with her husband, Alan, since 1992. She is passionate about learning and teaching from the Bible. In her free time, she enjoys basketmaking and hiking. Karen was president of American Baptist Women's Ministries from 2000–2003. (43, 89, 200, 215, 308)

Kelli Shermeyer is a thirteen-year-old who lives in Newark,

Delaware with her parents, Cindy and Chuck, and her little brother, Andrew. She attends Newark United Methodist Church and enjoys soccer, acting, writing, and listening to music. (19)

Julia D. Shreve is a Lutheran pastor and chaplain. At times she is also an artist, writer, singer, and dreamer of dreams. (124, 129, 181, 357)

Peggy Shriver is an Iowan, a Presbyterian, and a Christian—in ascending order. Mother of three, wife of the former president of Union Theological Seminary in New York, she has been a church executive since 1973 and has served in the National Council of Churches of Christ (USA) as a researcher and as an assistant general secretary. She is the author of *The Dances of Riverside Park and Other Poems.* (152)

Jane E. Shumway is an ordained American Baptist pastor. She serves the Almond Union of Churches, which is a union of American Baptist USA and Presbyterian Church USA, in Almond, New York. (298)

Martha Sobaje is minister of music and education at Phillips Memorial Baptist Church in Cranston, Rhode Island, and an adjunct instructor of music at Community College of Rhode Island. (265, 371)

Nancy J. Stelling, is a freelance writer living in Cary, North Carolina. She previously served as editor of *Lutheran Woman Today*, a publication of Women of the Evangelical Lutheran Church in America. (355)

Susan R. Street-Beavers is part of the executive leadership team for the Pension Fund of the Christian Church (DOC). She is founder and CEO of WTCE Inc. (Worldwide Training for Cross-cultural Empowerment), where she assists organizations with cross-cultural/diversity training, organizational development, and enhanced leadership skills. Dr. Street-Beavers has served as a senior pastor, and is a freelance writer and national and international speaker leading spiritual retreats and multicultural workshops. (40, 361)

Jackie Sullivan is director of pastoral care at Monroe Community Hospital in Rochester, New York. She is a graduate of Wells College, from which she holds a degree in Cross Cultural Sociology/Anthropology. She has also holds M.Div. and D.Min. degrees from Colgate Rochester Divinity School. She is the mother of three children—Jodi, Jennie, and Brian—and enjoys writing, sculpting (primarily portraiture), and gardening. (344)

Betty Susi, of Scarborough, Maine, is a mother, grandmother, and great-grandmother who is seeking after the Lord for a loving and growing relationship. (350)

Allison J. Tanner is a graduate of American Baptist Seminary of the West. She currently pastors at Lakeshore Avenue Baptist Church of Oakland, California, and directs an after-school program at St. Augustine's Catholic School, also in Oakland. (86)

Marilyn R. Taylor retired in 2003 from the position of associate regional minister for the Christian Church (Disciples of Christ) in Virginia. She held this position for more than fifteen years and is now looking forward to continued ministry as a church and community volunteer. (136, 266)

Janice I. Thompson is a Protestant chaplain at the Rhode Island Adult Correctional Institution, assigned to the Men's Medium Security. She is the wife of Dr. Vincent L. Thompson Jr., pastor of Community Baptist Church, Newport, Rhode Island. Currently, Janice is a D.Min. student at the Gordon-Conwell Theological Seminary in the track "Ministering In Complex Urban Settings." (164)

Becky Tornblom serves as pastor of First Baptist Church, Fitchburg, Massachusetts. (23, 84, 156)

Tawanda N. Tucker of Philadelphia, Pennsylvania, is a member of New Covenant Church. (7, 153)

Darla Dee Turlington is senior minister of the First Baptist Church of Westfield, New Jersey. She served as minister of Christian education and evangelism at First Baptist Westfield from 1991 –2000 and was active in denominational and community affairs, including the local ministerium, ABCNJ Ministers Council, and the board of the area's crisis hotline, CONTACT, We Care. (39, 48, 144)

Amy Turner is currently a graduate student at Denver Seminary completing a M.A. degree in Counseling. She holds a certificate in Evangelical Spiritual Guidance. She also teaches part-time in the area of spiritual formation and works with college students doing career counseling. She loves to travel, paint, and write in her free time. (292)

Adele Wilcox is a United Methodist minister who leads retreats for women's and church groups. She is the author of *Self and Soul: A Woman's Guide to Enhancing Self-Esteem Through Spirituality* and *Mending Broken Hearts: Meditations for Finding Peace and Hope After Heartbreak.* (195, 246)

Jeanne L. Williams lives in Denver with her husband and two sons. She is a therapist for urban, low-income children and adults and is a member of Garden Park Mennonite Brethren Church, where she serves as an elder and leads worship. (11, 82, 235)

Lois Wilson is a midwife, artist, and storyteller who resides in Philadelphia, Pennsylvania, with her husband, Tony, and their five children. She is a graduate of Eastern Baptist Theological Seminary and founder of Servant's Heart Ministries, a ministry dedicated to helping people encounter the Bible in new ways through the arts. (79)

Patricia A. Wilson-Robinson is an ordained American Baptist womanist theologian. She is an A.C.P.E. supervisor, Fellow in AAPC, and APC Board Chaplain. She serves as one of the associate ministers at Mount Zion Baptist Church in Seattle, Washington. (150)

Jo Ellen Witt is a graduate of William Jewel College in Liberty, Missouri, and has an M.Div. degree from Midwestern Baptist Theological Seminary in Kansas City, Missouri. She has taught school, owned a tax preparation business, and was minister of pastoral care and worship at Wornall Road Baptist Church in Kansas City prior to her current pastorate, of First Baptist Church in Marysville, Kansas, where she has served since 1995. She currently serves on the Ministers Council Senate. She has three children and two grandchildren. (38, 347, 372)

Marsha Brown Woodard is the pastor of Fellowship Christian Church (Disciples of Christ), Philadelphia, Pennsylvania and an affiliate professor at Eastern Baptist Theological Seminary, Wynnewood, Pennsylvania. (139, 287)

Penny B. Ziemer serves as minister of spiritual enrichment for First Christian Church, Goldsboro, North Carolina and teaches in the Religion and English Departments of Mt. Olive College, Mt. Olive, North Carolina. She is married to a wonderful man, Carey, and is blessed with two wonderful daughters, Carolyn and Laura. (83, 243)